Conversations with Tim Gautreaux

Literary Conversations Series
Peggy Whitman Prenshaw
General Editor

Conversations
with Tim Gautreaux

Edited by L. Lamar Nisly

University Press of Mississippi   *Jackson*

Books by Tim Gautreaux

Waiting for the Evening News (2010)
The Missing (2009)
The Clearing (2003)
Welding with Children (1999)
The Next Step in the Dance (1998)
Same Place, Same Things (1996)

www.upress.state.ms.us

The University Press of Mississippi is a member of the Association of American University Presses.

First printing 2012
Library of Congress Cataloging-in-Publication Data

Conversations with Tim Gautreaux / edited by L. Lamar Nisly.
    pages cm. — (Literary conversations series)
  Includes index. ISBN 978-1-4968-5214-4 (paperback)
    ISBN 978-1-61703-607-1 (cloth) — ISBN 978-1-61703-608-8 (ebook) (print) 1. Gautreaux, Tim—Interviews. 2. Authors, American—20th century—Interviews. 3. Authors, American—Southern States—Interviews. 4. Fiction—Authorship. I. Nisly, L. Lamar, 1968–
  PS3557.A954Z63 2012
  813'.54—dc23   2012000112

British Library Cataloging-in-Publication Data available

Contents

Introduction

In what is apparently Tim Gautreaux's first published interview, he tells his former student, Sheila Stroup, a humorous anecdote—that does not appear in his other interviews—about his becoming an English major. A student at Nicholls State University, in Thibodaux, Louisiana, he had planned to major in business, but then his five accounting books were stolen. "I went to see my adviser and told him to put me in something where nobody would steal my books," Gautreaux says. "He put me in English." It is a wonderful early story about his entry into the world of literature and, at the same time, may contain hints of Gautreaux's stated love of the frontier, tall-tale tradition. As he says in another interview, when he was a boy, he had a pen pal from Canada with whom he exchanged letters. "After a while, I ran out of things to talk about, so I started making up stuff." The interviewers, Jennifer Levasseur and Kevin Rabalais, wonder, "Was that your first experience in fiction writing?" Gautreaux responds, "Probably so. Lying to pen pals."

As suggested by these brief exchanges, Gautreaux's interviews not only offer insights into topics important in his writing and life. His voice also comes through clearly in these collected interviews, which span the period from 1993 to 2009. Always warm and courteous, he sometimes unleashes the droll humor that readers of his short stories might expect, trading witty one-liners with his interviewer. Other moments are much more contemplative, especially as he reflects on the moral focus he shares with fellow Catholic writers Walker Percy and Flannery O'Connor and muses about the darker themes of his later novels. Though many of the interviews are prompted by a new publication, one can see a consistency in theme and concern throughout the collection.

With two exceptions, the interviews printed here have all been published previously. Except for small errors, which have been silently corrected, the interviews are reprinted as they were originally published. Thus, the overlapping ideas and recurring stories present among these interviews are intentionally retained, for they provide a window into themes that have been important in Gautreaux's work and thinking. The two previously unpublished interviews, with Darlene Meyering in 2004 and Tom Ashbrook in

2009, were both conducted before a live audience. Meyering's interview took place before an audience at Calvin College's Festival of Faith and Writing; Ashbrook interviewed Gautreaux during his *On Point* call-in radio show for WBUR in Boston. Both of these transcriptions retain a more conversational feel and allow readers a sense of Gautreaux's easy give-and-take with an interviewer.

Though obviously less fully developed than in his later, longer interviews, the beginnings of important strands emerge already in his early interviews. Gautreaux points out prominent elements of his biography, particularly that he comes from a line of blue-collar workers and has inherited their love for machinery. He explains to Christina Masciere in 1998, "I collect antique machinery. . . . Part of it is genetic: My father was a tugboat captain, and my grandfather was a steamboat chief engineer. My great-uncle was a master mechanic. . . . My wife says I write fiction as an excuse to write about machinery." His love for antique machinery is connected as well, Gautreaux explains, to his storytelling roots. Since he was the "youngest child of a youngest child," as he says in various interviews, he had a chance to hear stories from older relatives who had worked on steamboats and other older machinery. Though the subject emerges many times, one of Gautreaux's most developed versions of the storytelling by relatives who, from a boy's perspective, seemed as these "very old men" occurs in Levasseur and Rabalais's interview: "They were retired riverboat men, tugboat pilots, or railroad men. . . . They would tell fascinating stories about what they used to do with their trains and their boats. There was a type of structure to the way they would tell their tales. The stories were spontaneous. . . . There would be this fantastic interweaving of stories because one man would make up facts, and the others would catch him, and their 'facts' would throw the story off on a tangent. It was great. These sessions taught me about the spontaneity, the organic structure, and the emotion that is involved in storytelling." Such a comment provides a useful window into the easily flowing narratives that Gautreaux develops in his stories and novels.

Since Gautreaux was for many years a teacher of creative writing at Southeastern Louisiana University, interviewers often ask him how he instructed his students. Many times he responds with versions of the lesson that students should depict the culture from which they come, as in this interview in *The Atlantic Online*: "What I do with students is try to put them in touch with where they're from. Everybody's heard the cliché, 'Write what you know,' and as is the case with most clichés, there's a great deal of truth in it. . . . They've been given a little piece of territory all their own, consisting of their family and neighborhood. If they're going to write, they've got to write about characters based on people they know: aunts, uncles, the eccentric guy down the block, and they've got to write using the unique language patterns of that landscape they own. Once I get them to use their own culture, everything starts to gel: the way people talk, the way things look, the way people value things." Gautreaux often illustrates this point by noting students who have skillfully rendered "mall-rat" or subdivision culture. In one early profile that is not included in this volume, Gautreaux notes that he typically includes in his fiction either a "South Louisiana Acadian voice or there's a voice from the central or northern part of the state."[1] Drawing on his love for machinery, Gautreaux also frequently invokes an engine metaphor as he discusses the need for careful plot construction. In his version on NPR's *All Things Considered*, host Elizabeth Arnold's laughter clearly indicates that she is enjoying his metaphor: "A short story—I like to tell students that a short story is like an automobile engine. There are no redundant parts. If you lift up your hood and you look at your car, you don't find extra spark plugs scotch-taped to the side of the engine [LAUGHTER] with a note from someone at the factory saying, 'we just found this on the floor. Thought you'd like to have it.' [LAUGHTER] Everything in the story has to have some kind of a function. And this means that what determines a good story is not so much what's in it, but what's not in it. It's important to know what to cut."

As is typical in many conversations with writers, Gautreaux's interviewers were interested in his writing practices. Though he describes no one fixed schedule for his writing, he does numerous times describe his process of editing. This account, from his 1997 *Atlantic Online* interview, sets out an approach that he reiterates in various interviews:

> I compose on a word processor, print out a first draft, and read for sentence structure. After edits I show it to someone (generally my wife or a graduate student I've worked with), and then I make five additional passes—each pass lasting about two and a half hours—before the manuscript is sent out for publication. On the first pass, I concentrate solely on language—vocabulary and authenticity, that is. The second pass consists of looking for all the tropes, metaphors, and similes in order to make sure they're integral to the story. Then, after letting it age a few days, I go through a third time and check all the punctuation and thin out anything extraneous. In the fourth pass I expand on the material still there. The final pass is an edit of anything that has been added. The process is a bit mechanical but very effective; it produces a clean manuscript.

In addition, he commonly mentions his appreciation for comments and directions from editors, saying that he will readily make changes as requested to a story.

Beyond the particulars of his writing approach, another important topic concerns Gautreaux's Cajun background and Louisiana setting for his stories. In Susan Larson's 1998 interview, though he is speaking specifically about his novel *The Next Step in the Dance*, his comments resonate about the small Louisiana towns present throughout his fiction:

> What I like about these places is that everyone knew everyone else, everyone was Catholic, I like the fact that everyone eats the same things. They share a common heritage so they make all sorts of assumptions about each other. . . . I can remember getting a haircut on Front Street in Morgan City [Gautreaux's home town] when I was about forty. It was a rundown place and the barber was on his last legs, and as he started cutting my hair, he said, "Aren't you a Gautreaux? I remember when your uncle drowned in the river trying to swim across and everyone was so upset." Now this conversation took place maybe around 1985 and my uncle had drowned in the mid-20s and he was talking about it as though it had happened last year.

Because of his Cajun background and the setting of much of his fiction, such elements of small-town Cajun life regularly are discussed in his conversations. Pointing out the prevalence of Catholicism throughout southern Louisiana, he frequently tells an illustrative story about his childhood memory of ordering in restaurants, as he explains here to Darlene Meyering: "But when I was a kid if you walked into a restaurant and you were maybe fifteen years old and ordered a hamburger, even a Protestant waitress would ask you, 'Well, do you remember that it's Friday?' They'd look out for you—you weren't supposed to eat meat on Friday in those days, you see." Such recurring images from his childhood experiences pepper his interviews.

The particularities of his experience in southern Louisiana may contribute to his resistance to having the broad "Southern writer" label attached to him. To the frequently recurring question of how he fits into the South's literary heritage, he explains in interview after interview that he sees such a label to be limiting. In a response to Christopher Scanlan, Gautreaux appeals to a quote from Walker Percy that he often cites: "Not calling myself a Southern writer is a trick I play on myself. If people tell you you're a Southern writer and you believe it, you put yourself in a little claustrophobic room, you restrict the way you look at the world and when you go to write, you say to yourself, 'Let's see, I've got to have some alligators in here and some French accordion music and a sheriff with mirrored sunglasses.' In other words, you start thinking in clichés. You can't let yourself think like that or else you'll be, as Walker Percy once stated, in the business of amazing Yankees. So I'm not a Southern writer. I'm just a writer who lives in the South." Similarly, though he often cites such writers as Annie Proulx and Cormac McCarthy as writers he admires, he finds any groupings among writers to be more limiting than helpful. Such a position comes through in his sardonic comment in 2005: "I don't know of many writers of literary fiction who consider themselves part of a 'school.' That depressing word reminds me of the dozen big goldfish one sees in the fiberglass pond outside of a Chinese restaurant. That's a school. They're all alike and I'd wager they all wish they were somewhere else."

In contrast to Gautreaux's resistance to a "Southern" identification, he readily articulates the importance that his Roman Catholicism has had on his writing. During one section of a very helpful, far-ranging interview, Margaret Bauer asks Gautreaux about his embracing of religious rather than regional identity as he thinks about himself as a writer. Gautreaux says, "In south-central Louisiana, I never really ran across many people that considered themselves southerners in the sense that Georgians or Mississippians consider themselves southerners. And I don't consider myself to be any kind of alligator-eating Cajun type. As I said, that's kind of superficial. But I've always been a Roman Catholic, since baptism, since birth."

This religious identification links directly with one of the most frequently discussed elements of his writing life: his initiation into fiction writing through a 1977 Loyola University seminar with Catholic writer Walker Percy. Percy selected twelve students to study fiction writing, as he read and commented on the students' work. The importance of Percy to Gautreaux's development as a writer becomes clear in his response to Maria Hebert-Leiter's question about what writer has influenced him the most:

> Probably Walker Percy from the standpoint of ideas. . . . What was interesting to Percy is not that people did things but why people did things. That carried over to his teaching of fiction. He would lead us in class to think not how we wrote, but why we wrote. There was always this moral foundation to whatever he wrote. And he was never didactic or preachy. He was always asking us, his readers, to think about why we did things. And when he taught me (a novel writing course in 1977, at Loyola), he was not very opinionated as to what we should write about, but he was very adamant in letting us know that we're all on some kind of a quest.

> The writer is always looking for something, the characters are always looking for something. It's an exploration. An exploration of what? Well, for Percy, it was, at least in part, always spiritual.

As this comment makes clear, Percy's approach as a teacher and the moral framework in his writing both shaped Gautreaux's own understandings of fiction. More succinctly, he enunciates in 1997 his basic stance: "I consider myself to be a Catholic writer in the tradition of Walker Percy. If a story does not deal with a moral question, I don't think it's much of a story." Or again, in Susan Larson's 1998 profile, he explains, "I'm not a philosopher like Walker Percy. . . . I'm just a Catholic from the bayou. But it's one of the rhythms of life." Percy's model, both in being a successful fiction writer and in modeling a committed Catholic stance, is one that Gautreaux cites often throughout his interviews and seems to have influenced his own self-identity as a Catholic who writes.

Given that deep connection with his fellow Louisiana and Catholic writer, it is probably hardly surprising that the other author Gautreaux regularly cites as having influenced his writing is another writer who openly embraced her faith, Flannery O'Connor. Often his praise for her centers on her technique, noting her common use of humor even in situations that seem not obviously to be funny. He explains to Masciere, "This is what a writer is always looking for, that situation that blends humor and pathos evenly. And you've got to hit it just right, because if you miss it, it's hokey or sentimental—both of which are just awful things to do to a reader. That's what Flannery O'Connor does so well. She has these characters that you laugh at, but that you can feel sorry for at the same time, or at least you're amazed at what a terrible experience they're going through while you're laughing at them." At times, though, he makes clear that his appreciation for O'Connor goes beyond her technical excellence as a story writer. In a comment to Hebert-Leiter, he notes, "Well, naturally an influence on just about everybody writing in the South was Flannery O'Connor. She's probably the country's premier short story writer. If you analyze her stories you see she was working with tragedy, and humor, and irony. And putting all of these elements together in a technically perfect way, and that was because she really took to heart what the instructors at Iowa gave her in the way of how to put a story together. She was *very* expert in the way she assembled her story structure. Also, you know, she was Catholic, and I can relate to that because I'm Catholic."

This moral angle that he embraces leads to a fictional approach that Gautreaux often describes as being different from the standard *New Yorker* stories, where, as he says to Julie Kane, "all is doom is gloom and nothing means anything, not even the narrative." In contrast, Gautreaux sees himself as offering glimpses of hope in his writing. He says to Masciere, "there's a lot of depressing stuff in my fiction, but personally I don't believe that you have to constantly remind people that life sucks, then you die, because everybody knows that. This idea that some, particularly young, writers have that life is just some dark journey and then you die is a myopic way of looking at things." In a longer response to Bauer, he explains that realism can demand difficult or dark themes but such approaches should not be the only tones in fiction:

> Where are the short stories about the small successes that people have dealing with their problems? Well, they're not out there because they're hard as hell to write without making them seem simple-minded or clichéd or insipid or sentimental. The most frightening thing in the world to an intelligent writer is sentimentality. He doesn't want a molecule of it in his fiction. But I think if you read enough and you understand how to blend humor and irony and the right tone in with the bad stuff, you can write a story that carries an emotional load yet is not sentimental in the least. If anybody wants to know how to deal with this type of thing, he can read my stories. I'm not exactly sure how I do it myself, but it's a conscious mixing of comedy and tragedy, of irony and straight non-ironic storytelling. A lot of it's like tap dancing or jitterbugging or singing: either you got it or you ain't.

While many of these themes about his life and influences on his writing recur, a shift in the depth of his interviews occurs in 1998 when the first literary journal interview appeared in the *New Delta Review* followed quickly by one in *The Mississippi Review* (that was later republished in a condensed form in *Novel Voices*[2]). Since *The Next Step in the Dance* had just been published, themes and elements from that novel figure prominently into these interviews—Colette and Paul's relationship, the fights in bars, the cultural geography of the setting. Besides some new details in the *New Delta Review* (what is the game bourré?), *The Mississippi Review* interview with Levasseur and Rabalais in particular covers new territory. Gautreaux details how he came to study poetry in graduate school with the poet James Dickey, who read Gautreaux's prize-winning poem at the Southern Literary Festival and ordered that Gautreaux be offered an assistantship to study at the University of South Carolina. He discusses what poetry he teaches in his classes, stating his aversion to T. S. Eliot's *The Waste Land*. He explains the difference between the genesis of a story and a novel, since "a story is driven by event and a novel by character" and describes the basis of various short stories.

Julie Kane, author of Gautreaux's biographical profile in *Dictionary of Literary Biography*, explores with Gautreaux many elements of his life, growing up in Morgan City, the roles of women when he was a child. Though he makes clear that he does not tend to create autobiographical characters, Gautreaux suggests that Paul in *The Next Step in the Dance* has some parallels to him: "I guess Paul would be the closest to how I feel about certain things. He's a little thick-headed and slow to catch on, and that might be like me." Gautreaux also describes his experiences of studying under Dickey and Percy. Dickey was "garrulous and outgoing," seeming to know all the contemporary poets. Gautreaux notes, "he was very knowledgeable about poetry, and he never said anything about poetry that seemed to be wrongheaded. I have nothing but praise for him as a teacher." In contrast, Percy had a more laid-back approach in his classes: "Percy was very subtle, very instructive; he was not afraid to talk about basics; everything he said was relevant to what we were doing; he did not bloviate or expand upon certain theoretical approaches to fiction that were not really of any practical help to us—mainly he would ask us a lot of questions. We would workshop a story and he would just ask questions and, of course, in our answering them, we would be instructing ourselves, because the questions were very pointed and purposeful. He was very modest, very unassuming." As in other interviews, Gautreaux extols Percy's influence on his work, particularly as it encouraged Gautreaux to allow his moral sense always to be present in his fiction. "The business about value—what do you do with children, why do you do *anything* in life?—is always behind my fiction," Gautreaux explains.

The publication of Gautreaux's second novel in 2003, *The Clearing*, sparked several additional in-depth interviews. While Robert Birnbaum's interview circles among a number of familiar topics, such as Louisiana life and Gautreaux's Catholic perspective, it provides a particularly useful discussion of various elements of this 1920s lumber mill novel. Gautreaux notes the importance of his decision to write it from the point of view of two brothers from Pennsylvania, outsiders to the swampy Louisiana region where the novel is set; such a view "makes all the difference in the world— instead of this being another Southern novel where the artist has put together a bunch of uneducated deplorable folks and allowed them to self-destruct for four hundred pages." Gautreaux also acknowledges that the novel could have continued beyond its current ending, but that "I was afraid to lose the

focus of the world I had created down there at the lumber mill site." Birnbaum explores with Gautreaux the family connections to this novel, hints of
stories he had heard about ancestors who were a constable and a marshal.
Covering some of the same territory, The *Chattahoochee* Review published
an interview for which we were not able to secure reprint permission.[3] Particularly enlightening in this interview is Gautreaux's account of the influence his uncle's experience in WWI had in his creation of the character
Byron in *The Clearing*:

> One thing I remembered was my uncle who lived to be eighty-eight years old
> and was in WWI. As a matter of fact, he was in all eight major American engage-
> ments of WWI. He was shot up, he was gassed, he was captured by the Germans,
> he was tortured. He had a lung removed in a tent field hospital. He came back
> quite changed, quite ruined, and for the rest of his life was kind of a haunted man.
> He didn't talk about his war experiences much, but a sentence here, a couple of
> sentences there, and I could gather what had happened to him. . . . Now the char-
> acter in the novel, Byron Aldridge, the WWI veteran, is nothing like my uncle
> Clarence. But Byron's haunted nature, the ruined aspect, that comes from my
> uncle. (104–5)

Similarly striking is a passage in which Gautreaux discusses two of the villains of the novel, the mob boss Buzetti and the hit man Crouch:

> Buzetti and Crouch are bad people, but not because they're from the North.
> They were ruined in the war. . . . But they're not one-dimensional. As a matter of
> fact, if I could go back and work on the novel some more, one thing I would do
> is give Buzetti and his cousin a few more paragraphs of development, because
> Crouch, of course, is a tortured man and deserves development. His eye was
> burned out by an Austrian officer for sport. There is a key passage in the novel,
> where Byron is speaking with Buzetti, trying to run him off, and he asks about the
> war, "Why did we do it?" And Buzetti says, "Because somebody gave us permis-
> sion. It's a nice thing, permission. I learned to give it to myself." That to me is the
> scariest line in the novel. (107)

Gautreaux's observations about the novel reinforce his comment to Birnbaum that *The Clearing* "is a novel that has been percolating perhaps twenty
or twenty-five years." His description of the novel's origins and his own reflections on its complications enrich a reader's interaction with this grip-
ping, disturbing novel.

Three longer interviews, conducted in the next couple of years, provide reinforcement of familiar themes as well as new directions. Darlene Meyering's interview of Gautreaux is perhaps most intriguing for its conversational style as she explores with him an array of his stories and the questions that emerge from their content. For instance, when Gautreaux explains that he worked as a piano tuner in the summers, Meyering asked him if a woman had ever come on to him, as occurs in his story "The Piano Tuner." Gautreaux jokingly responds, "Alas, no." More substantively, he explains his attitude about including racy material in his writing, pointing out that "I don't go out of my way to titillate or arouse." Maria Hebert-Leiter's interview is particularly enlightening in its exploration of Gautreaux's depictions of Cajun culture, an emphasis not surprising given that the interview factored into Hebert-Leiter's research for her book, *Becoming Cajun, Becoming American: The Acadian in American Literature from Longfellow to James Lee Burke.*[4] Gautreaux describes how he became more aware of Cajun culture when he left the state for graduate studies:

> If you would have asked me when I was twelve years old, "Are you a Cajun?" I would say, "I don't know." It was when I moved away to South Carolina when I was maybe twenty-one, twenty-two years old (for graduate school), that I found myself in a different culture at that point, and realized how different Louisiana was, south Louisiana in particular, from the rest of the country. When I moved to South Carolina, the food was totally different, and the religion was different, the politics was different, everything was different. Attitudes were different. At that point it began to be clear to me what being Cajun was. And it had to do with attitudes, the value of food, the value of religion, and things of that nature. And it's sort of an attitude about life.

Two topics of particular interest that arise in my interview with Gautreaux are his descriptions of his Catholic background, particularly his experience being educated by Marianite nuns, and his discussion of how to deal with violence in fiction. Though he is speaking specifically about *The Clearing*, the comments seems to apply equally well to his next novel, *The Missing*: "Much violence in movies is presented in such a way that the anguish of those who love the victim is invisible or far in the background. The anguish of the person causing the violence likewise seldom figures in the plot. The violence just happens with the significance and effect of a summer fireworks show. If violence is to be justified in a literary work, it has to have a purpose beyond the spectacular display, and one way for a writer to make violence purposeful is to show the effects or lack thereof on both sides of the act it-self." Gautreaux's concern with questions of violence and vengeance become particularly important in his later interviews, a very reasonable occurrence given the subject matter of his later novels.

Since the final three extensive interviews occur after Gautreaux had written *The Missing*, one of the rich additions to these conversations is his reflections on that novel. Given that Margaret Bauer wrote the first full-length examination of Gautreaux's work,[5] it is hardly surprising that her interview covers a broad swath of territory and invites Gautreaux to reflect on some new topics. For instance, Bauer focuses on whether Gautreaux has written an autobiographical novel, how Mark Twain and William Faulkner have influenced his writing, and how it is that his latest two novels deal with WWI. Additionally, because this interview occurred after Bauer had read *The Missing*, she encourages Gautreaux to explore that novel alongside *The Clearing*:

> really, the novels can be analyzed side by side because in one, we have a protagonist severely damaged by his experiences in World War I, and in the second we have a protagonist who arrives in France on the day the armistice is signed and doesn't get to shoot anybody at all. . . . Then we follow him through the rest of his experiences in *The Missing*, and we see that he behaves differently from Byron in *The Clearing*, has a different life, a different outlook. The novel is negative definition: Sam, the main character in *The Missing*, is defined by what he does not do. If I had had him show up two months earlier on that troop ship, while the killing was still going on, it would have been a different novel. I think the whole narration is propelled by the fact that he did not have to shoot anybody in France, that he showed up by an incredible stroke of luck on the day the armistice was signed.

Gautreaux's interview in *Image* reinforces some familiar topics. Yet his former student, Dayne Sherman, leads Gautreaux to offer an incisive analysis of *The Missing*. Gautreaux notes that his novel "goes against contemporary American culture" because it resists the "template of offense followed by justified violence." Gautreaux praises Clint Eastwood's movie *Gran Torino*, in which the "path of self-sacrifice was chosen to great purpose." Gautreaux reflects, "I hope *The Missing* sets some writers free from the idea that if offense is given then offense must be taken." In similar manner, Tom Ashbrook's radio interview/talk show is primarily concerned with *The Missing*. Ashbrook asks Gautreaux many questions about the steamboat and jazz era portrayed in the novel, though he also turns to the novel's theme of vengeance. As the calls suggest, Gautreaux's depiction of a bygone era on the river connected with the nostalgia of listeners, even though the novel itself shows much of the brutality and pain of life in the 1920s.

Reading through Gautreaux's interviews provides an enlightening window into details of his life and themes of his writing that are important to him. At the same time, the successive interviews also reveal a growing acceptance of his rising fame as a writer. In his first interview he says ruefully, "After being ignored for twenty years, I get fan mail. . . . People writing from Pennsylvania for advice is sort of unnerving." Sixteen years later he seems perfectly comfortable handling calls on a syndicated call-in show on NPR. Similarly, the breadth of the subject matter in his interviews has increased, in part because of the longer venues for his comments but also because Gautreaux continues to explore and expand the shadowy moral questions in his fiction. He has found success later in his writing life, he believes, because writers need a long learning process to perfect the craft and gain the life experience necessary for rich fiction. Or, as he puts it more succinctly to Ashbrook, "No creative writing student is ever worth a damn until he's middle-aged." Gautreaux acknowledges various times, though, that writing is hard work, and he might find it tempting to rest in retirement, were it not for his Catholic guilt prodding him forward. While he is working on *The Missing*, he tells Christopher Scanlan, "the thing that's driving me to write it is basically religious guilt. If you have a talent, it's wrong not to exercise it." These interviews reveal a sense of Gautreaux—his humor, his love of family, his deep moral commitments—that serves to enrich our appreciation of this great talent revealed in his fiction.

Throughout this project, I have valued the support and direction provided by my editor at the University Press of Mississippi, Walter Biggins. My deep appreciation, too, goes to the many editors and interviewers who willingly provided permission for their interviews to be reprinted. I am particularly grateful to Tim Gautreaux for his generous consent for republication of interviews and for the photo he provided for the cover. My father, Paul Nisly, English professor emeritus from Messiah College, made helpful suggestions about the introduction and was supportive throughout the work. As always, my deepest gratitude goes to my children Jonathan, Elizabeth, and Annalise and to my wife Deborah for their faithful encouragement of my work.

LLN

Notes

1. Greg Langley, "Gautreaux Doesn't Need a Label Other than 'Writer,'" *The Advocate Online* 10 October 1999.

2. Tim Gautreaux, interview with Jennifer Levasseur and Kevin Rabalais, "Mining Literary Heritage," in *Novel Voices*, ed. Levasseur and Rabalais (Cincinnati: Writer's Digest Books, 2003) 114-126.

3. Tim Gautreaux, "A Conversation with Tim Gautreaux," *Chattahoochee Review* 24/1 (Fall 2003).

4. Baton Rouge: Louisiana State University Press, 2009.

5. Margaret Donovan Bauer, *Understanding Tim Gautreaux* (Columbia, SC: The University of South Carolina Press, 2010).

Chronology

1947   Timothy Martin Gautreaux is born on 19 October to Florence Ella and Minos Lee Gautreaux in Morgan City, Louisiana. His father is a tugboat captain.

1969   Graduates from Nicholls State University in Thibodaux, Louisiana, with a major in English. One of his creative writing professors enters some of Gautreaux's poems into a Southern Literary Festival contest at Knoxville, Tennessee. Poet James Dickey reads Gautreaux's winning poems and directs that Gautreaux be offered an assistantship to study at the University of South Carolina under Dickey.

1972   Completes Ph.D. from the University of South Carolina by writing a poetry manuscript for his dissertation, "Night-Wide River." He accepts a position teaching English at Southeastern Louisiana University in Hammond, Louisiana. Gautreaux marries Winborne Howell, who is a master's student in American literature at the University of South Carolina. They have two sons, Robert and Thomas.

1977   Selected by novelist Walker Percy to participate in a fiction-writing seminar at Loyola University, New Orleans. Gautreaux frequently credits this seminar with Percy as launching his fiction-writing career.

1983   Publishes his first short story, "A Sacrifice of Doves," in *Kansas Quarterly*.

1992   Has "Same Place, Same Things," originally published in the *Atlantic Monthly*, chosen for inclusion in *Best American Short Stories, 1992*.

1993   Receives National Endowment for the Arts literature fellowship.

1995   Wins the National Magazine Award for fiction for "Waiting for the Evening News," published in *Story*. "The Bug Man," first printed in *GQ*, is chosen for *New Stories from the South: The Year's Best, 1995*.

1996   Publishes *Same Place, Same Things* with Picador/St. Martin's Press. "Died and Gone to Vegas," which first appeared in the *Atlantic Monthly*, is included in *New Stories from the South: The Year's Best, 1996*. Gautreaux is appointed to the John and Renée Grisham

Southern Writer-in-Residence position at the University of Mississippi for the fall semester.

1997   Has "Little Frogs in a Ditch," first published in *GQ*, chosen for both *New Stories from the South: The Year's Best, 1997* and *Best American Short Stories, 1997*. Gautreaux is named writer-in-residence at Southeastern Louisiana University and given a reduced teaching load.

1998   Publishes *The Next Step in the Dance* with Picador/St. Martin's Press. "Welding with Children," first published in the *Atlantic Monthly*, is selected for *Best American Short Stories, 1998*. "Sorry Blood," originally printed in *Fiction*, is included in *New Stories from the South: The Year's Best, 1998*.

1999   Publishes *Welding with Children* with Picador/St. Martin's Press, chosen by the *New York Times* as a notable book of the year. *The Next Step in the Dance* wins the Southeastern Booksellers Association Novel of the Year award. "The Piano Tuner," first published in *Harper's*, is selected for inclusion in *Best American Short Stories, 1999*.

2000   Has "Easy Pickings," originally published in *GQ*, selected for inclusion in *Prize Stories, 2000: The O. Henry Awards*. "Good for the Soul," originally published in *Story*, is chosen for *Best American Short Stories, 2000*. "Dancing with the One-Armed Gal," first printed in *Zoetrope*, is included in *New Stories from the South: The Year's Best, 2000*.

2003   Publishes *The Clearing* with Alfred A. Knopf. Gautreaux retires from teaching at Southeastern Louisiana University.

2004   Writes the preface for *New Stories from the South: The Year's Best, 2004*.

2005   Wins the John Dos Passos Prize for literature at Longwood University. Gautreaux is also awarded the Heasley Prize from Lyon College.

2007   Has "The Safe," originally published in the *Atlantic Monthly*, selected for *New Stories from the South: The Year's Best, 2007*.

2009   Publishes *The Missing* with Alfred A. Knopf. Gautreaux receives the Louisiana Writer Award.

2010   Publishes *Waiting for the Evening News* with Sceptre Publishing (UK). This volume combines the stories earlier published in *Same Place, Same Things* and in *Welding with Children*. Gautreaux's story "Idols," first printed in the *New Yorker*, is selected for inclusion in *New Stories from the South 2010: The Year's Best*.

Conversations with Tim Gautreaux

He's Got the Write Stuff

Sheila Stroup/1993

From the *Times-Picayune* (26 January 1993). © 2011 The Times-Picayune. All rights reserved. Reprinted with permission.

It felt strange to be sitting in Tim Gautreaux's office, taking notes in a reporter's notebook instead of a three-subject one. He's moved up in the world since he was my writing professor.

For one thing, he has a window in his office now. A room with a view isn't easy to come by in the Southeastern Louisiana University English department.

For another, his story "Same Place, Same Things" (originally published in the *Atlantic*) was included in *The Best American Short Stories, 1992*. In the world of the short fiction writer, that's about the highest honor there is.

"After being ignored for twenty years, I get fan mail," he said, turning up a letter among the beginning-of-the-semester stacks of student papers on his desk. "People writing from Pennsylvania for advice is sort of unnerving."

He's been teaching at SLU for twenty-one years and writing stories even longer. He didn't set out to do either.

He planned to be a business major at Nicholls State, but then someone stole five of his accounting books. "I went to see my adviser and told him to put me in something where nobody would steal my books," he said. "He put me in English."

It was the place for him to be.

Except for the gray in his moustache, he's much the same as he was when he was my teacher ten years ago—thin as a rope and still popping Tums like they were after-dinner mints. "My stomach hurts all the time," he said. "I think it comes from teaching at a Louisiana college."

But he likes to teach. He likes marking the places where you got the words just right, helping you shape them into something fine. And he likes talking about writing.

He still has that slow deliberate Louisiana way of speaking. And he's one of those rare writers who can read his own work and bring out the emotion and humor in it.

He credits that ability to liking to tell stories and to reading the *Catholic Messenger* out loud when he was in elementary school in Morgan City, Louisiana. He read so well that one time his third-grade teacher took him upstairs and had him read to the sixth-graders, to show them how it should be done. "For years, a classroom of thirty kids all hated my guts," he said.

"Same Place, Same Things" came about in 1989 after Gautreaux got a grant to write stories about the Florida Parishes.

It was the first time he really followed the advice he's been giving his students for years: Write what you're interested in; write what you know.

He's always been fascinated by obsolete machinery, so he set the story in the strawberry fields of Tangipahoa Parish during the Depression and wrote about a man who repaired the gas engines that powered well pumps.

The tale seemed to take shape almost on its own, powered by ancient machinery and the drought-plagued farm land.

"It made me realize that fiction can come out of any place," he said. "That fiction happens in your own back yard."

Several of his Louisiana stories have been published, and on the strength of them he has received a number of grants, including a plum—$20,000 from the National Endowment for the Arts that will allow him to take off and write full time for a semester.

He has his office door decorated with rejection slips—to show his students that writing is a life of hard work and to keep success from going to his head. He's not too comfortable with fame.

"A lot of people are buying the short story book and asking me to autograph it," he said. "But I never have any idea what to write."

Pelican Briefs

Susan Larson/1996

From the *Times-Picayune* (15 September 1996) © 2011 The Times-Picayune. All rights reserved. Reprinted with permission.

When Tim Gautreaux writes his critically acclaimed short stories about Louisiana, recently published in the collection, *Same Place, Same Things*, he's not writing about the land of dreamy dreams. His Louisiana is a tough place, where it's hard to make a living. It's a place where the land is swamp or scorched fields, where small towns have fallen on hard times, where heavy machinery, all too often broken, litters the landscape, and the water comes right up to the road. The names of his characters—Robicheaux and Thibodeaux and Bergeron—and his towns—Gumwood and Pine Oil and Grand Crapaud—are straight out of Louisiana.

Gautreaux eyes this tough scenery with a keen sense of objectivity tempered with the wisdom of long acquaintance, as well as a native son's affection. Born in Morgan City, the son of a tugboat captain and the grandson of a steamboat engineer, he knows the world of men and machines like the back of his hand. Or the back of his yard for that matter.

"I collect antique machinery. I've got three or four old antique tractors, old John Deere tractors, around the place that I'm always working on," he said. "I'm a collector. I like antique railroad lanterns. I've got a lot of vertical steamboat whistles. We've got an Acadian back in the woods on a couple of acres and a lot of land behind us that we don't own but we play on. That, of course, is the advantage of living out in the woods. You can do what you want. I can set off a steam whistle off the compressor and not disturb the neighbors 'cause we don't have much in the way of neighbors."

When he's not setting off whistles, Gautreaux is listening to the noise of favorable reviews of his new book and enjoying a new position. This semester, he's taken leave from his teaching duties at Southeastern Louisiana

University in Hammond to be the first John and Renee Grisham professor of creative writing at the University of Mississippi. His temporary life in Oxford seems to suit Gautreaux just fine.

"I got a phone call from Barry Hannah and he said, how would you like to come up here and live rent-free in this nice house in Oxford, Mississippi, and we'll pay you $25,000," Gautreaux said. "I wouldn't say yes, because I thought there had to be a catch. But the duties are very light. The idea is to give a writer such as myself time to produce and that's always what I sorely need because I usually teach such a heavy load. It's been a very, very welcome respite and I'm profoundly grateful."

And no, he hasn't met his famous benefactors in person, and no, he hasn't read any of Grisham's work, though he plans to. He's using the time to revise a novel, *Machinery of Dreams*, set in the Louisiana oil patch during the big bust, drawing once again on his own memories of growing up.

"Morgan City was just a rough little town that had about thirty barrooms and twenty churches. No, there were probably about ten churches," he said. "It's not really a Cajun town, it's a kind of hybrid place. I knew it was a rough place. It still is, but it's a real place.

"People would sit around in my family and tell stories and that's important. Particularly the men, when they'd get a few beers in 'em, would start telling river stories and steamboat stories. And of course, I was the youngest kid, by myself, nobody to play with, and I'd listen to the old guys.

"People are always asking me how I know all this stuff about machines and find it really amazing," Gautreaux said. "If your father and your mother were white-collar workers, you were never exposed to your father working on a machine or having a little machine shop. You have no idea what things are called, what a certain type of glue is called, how long it takes to set up, why it's better or worse than another kind, what that screw is, how many threads to the inch . . . and of course all that stuff is second nature to me.

"I tell writing students, if you're going to describe setting, if you're going to set a story in a particular area, you've got know what the bushes are called. When I was a kid in the 4-H club, I got a thing called Louisiana Trees, a little brown pamphlet. I still have it and I never have it more than two feet away from my word processor because it tells me things like when things are in bloom. If I'm describing some old lady's yard, and I mention pyracantha berries, I can check and see if those berries would be out."

He cherishes his culture, even as he is taken aback by its commercialization. "The rest of the country is getting so homogenized. You hear about Cajun food and Cajun dancing . . . hell, we used to eat crawfish one day, and crabs the next and gumbo the next and white beans and rice and we didn't even know what a Cajun was. And I can trace my roots all the way back to Nova Scotia."

What resonates with readers is Gautreaux's absolute authority over the landscape, his intense understanding of its people. "I just try to deal with what is," he said. "My stories are set in west Louisiana and I just try to go back to what I remember, and when I feel I'm losing touch, I go off to Fred's Lounge in Mamou on Saturday morning and listen to the band and watch 'em dance."

"It's so hard to find the real thing, whatever the real thing is," Gautreaux said. "But when you stumble across it, you know it, don't you?"

He knows it all right. It's in all his stories.

A Conversation with Tim Gautreaux

Katie Bolick and David Watta/1997

From the *Atlantic Online* (14 March 1997). Copyright 1997, The Atlantic Media Co. as published in the *Atlantic Online*. Distributed by Tribune Media Services.

In a world characterized by increased transience, Tim Gautreaux is a writer with a strong sense of place. His accurate prose, both visual—"a yellow butterfly playing in a clump of pigweed"—and vernacular—"Whoo. Grendaddy can bust a move"—is culled from a lifetime spent keenly observing the South, beyond the anesthesia of cultural homogeneity.

"Welding with Children" (March, 1997, *Atlantic*), is Gautreaux's third *Atlantic* story. His fiction has appeared in, among other journals, *Harper's*, *GQ*, and *Story*, and been selected for publication in *New Stories from the South* and *Best American Short Stories*. The recipient of a National Endowment for the Arts fellowship and the National Magazine Award for Fiction, Gautreaux has directed the creative writing program at Southeastern Louisiana University for more than two decades. St. Martin's Press has recently published his book of short stories, *Same Place, Same Things* (1996), and will issue his novel, *Machinery of Dreams*, early next year.

Gautreaux recently spoke with *Atlantic Unbound*'s Katie Bolick and David Watta.

Character Sketch

Home
Hammond, Louisiana.

Education
Ph.D., English Literature and Creative Writing, University of South Carolina.

Age
Forty-nine.

First Publication
"A Sacrifice of Doves," a short story published in *Kansas Quarterly*.

Last Book Read
Heart Songs and Other Stories, by E. Annie Proulx.

Advice to Writers
"Listen to how those around you speak. Authenticity of dialogue is magic for a reader."

Bolick and Watta: The majority of your writing is based in Southern Louisiana, where you have spent a great deal of your life. Although location never overwhelms your characters, it certainly determines some, if not all, of who they are and will be. Does the same hold for you as well?

Gautreaux: I think every writer is limited by where he's from, particularly someone who has spent his entire life in one region. This is, of course, a mixed blessing. You get to know a place very well but you don't know others at all. A writer who has lived only in Nebraska, for example, has to write about Nebraska. This is not a problem to be lamented but it is a determiner of who your characters will be.

Bolick and Watta: What would you say the differences are, if any, between the preoccupations of a "Southern" writer and other American writers? And how do you feel your work fits into the Southern tradition?

Gautreaux: I don't really understand what a "Southern" writer is. Writers just tend to write about their environment. If the South tends to be more poverty stricken, or has a less-educated population, or the politicians seem more arrogant, or there's a more intense devotion to religion, that's just the way it is.

Perhaps the only difference I can perceive between a "Southern" writer and a non-Southern writer is that maybe the "Southern" writer loves where he lives more than other writers. When you read Eudora Welty or Walker Percy you sense they really enjoy the details of where they live, warts and all. This quality doesn't seem to surface as much with non-Southern writers.

I would rather be classified in the Frontier tradition than the "Southern" tradition, because I can see elements of the old tall tale and frontier humor in my writing. Much of my early reading was devoted to folklore and the likes of Mark Twain. Tall tales, with their hyperbole and outlandish plots, seem to have had an effect on my writing.

I hearken back to the days when television was a minimal presence in American life. People used to sit around and tell tales, particularly the older relatives who would come over and entertain with stories. This is something that Ernest Gaines writes about—he used memories of his aunts sitting on the porch and telling stories to provide the rhythms for his characters' dialogue. For me, it was a little different: I listened to retired tug-boat captains and oil-field workers try to outdo each other in stories.

Bolick and Watta: The themes you choose to write about seem to rise from regional roots to encompass universal concerns. Which come first, the characters or the themes?

Gautreaux: Themes rise out of character organically. A writer who sits down and thinks "I'm going to deal with a theme," rather than "I'm going to tell a story," is not a fiction writer but an essayist in disguise. I think no matter what character a writer chooses he's going to write about the same themes, because a writer's favorite thematic concerns arise no matter what the story line is, no matter what characters are chosen. I just set a couple characters against each other on the first page, and next thing I know, the story is "about" some idea that interests me—and that is the theme.

Bolick and Watta: Your characters are so real and so vividly rendered that they seem to live on long after the story is finished. How do you approach characterization?

Gautreaux: When people say, "Your characters are memorable," they are remembering what the characters say and how they say it. For description, as far as characters are concerned, I try to use unique details rather than a bland inventory of a character's experience. I like to do that in a very minimalist fashion—two or three carefully chosen details that quickly give the reader an idea of what this character is about. I pay a lot of attention to little body movements: the way people move their hands, position their feet, what they do with a cigarette. Movement becomes a language unto itself.

Bolick and Watta: The names you use are interesting—Moonbeam, Nu-Nu, Pig, Bullfinch, Fernest, to name but a few. How and why do you choose the names you do?

Gautreaux: I have no particular method in mind when I choose names.

Striking names are hard for a reader to forget. But the names that appear in my stories are the types of names found in rural Louisiana.

Bolick and Watta: Most of your stories seem to pivot on moral questions. Could you talk about moral weight as an aspect of fiction, and its importance in your work?

Gautreaux: I consider myself to be a Catholic writer in the tradition of Walker Percy. If a story does not deal with a moral question, I don't think it's much of a story.

Bolick and Watta: You have been both a professor and editor while continuing to write. How do these different roles inform your fiction? How justified do you feel about asking others to revise and how do you feel about changes that are suggested to you?

Gautreaux: When you teach creative writing, you're always telling people what to do, and this constant discussion of technique has an effect on your own writing. When you're an editor, you're micro-managing other people's manuscripts, and it's similar to being a teacher. What you end up telling the person whose manuscript you're looking at is something you're basically teaching or telling yourself. It's a learning process both ways.

As far as feeling justified about asking others to revise, my take is, "How can I help this person to make a better manuscript?" That's the sole thought I have in my head when I read others people's work. With regard to recommendations about my own work, I generally always follow them. If a writer or editor takes the time to make a recommendation, he must care about my work and want to make it better. If someone tells me to cut a thousand words, I'll do it in a heartbeat. It's okay for story writing to be a collaborative art.

Bolick and Watta: How would you describe your writing habits?

Gautreaux: I'm very erratic in the way I write. I have no particular schedule I adhere to. I simply write whenever the urge hits. I compose on a word processor, print out a first draft, and read for sentence structure. After edits I show it to someone (generally my wife or a graduate student I've worked with), and then I make five additional passes—each pass lasting about two and a half hours—before the manuscript is sent out for publication. On the first pass, I concentrate solely on language—vocabulary and authenticity, that is. The second pass consists of looking for all the tropes, metaphors, and similes in order to make sure they're integral to the story. Then, after letting it age a few days, I go through a third time and check all the punctuation and thin out anything extraneous. In the fourth pass I expand on the material still there. The final pass is an edit of anything that has been added. The process is a bit mechanical but very effective; it produces a clean manuscript.

Bolick and Watta: You once wrote, about teaching fiction: "I'm big on telling students to incorporate their own fascinations into the fabric of their writing, whether it's mounting butterflies or collecting toilet bowls. I've also taught them that they should write about what goes on in their own back yards." What's your approach to the teaching of fiction?

Gautreaux: What I do with students is try to put them in touch with where they're from. Everybody's heard the cliché, "Write what you know," and as is the case with most clichés, there's a great deal of truth in it. One of my big problems with beginning writers is that they act like they're all from Los Angeles or New York, and that's because they've been bombarded by everything from MTV to Burger King ads to Hollywood stereotypes, all originally from those two places. My job is to tell them that no, this way of thinking is inaccurate. They've been given a little piece of territory all their own, consisting of their family and neighborhood. If they're going to write, they've got to write about characters based on people they know: aunts, uncles, the eccentric guy down the block, and they've got to write using the unique language patterns of that landscape they own. Once I get them to use their own culture, everything starts to gel: the way people talk, the way things look, the way people value things.

Best American Short Stories 1997

Elizabeth Arnold/1997

Robert Siegel, host: This is *All Things Considered*. I'm Robert Siegel.
Elizabeth Arnold, host: And I'm Elizabeth Arnold.

A consistent top seller during the holiday season is the *Best American Short Stories*. Every year since 1915, it's provided a roundup of the best short fiction to have appeared in print the previous twelve months.

About a hundred stories make the first cut, then they are passed on to a guest editor. This year it was writer E. Annie Proulx. Among the twenty-one stories she chose for the 1997 anthology is "Little Frogs in a Ditch" by Tim Gautreaux.

Gautreaux has taught creative writing at Southeastern Louisiana University for the last twenty-five years and is recognized as a master of the short story.

Gautreaux: I think something that gets out of the box pretty quickly is one thing I try to produce; something that grabs the reader. Rust Hills said that every story starts with something called moving action, something out of the ordinary happening in a person's life. And that point is where many great artists, down through literary history, start.

Shakespeare, for example, starts *in medias res*. And that's what I like to do, start right with that change in a character's life, that out-of-the-ordinary thing that happens to a person.

Arnold: Although it seems attractive at the outset, I would think that the short story would actually be a difficult literary form, requiring more in the way of discipline and balance and control than a longer work.

Gautreaux: Well, this is true. Every line, every sentence has to have some sort of a connection with what you're trying to do in the way of theme or in the way of the narrative.

A short story—I like to tell students that a short story is like an automobile engine. There are no redundant parts. If you lift up your hood and you look at your car, you don't find extra spark plugs scotch-taped to the side of the engine . . .

(LAUGHTER)

. . . with a note from someone at the factory saying, "we just found this on the floor. Thought you'd like to have it."

(LAUGHTER)

Everything in the story has to have some kind of a function. And this means that what determines a good story is not so much what's in it, but what's not in it. It's important to know what to cut.

Arnold: You know, you must look at a lot of students' work. In the introduction to this collection that E. Annie Proulx writes, she talks about the stories that didn't make it into the collection.

And she writes, "some were weak anecdotes, not stories at all. Not a few were written in chatty, slangy, conversational style, a kind of TV dialogue-like jabber, characterized by short, hard little sentences with the rhythm of a woodpecker in a dead tree."

Does this sound familiar to you?

Gautreaux: Yes. It's hard to turn students on to authentic dialogue, to make them pay attention to the way people around them actually speak—their aunts and their uncles and the people in their neighborhood—and to make them realize that people in Minneapolis do have a slightly different way of speaking than people in any other place, even in the Midwest.

But students have absorbed so many—really tens of thousands of hours of television script dialogue by the time they're eighteen years old—that this is embedded in them, the fact that everybody talks the way Hollywood script writers had them talk.

Arnold: Hmm.

Gautreaux: And they don't really listen to the people they grow up with.

Arnold: How do you approach a story? I mean, let's talk about the one in this collection, "Little Frogs in a Ditch." Where did that come from?

Gautreaux: Stories very often are found things. That one came to me entire while I was overhearing a radio broadcast. I listen to a lot of local talk radio.

Arnold: Uh-huh.

Gautreaux: And one morning the subject was the meanest trick you ever played on anyone as a kid. And this fella called up and said that he actually took an ad out in the local newspaper saying that he could sell homing pigeons, instructions included, $10.

And what he was doing is actually just getting ordinary pigeons off somebody's shed roof and selling them as homing pigeons with this incredibly difficult regimen of how to train the bird. It took two weeks.

Well, by the time the person bought the bird and made a fool out of himself by doing this, they wouldn't bring it back, complaining. And of course, when they turned the pigeon loose, it would never show up again. It would disappear.

I thought, "What an incredibly mean thing to do. And what would it be like to have someone like that in your family?" And that was the beginning of that story. It was totally found. And many of my stories are like that.

Arnold: What do you tell students who are struggling with the short story form?

Gautreaux: That it takes a lot of practice. It takes a long time to learn the trade. And it's an art form, just like ice skating or painting. You don't get good overnight.

It takes a long time. It takes a lot of rejection. And I try to teach them that they should thrive on rejection.

Arnold: One last question. How do you write? I mean, are you disciplined? Are you lazy and sporadic? Are you—do you sit down in the morning? How do you write?

Gautreaux: I write a lot late at night. And basically, my method is rewriting. I'll come out with a first draft and, of course, I'll go over it and then cut it. Everything that's extraneous goes.

And then I'll go over it, sentence by sentence, looking for structure of each individual sentence. Then I'll put it aside and go over it, looking at all the tropes—the metaphors, the similes, everything in the way of figurative language—to make sure everything is right there.

And then, of course, I send it—I give it to my wife. And she reads it and tells me what she thinks of it. And several people see it.

And then I set it aside and let it age like a cheese or something and then a month later look at it. And what I thought was ready to send off to my agent still has a lot of problems. And I'll go over it again.

And that's kind of, really, a brief version of what I do to a story. I make—I mean, I make specialized passes. I—and it—the myopia of it helps me really make a story take on a certain type of polish.

That's one thing—students think they can very often turn out an excellent story on one pass, but that's not the case with me, anyway.

Arnold: Tim Gautreaux, thanks so much for talking with us.
Gautreaux: You're very welcome.

Arnold: Tim Gautreaux is a writer who lives in Hammond, Louisiana. His stories appear in numerous literary collections, including this year's *Best American Short Stories.*

He joined us from WEZB in New Orleans.

Novel Approach: Tim Gautreaux Takes "The Next Step"

Christina Masciere/1998

From *New Orleans Magazine* 32.6 (March 1998). © MC Media. Reprinted courtesy of *New Orleans Magazine*.

Hot off the success of his *Same Place, Same Things* collection of short stories, Morgan City native Tim Gautreaux debuts his first novel this month. *The Next Step in the Dance* (Picador) explores the rich and timeless Cajun culture of South Louisiana in a seriocomic tale that explores marriage, family, and sense of place.

A recent Southern Writer-in-Residence at Ole Miss, Gautreaux has won a National Endowment for the Arts fellowship and the National Magazine Award. His lyrical short stories have appeared in magazines including *Atlantic Monthly, Harper's,* and *GQ* as well as in the recent anthologies *New Stories from the South* (Algonquin) and *A Few Thousand Words about Love* (St. Martin's Press).

Gautreaux, a professor of English at Southeastern Louisiana University for twenty-six years, recently took time out to talk about his writing. Look for him at this month's Tennessee Williams Festival, where he'll teach a master class and speak on two panels.

Masciere*:* Besides length, what's different about writing a novel?
Gautreaux: The short story is something you have to work over in a microcosmic way. You can't really make a bad sentence in a short story. Everything has to be right. With a novel, of course, you've got to get it as right as you can, but a publisher will be more understanding if there is a bad page or something that is not quite logical or is underdeveloped. If he sees that you've created characters that a reader will be sorry to have finished read-

17

ing about at the end of the book, he will work with you on all of the other problems.

Masciere: There are many religious motifs in your work, and you've said that you switched from poetry to stories after taking a seminar with Walker Percy. Do you consider yourself a Catholic writer, like Percy?

Gautreaux: Yes, I would say so. First, it's impossible to write about South Louisiana culture without writing about the Catholic Church, because it permeates everything—from wedding ceremonies to industrial fishing to the sugarcane industry to the way people think about eating on Friday. A lot of my stories have priests in them, or references to going to Mass or confession, and that's because of what I'm writing about.

[Themes of moral dilemmas and redemption] come out more or less subconsciously. Each of us has a type of ingrained, almost instinctual interest in a theme, whether it's pollution or child abuse or alienation or depression. No matter what story you write, no matter what plot you choose, that theme is going to be in there. It's almost inevitable that a writer can't escape the themes that are in his soul.

Masciere: What about the recurring motif of machinery? I see it as a parallel to Catholicism—the possibility of fixing things.

Gautreaux: I collect antique machinery, so I relate to that. Part of it is genetic: My father was a tugboat captain, and my grandfather was a steamboat chief engineer. My great-uncle was a master mechanic. Machinery has a particular metaphorical function, and sometimes I'm working with it a little bit obviously, but most of the time it's subconscious. My wife says I write fiction as an excuse to write about machinery.

Masciere: Many of your characters are pathetic but funny at the same time.

Gautreaux: This is what a writer is always looking for, that situation that blends humor and pathos evenly. And you've got to hit it just right, because if you miss it, it's hokey or sentimental—both of which are just awful things to do to a reader. That's what Flannery O'Connor does so well. She has these characters that you laugh at, but that you can feel sorry for at the same time, or at least you're amazed at what a terrible experience they're going through while you're laughing at them.

Masciere: Do you consider yourself a Southern writer?

Gautreaux: I don't know if the term has much meaning. The more I think about it, the less I understand it. After *The Shipping News*, would you call Annie Proulx a Newfoundland writer? Would you call Sherwood Anderson a Midwestern writer? Ultimately, I consider the term "Southern writer" to be pretty empty. I'm just a writer that lives in the South.

The only real tradition in which I'm operating would be that of the frontier humorists. When I was a kid, what I read most of all was things like folktales—stories in which men sat around and told obvious lies. I grew up listening to a lot of old men tell stories to each other about their jobs.

Now, you're going to get into this question of well, aren't we greater storytellers in the South? I don't know. I bet if you walk into steelworkers' bars in the Northeast, you're going to find people who are telling stories. It's not only a Southern tradition or a Western tradition.

Masciere: Dialogue in your books rings so true. How do you approach it?

Gautreaux: There is still a rich creative metaphorical magic alive, and it's in the mouths of uneducated people. Educated people tend to speak a standard English which is not creative and which is not conducive to storytelling or bull-shitting or any verbal color at all. We go to a university, we get a degree, we get educated, we get a standard vocabulary and idiom, and then we use it like insurance salesmen. People who are uneducated basically have to make up an idiom as they go along. These are the people I like to listen to, because they're very acrobatic with the way they use the language.

Until I went to college I had a Cajun accent, and not much in the way of vocabulary. But I liked to talk, I liked to tell stories, because I was raised listening to people tell colorful stories. I liked to make up stuff and lie. That's where I got my verbal skills.

Masciere: After attending Nicholls State, you studied under James Dickey at the University of South Carolina. Was graduate school the only time you've lived outside of South Louisiana?

Gautreaux: Yes, I guess a lot of states are fairly homogenous as far as language is concerned and manners, things like that. I take care with "homogenous" because every place has its little nuances. But in Louisiana, you have such a strange hodgepodge. Maybe one thing that makes the South different from other parts of the country is that there's such a mixture of values, levels of society, understandings.

Masciere: How does teaching affect you and your writing?

Gautreaux: It's a two-edged sword. One, teaching keeps you reading contemporary fiction, because you have to teach it. But it takes a lot of your time to teach a twelve-hour load. It keeps you from writing as much as you could. But then there are a lot of things that keep you from writing as much as you could, things that are just as important. I raised two boys and taught twelve hours and pursued a lot of hobbies.

One of the most important reasons I write is the feeling that I *can* write. People tell me that I do it well, and I actually believe it would be evil for me to not do what I can do well. Whatever you can do well is a gift, and if you don't exercise it, then you're doing something wrong. That's one of the main reasons I write.

Masciere: What writers do you enjoy reading?

Gautreaux: I like Annie Proulx. I like Cormac McCarthy's later books. He's the last guy in America who can handle grandiose dialogue. His earlier novels are very, very dark, not really what you'd call commercial fiction.

You've got to ask yourself, what do you want to do? When your publishers tell you that they need likeable characters in a novel, and you put likeable characters in there, are you really perverting your art? Whenever a publisher puts a hurdle in front of me and says that my writing is too dark, that I have to change it, I try not to make a directive like that from a publisher or agent something to surrender to. I just consider it a hurdle that I have to use my art to get over.

I have to do what I want to do, but I have to keep the public in mind. People don't want to be bombarded constantly with depressing things. I mean, there's a lot of depressing stuff in my fiction, but personally I don't believe that you have to constantly remind people that life sucks, then you die, because everybody knows that. This idea that some, particularly young, writers have that life is just some dark journey and then you die is a myopic way of looking at things.

Masciere: How do you define yourself?

Gautreaux: I write, but I don't look at myself as a writer. I've heard people introduce themselves as writers. That's the last thing I would ever say. I would rather say, "I'm Tim Gautreaux, and I'm a collector of antique steam machinery" or something. Or, "I'm an English teacher." I think it's almost important not to think of yourself in that one dimension. I do lots of things; writing is one of them. Ambition has never been my long suit, and that's one thing that marks me as a Louisiana native. It's nice that the appreciation of what I do as a writer happens. Yet if nobody ever published any of my stuff, I would still write.

Masciere: How did the success of *Same Place, Same Things* affect you?

Gautreaux: It made me work harder on the novel manuscript for *The Next Step in the Dance.* St. Martin's bought it with no qualms. This, of course, got the administration of my college thinking, "Hm, this guy's published nationally, maybe we ought to give him more time off to write." And so they gave me an official title of writer-in-residence and cut my workload in half, to six hours a semester.

Masciere: What are you working on now?

Gautreaux: I have another novel in mind that's set in Morgan City, Louisiana, in the 1920s, and it deals with the lumber industry down there. So I'm doing historical research on that. I've got a contract for a book of short stories. And I haven't signed it yet, but I've got a contract coming for a cowboy movie of some type—I'm writing a script.

Masciere: What advice do you give to your creative-writing students?

Gautreaux: A writer has a duty to get in touch with his culture, whatever that culture is. My students will say, well, I was basically a mall rat; what can I write about? I say, that's your culture. If you choose to be interested in the culture that God has given you, it's just as exotic as living in Istanbul. Everything is exotic—that's my view about life. It's not what you write about; it's how you write it. I gave that speech one time, and this kid wrote a story about his neighborhood near the Esplanade Mall. It was dead-on. It was Flannery O'Connor gone to Kenner. And when I can do that, I know I've taught him something.

The Writer Next Door

Susan Larson/1998

From the *Times-Picayune* (15 March 1998). © 2011 The Times-Picayune. All rights reserved. Reprinted with permission.

When Hammond writer Tim Gautreaux set out to write a novel following his critically acclaimed, Louisiana-set story collection, *Same Place, Same Things,* he knew what his subject would be—the oil bust of the '80s. "It was a tremendously interesting time. So many people had to pull up stakes and move out of Louisiana. So many people suffered and stepped down several levels in their employment and in the amount of money they were making. It was really a time of great trauma for this state and certainly deserved a literary piece to memorialize it."

That newly published novel is *The Next Step in the Dance,* which chronicles the romance of Colette Jeansomme and Paul Thibodeaux, citizens of Tiger Island, Louisiana. Their marital difficulties spring out of that same period. "A lot of marriages broke up during the oil bust," Gautreaux said. "It put tremendous stresses on the population of Louisiana. I just felt it had all sorts of things going for it—a sense of culture, a sense of place, and not a place in stasis, but a place in turbulent movement. It's nice to have reality on your side."

A sense of the reality of Louisiana—the place and its people—is one of the distinguishing characteristics of Gautreaux's fine fiction. He grew up in Morgan City, the son of a tugboat captain and the grandson of a steamboat engineer. After graduating from Nicholls State University and getting his doctorate from the University of South Carolina, he came home, and he's been teaching at Southeastern Louisiana University for twenty-six years. So when it comes to Louisiana, he knows whereof he speaks.

"Tiger Island is really a composite of three or four little towns—Morgan City (the first name for Morgan City back in the 1840s was Tiger Island),

22

Donaldsonville, Houma, and Thibodeaux—those are the towns I have some experience with," he said. "What I like about these places is that everyone knew everyone else, everyone was Catholic, I like the fact that everyone eats the same things. They share a common heritage so they make all sorts of assumptions about each other.

"It's nice to be known, although young people tend not to want that. They want to get away to meet people that they don't know. But when you get older you see that it's nice to be known . . . I can remember getting a haircut on Front Street in Morgan City when I was about forty. It was a rundown place and the barber was on his last legs, and as he started cutting my hair, he said, 'Aren't you a Gautreaux? I remember when your uncle drowned in the river trying to swim across and everyone was so upset.' Now this conversation took place maybe around 1985 and my uncle had drowned in the mid-20s and he was talking about it as though it had happened last year."

Gautreaux lives outside Hammond in an Acadian home in the woods. If you've read his work, you recognize signs of his passion for machinery—the tractors in the back, the locomotive on the mailbox and the railroad sign on the workshop. His collection of railroad lanterns and steamboat whistles, polished to perfection, adorns the mantel in his living room and the desk and bookshelves in his office, along with his collection of books about antique machinery, ranging from *The Locomotive Catechism* to *The Piston Engine* to a hardware catalog from 1918. This is a man who likes to know how things work. "I was born in 1947 and I remember steam locomotives charging through town. Southern Pacific used them up until 1955," he said.

But he doesn't dream of going away. Gautreaux's found everything he needs to write about right in his own back yard. "Louisiana's not going to stop being a good place to write about. It's going to be hard to exhaust this state because it's so rich. It comes out of its diversity of cultures and values and all these things are going to be changing." He laughs. "I saw a sign in a butcher shop the other day for 'diet hogshead cheese,' made with turkey instead of pork. So things are constantly changing."

The Catholic aspects of this culture also appeal to him. "I'm not a philosopher like Walker Percy," Gautreaux insists. (He took a novel writing class Percy taught at Loyola in 1977.) "I'm just a Catholic from the bayou. But it's one of the rhythms of life."

His mother, who is ninety years old and lives in Morgan City, has read her son's newest work. "It was a little racy for her," Gautreaux said. "She told me, 'Well, I read your book and now I feel like I have to go to confession.'"

Gautreaux will have another short story collection coming out next year, and right now he's hard at work on a script for a cowboy movie for his nephews, film directors Josh and Jay Pate, set in Texas in 1875. And he's working on another novel set in Louisiana in the '20s, based on stories of the lumbering industry back in the swamp.

Gautreaux writes every day, but he's easily seduced away from his word processor or legal pad. "I can be spirited away by the need to go polish a steam whistle or build a cabinet or rake the lawn."

And what about dancing? His main character, Paul Thibodeaux, is an expert dancer, there's a Beau Jocque disk on the open CD player in the kitchen, and some of the best passages in the book take place in Cajun dance halls. "Well," said Gautreaux, with his characteristic dry understatement, "I dance."

An Interview with Tim Gautreaux

Christopher Joyal/1998

From *New Delta Review* 16.1 (1998), 87-97. © *New Delta Review.* Reprinted courtesy of *New Delta Review.*

Tim Gautreaux was born and raised in Morgan City, Louisiana, a blue-collar, Gulf Coast city tied to Acadian culture. He lives in Hammond, Louisiana, with his wife, Winborne, where he is Writer in Residence at Southeastern Louisiana University. Gautreaux stories have appeared in *Harper's*, the *Atlantic Monthly*, *GQ*, and *Story*, winning a National Magazine Award for fiction and an NEA Creative Fellowship. He also has had stories appear in *New Stories from the South* and *Best American Short Stories*. Gautreaux's first book, a collection of stories titled *Same Place, Same Things*, chronicles the lives of blue collar workers placed in sometimes extraordinary and often humorous situations. Once put to the test, his characters frequently display a basic humanity and decency sometimes derided in more cosmopolitan fiction.

Gautreaux's new novel, *The Next Step in the Dance*, published in 1998, is about a machinist named Paul, who wants nothing more than a pleasant and comfortable life in Louisiana. His wife, Colette, however, leaves him and travels to California, hoping to find a life and a lover with more ambition. With a rare combination of mechanical precision and a sympathetic understanding of south Louisiana people and culture, Gautreaux explores the difficulties of marriage and true commitment, the conflict between big city ideals and small town morals, and the difference between men and women in an almost mythological setting—a land of snakes, alligators, epic bar room brawls, and rifle contests—the setting Tim Gautreaux calls home.

CJ: The female protagonist in your novel, *The Next Step in the Dance*, Colette, says that she wants to leave Louisiana because it's a foreign country.

Another character in a story from *Same Place, Same Things* has a mother who leaves for a similar reason. Do you think of south Louisiana as a foreign country relative to the rest of the United States?

TG: People realize that this place is kind of different. Not too many states allow drive-thru daiquiri windows or sell hard liquor at filling stations.

CJ: Your books show a fascination with machines. The main character in your novel, Paul, for example, repairs old machinery.

TG: I come from a blue-collar family, and everybody was always talking about machines when I was a kid because my family was made up of tug-boat captains, oil rig workers, and railroad workers. They'd talk about their trades.

CJ: We often talk about how television and movies homogenize culture, but in literature departments there is a large interest in literature specifically about ethnicity and gender. Do you think that regional writers represent a reaction against homogeneity?

TG: I try not to think about that too much. I just accept what I write as an unavoidable part of who I am. I write about Acadian culture or blue-collar families here in the South because it's where I'm from. It's just a fact that I was raised in a rough oil-patch town on the gulf, Morgan City. We had thirty-two bars and eighteen churches. That's my territory as a writer.

CJ: I wanted to ask you about religion in your work.

TG: Religion was also very much a part of my culture. I went to Catholic school, and I'm still Catholic. I was educated by Marianite nuns in the 1950s. Religion was part of the fabric of small Louisiana towns. We did things in terms of the liturgical calendar sometimes. Even government events would be scheduled that way. When I was at college, at Nicholls State, in those days they would cancel *class* on holy days of obligation so the Catholic students wouldn't miss mass. And if you went into a restaurant in Morgan City in the 1950s and ordered a meat dish on Fridays, the waitress would ask if you knew it was Friday. In those days, you didn't eat meat on Friday.

CJ: Coming from a blue-collar family, what did your folks think about you becoming a writer?

TG: They were very supportive. Of course I never told anybody I was going to be a writer, because I didn't know that. I was just a student or an English major. I was going to teach somewhere.

CJ: So you didn't feel any of the pressure that Colette feels to leave Louisiana for lofty goals.

TG: No. There wasn't any pressure like that. My father gave me the option of traveling with him on the tugboat up the Mississippi, but he never pressured me to do one thing or the other.

CJ: When you visited one of those thirty-two bars, did you ever get in any of those fights like you describe in *The Next Step*?

TG: No, but I used to see a lot of those fights. You started going to bar rooms very early in the 50s, when you were sixteen or seventeen. In fact, it's probably like that today. You used to see a lot more fist fighting in those days. Nowadays, you have to worry. In those days it was sort of a benevolent adventure among high school kids. Today, if you have one of those big brawls, it's frightening. Someone could pull out a firearm.

CJ: It's not just a game.

TG: Right. Years ago, a few friends would go out on a Saturday night looking for boys from another town to get into a fight with, and if they couldn't find someone to fight with, they'd fight each other.

CJ: One of the reviewer's of your first book described your characters as "mired in life." Are your characters mired in life?

TG: No. (Laughs.) If you have that attitude, I guess everybody is sort of trapped by life, mired in life, whether you like it or not.

CJ: But the world beats up on your characters pretty hard. I guess I was asking about the pride your characters feel toward where they're from.

TG: The world beats up on everybody. It just beats up on blue-collar folks in different ways. Not a lot of people write about that.

CJ: What role does humor play for you as a writer?

TG: Humor has to be in everything I write, and I believe, since Flannery O'Connor, that most writers understand humor is a tool that a writer just about has to use. I'm not sure quite why that is—I don't know whether it's the ironic or sardonic stance that writers take—but if you scan the stories that appear in the major journals—*Atlantic*, the *New Yorker*, etc.—every one of them has humor in it. Even if it's about a person dying from cancer. Look at that John DuFresne novel, *Love Warps the Mind a Little*. It's a very funny book, but it's about a person dying of cancer. There's humor in everything.

CJ: In *Next Step*, Colette wants to leave Louisiana, and Paul is happy where he is. To an outsider Paul would be the guy "mired in life"—not well-educated, unambitious. He ends up getting what he wants—he even has the chance to work for Disney in California. What attracts you to Paul as a character?

TG: The fact that he isn't ambitious. He takes what he can get from life, but he is not unhappy with what he does not have. That's typical of a lot of Acadians. They're satisfied with what they have, and they don't make themselves unhappy about what they don't have.

CJ: So in a real sense, Colette's need for a big Mercedes goes head to head with small-town values in Los Angeles?

TG: Well, I would never own a Mercedes because I can't understand why it's one ounce better than a Ford Crown Victoria, for example. My blue-collar mindset. I can't see throwing away an extra thirty-thousand dollars like that.

CJ: As someone with those values, was it difficult to write from Colette's point of view?

TG: The challenge was that I had to revise Colette's character and make her continually softer because she was originally a very hard character and not very likable, thus not very marketable to the reading public. Readers like to identify with a character. I had to make the reader understand Colette and sympathize with her. The Colette in the first revision of the novel was a holy terror. I still think that she is in this novel, so you can imagine what she was like before. But when I was growing up, it was understood that girls were mean. At recess, if a girl liked you she threw rocks at you. You just dealt with it and tried to understand it.

CJ: Do you plot your novels ahead of time or write it as it comes?

TG: You have to plot them out. You can't risk being lost in a novel manuscript and writing thirty-thousand words and having to throw it all away because it's irrelevant. What novelists do, I guess, is turn out about seven thousand words, figure out where it could be going, and come up with an outline.

CJ: My favorite story in *Same Place, Same Things* is "Died and Gone to Vegas," about a group of card players trying to outdo each other both in a card game called *bourre*, and the yarns they tell while playing it. What is *bourre*?

TG: Bourre is *the* game among south Louisiana people. It's like hearts, but it's only played with five cards, and there are five tricks to be taken. Whoever gets three tricks wins the pot. If you don't take any tricks, you are *"bourre-ed"* and you have to match the pot or pay a pre-agreed sum.

CJ: What does it mean in French?

TG: I think the old word in French means a very fast dance, and I think it has something to do with the way people play. People who have played with each other a long time just fling the cards constantly. Everybody gets their hand and then draws, and then the cards just fly, like a dance. I grew up playing it.

CJ: So you'd have no problem cleaning me out?

TG: No.

CJ: If Louisiana seems like a foreign country, do you use that as a joke on outsiders—you know, mythical battles with alligators and water moccasins and so forth? When does setting become myth for you?

TG: Well all of that is based on things I've seen in the culture, and it is hard to tell when a writer is engaging in tall-tale sport or whether he's actually replicating things that he's seen—how much is exaggeration and how much is true. As long as the reader wonders, you're winning the game. If the reader says, "No, that's impossible!", then you've lost the game. Walker Percy said that all southern writers are in the business of "amazing Yankees," and so that's always in the back of your head when you're writing something with strong regional flavor. It's a good warning too, because you don't want to be writing hokum. You don't want the writing just to be regionalism or local color, but I've never been accused of that so far.

CJ: A writer's habits and the conditions of his workplace have always interested me. How do you work?

TG: One thing that I've done recently is to move my office into a small and plain area so that there is nothing to look at. I'm easily distracted, and I think a lot of people are. The office I did have was full of books and collector's items. I was constantly wandering away from the computer screen and looking at something else: an old railroad steam whistle or a lantern. My wife told me, "You have too much junk in this room. You've got to do something." So I confiscated her little closet of an office and gave her my office. It's a lot more productive. Fewer distractions, fewer windows.

CJ: So now she gets to stare at all of your lanterns and whistles?
TG: No, she doesn't do that at all. She's very focused.

CJ: You teach writing at Southeastern. What do you think M.F.A. programs have done for modern writing? Are they good for writing, or do they kill original voices with too much craft?
TG: I don't see any detrimental effect from the M.F.A. programs at all. I hear people talk, snatches of conversation among academics about "the work-shop poem," and "the workshop story," but I have absolutely no idea what that is. The point of taking a creative writing workshop is to better your craft, to tell a better story. I don't see how studying the genre is going to be detrimental to your writing. The best short story writer we've had, as far as technique is concerned, is Flannery O'Connor, and she was an M.F.A. gal. She went through the program at Iowa.

CJ: You mentioned O'Connor and Percy already. What other writers are your touchstones?
TG: Cormac McCarthy. Especially *All the Pretty Horses.* His early stuff is too hairy for me, but the Border Trilogy is exceptional. *The Shipping News* by Annie Proulx, which I liked for the story and the author's love of place. Those are the ones which are very exciting to me. Stories that excite me are things like Tobias Wolff's "In the Garden of the North American Martyrs," which is a wonderful story. I still like Joy Williams's story "Taking Care." Those are stories I still reread when I really forget how language can be special. I never read Faulkner.

CJ: I find you end up writing like him when you read too much of him.
TG: People say that. I guess that it's possible. I have a tendency to write dark things, and what keeps me from doing that is one, my wife, and two, nobody will ever publish anything dark that I write.

CJ: Why?
TG: Particularly the big magazines don't like dark stories. That's under-standable.

CJ: But a lot of times young writers like that tragedy and dark material. Do you think that's one of the reasons young writers have such a hard time? We have to learn what life's about before we can move on and get over it?
TG: Yeah, I think that's true. A lot of young writers in their twenties and

thirties write about subjects that are extremely dark and the message be-hind this writing is that life really sucks, and it's scary. Of course the older reader in his forties and fifties finds such fiction very tedious because his response is, "What was your first clue?" You live about fifty years, and then your health declines, and then you die. (He laughs.) What's your first clue? Dark writing for readers in their fifties and sixties often seems excruciat-ingly naive. Conrad's been there and done that.

CJ: But when we think about the "great American novel," a large number of them are tragedies. Faulkner's best work, for example, *Gatsby* . . . when we think about short stories, is that the case? Is the novel better suited for tragedy?

TG: Nobody can write grandiose, dark poetical prose like Faulkner any-more, except maybe Cormac McCarthy. He is our last writer developing dark themes on the grand scale. If an author wants to make a serious explo-ration of some important dark theme, the novel is the place for it.

CJ: So then what makes a good short story? Why do people read them?

TG: Gee, that's a hard one. That's like asking me what makes a good Pres-byterian.

When we were talking about stories that are important to me, I almost forgot James Allen McPherson's "Solo Song for Doc." That's an outstanding story. It's about an old black waiter who works in the dining car of a train. I remember riding trains thirty, forty years ago. The dining car was something else, and the service was excellent. The waiters knew they were giving great service—Amtrak ruined all that. But this story is about a railroad inspector who tries to make Doc perform very difficult tasks. He's trying to get Doc fired. The reader knows it, and Doc knows it too.

By the time the confrontation takes place, we have so much emotional in-vestment in Doc that it's like Beowulf and Grendel duking it out. I mean, the battle feels epic, but it's only about a simple waiter and a railroad inspector. That story made me realize that I could write compellingly about blue-collar subjects. An uneducated, poor person still has a significant life.

CJ: How long ago was that?

TG: Fifteen years or so.

CJ: You started publishing soon after that, right?

TG: Yes.

CJ: So what else do you look for in your short stories?

TG: People don't like to be bored. Listeners don't like to be bored. When I'm writing a story, I pretend I'll be reading it to a rather fidgety audience that doesn't particularly want to be in the hall listening to me. So what happens is that in a manuscript every sentence becomes about capturing and holding attention. There's nothing worse than the feeling of being ignored or people falling asleep in front of you while you're reading or speaking to them.

CJ: Creative humility?

TG: Why on earth would anyone want to come into a room to listen to you talk? You have to reward them with something that is uplifting or amazing or entertaining, something.

CJ: I'm from New Hampshire, so maybe you've tried to fool me as a Yankee, but not many literary scholars and writers know much about machinery. Is that a foreign country along with Louisiana? Is there any sort of connection for you between the repair of machines and the repair of a culture beat up badly by modern times?

TG: Sometimes machinery functions as a metaphor in my stories, and I'm aware of that during revision. Then I forget about it once a story is published. So when people ask me if machines in the story, "Same Place, Same Things," are a metaphor for something, my response is generally, "I forgot." That's the kind of stuff I let critics handle as they analyze the story. But machinery, big machinery is a fascination of mine. My wife says that the only reason I write fiction is that it gives me the chance to describe big machines. I tie machines to people.

I grew up with folks who talked about machines as if they had personalities. If my father's tugboat engine wouldn't operate, he couldn't go anywhere. He was always talking about its idiosyncracies. Also, when men can't understand people, they relate to things they can understand, like mechanical devices. Maybe that's one of the reasons some men are so mechanical; other parts of life mystify them so much.

CJ: And that's one of the central conflicts between Colette and Paul.

TG: Paul does not understand his wife, but he understands the machine shop and the milling machines, the lathes and diesel engines.

CJ: I'm interested in how you conceive your stories. What comes first: the character or the story? Your characters seem to take over the story.

TG: Everything for me is propelled by narrative. As far as the genesis of a story is concerned, there is no one way a story starts. "Deputy Sid's Gift" started with that phrase. I was sitting around thinking one day, maybe in the shower, and that phrase, "deputy Sid's gift," came into my head. I liked the assonance of it. I wrote a piece of the story and decided I didn't like it, so I started again. The final story about Sid's kindness came solely out of that title. Now another story "Waiting for the Evening News," grew out of me reading the newspaper one morning. There was a train derailment in Louisiana, and then there was a passenger derailment in Mexico where the engineer ran away. Exxon *Valdez* was going on at the time. So I put the events together, and it all coalesced into this business of the ordinary man involved in an accident who runs off, instead of staying around and fessing up so his troubles would be over in a few days.

CJ: Again, a character who was beaten up by fate. I mean the train should have stayed on the tracks. Something simply went wrong, and he finds himself a villain on national television.
TG: It's all a big accident of fate because he had no control over what caused the accident.

CJ: But he accepts that.
TG: He can't deny the fact of his notoriety. I mean, he has literally been transmogrified by the media, and now he has to deal with it.

CJ: Do you consider yourself a moral writer?
TG: I am a moral writer. I don't remember who said this, either O'Connor or Percy, but one of them said that if a story doesn't in some way involve a question of morals or ethics, it wasn't much of a story. I kind of follow that idea.

CJ: In the first draft of *Next Step in the Dance*, was Colette still a nutria-hunting, sharpshooting dynamo?
TG: She was not as believable in the first draft. When I recrafted her in later drafts, I put in details that made her ability to navigate the swamps more believable, so she wasn't just some spoiled bank teller who started shooting rats well. If you read the novel you see little things that foreshadow her success.

CJ: Like shooting rifles when she was younger.
TG: Yes, with her uncle. Details like that are added in revision. In high school she cut up chickens in a grocery, so she knows how an animal comes apart.

CJ: Do you write every day?
TG: I try to.

CJ: Do you set goals for yourself, a certain number of pages or a word count?
TG: When I was writing the novel I had to. When you are dealing with a really big manuscript you have to put yourself on a daily schedule, otherwise you forget what you are doing. You lose contact with your characters. With a short story, it's helpful to put it aside for a week and return to it with fresh eyes. That doesn't work with a novel manuscript, but it works with short stories.

CJ: Are you a fanatic editor?
TG: Yeah, very much so. I just comb the stories and cull the stories constantly. When a photograph develops on your computer, you see a bar code pass down over the screen, and every time that line passes, the image gets sharper. Revision is like that for me. The more I work, the sharper the story becomes.

CJ: It's the same way with machines?
TG: I like to take machines apart and put them back together. It's almost ridiculous. If I have a lawn mower that doesn't work, I'll take it completely apart and put it back together. If it still doesn't work, I'll keep at it. Even if I quit for a few days, it will bug me that it isn't running. Eventually, I'll get it to work. I gladly put a thousand dollars worth of labor into a five-hundred-dollar tractor. Eventually a story I keep revising will sell. It's all the same thing, isn't it?

Interview with Tim Gautreaux

Jennifer Levasseur and Kevin Rabalais/1998

From the *Mississippi Review* 27.3 (1999), 19-40. © Jennifer Levasseur and Kevin Rabalais. Reprinted courtesy of Jennifer Levasseur and Kevin Rabalais.

Tim Gautreaux, author of a collection of stories, *Same Place, Same Things*, and a novel, *The Next Step in the Dance*, was born in Morgan City, Louisiana. He studied English at Nicholls State University in Thibodaux, Louisiana, and received his Ph.D. from the University of South Carolina, where he studied under George Garrett and James Dickey. Gautreaux is writer-in-residence at Southeastern Louisiana University. His short stories have appeared in the *Atlantic Monthly*, *GQ*, *Harper's*, *Story*, *The Best American Short Stories 1997* and *1998*, and *New Stories from the South*. He is the recipient of a fellowship from the National Endowment for the Arts. Jennifer Levasseur and Kevin Rabalais met with Tim Gautreaux in his home in Hammond, Louisiana, on March 20, 1998.

Interviewer: You have said you think every writer is limited to where he is from. How does this apply to your own work?

Tim Gautreaux: I think everybody owns the territory he was born into. That's what can be used best, the richest ore that can be mined. That sounds like a theory, and there are exceptions to anything anybody comes up with in the way of a theory. But that is what I teach. Get in touch with where you're from, your aunts, your uncles. I teach creative writing students that no matter where they are from, even if it's a subdivision in Kenner, Louisiana, that that is their literary heritage. That's their culture. If they look at it closely enough, they will see that it is as exotic and unique as some Central or South American cultures in the mountains. It is what they are given to work with. I really can't understand these people who say that they can write about anything and any time if they do enough research, because when they say that, they cut themselves off from the speech of those they grew up with. Speech and dialogue and cadence and dialect are very important to me. Sometimes I try to set a story in another region of the country, and it's harder for me to write those stories. Such a tale might work, but there will be a richness of language, a whole dimension, that is left out.

Interviewer: In your novel, *The Next Step in the Dance*, you take two of your characters from Louisiana to Los Angeles.

TG: But they carry their idiom with them. If I were just writing about two Los Angeles people in Los Angeles, I would have been helpless, and there would have been a whole dimension missing from their language.

Interviewer: Do you see yourself eventually departing from a Southern setting and researching other regions and setting stories elsewhere?

TG: The projects I have planned now are all Louisiana projects. I think a writer forms most of his opinions and absorbs most of his nuances in the first fifteen years of his life. Somebody with creative sensibility is someone who was born with a lot of antennae. A teacher can tell you that children are much more receptive up to seventh grade than they are after. The little seven-, eight-, and nine-year-olds'—information is just pouring into them because they are wide open to all sorts of things. I think that's why when they grow up to be writers, their youth is what they mine.

Interviewer: There are many writers today who try to achieve a Southern dialect, yet they often end up writing in clichés. With your writing, the dialect is genuine, but you obviously do not speak that way. From where did this foundation come?

TG: I did speak that way up until the time I became educated. One thing you've got to understand—I mean, you've opened up a really complicated answer here—is that uneducated people have a much richer language than educated people, and it is because they are forced to improvise. After you go through four years of college, you have standard, formal English you are supposed to speak. And those people who are raised with parents and in a neighborhood where everyone speaks standard, formal English really don't understand the richness of nonstandard speech. One thing about growing up in Louisiana (where pretty much everybody around me was poor) is that I was exposed to many different levels of language. Next door to me when I was growing up was a Cuban family. On the other side were black children that I played with. I'm talking about when I was three, four, and five years old. Living behind me were some hillbillies. Across the street were old Creole black ladies who talked with a French accent. My father worked for a tugboat company in Texas and picked up a Texas accent. What happened is I got all these influences in my speech. When you listen to people from Morgan City, you can hear a combination of Texas, lots of a New Orleans–type accent, and a little bit of Cajun pronunciation. As a result, when I was a kid, I was good at mimicking people, changing my voice to various types of accents. It's helpful to me as a reader today when I'm reading characters from several different socioeconomic backgrounds in a story.

Interviewer: So this exposure you had at a young age to different speech patterns and dialects is still something you draw on?
TG: Very much so. And I still pick them up. I've discovered that the east St. Tammany Parish dialect is different from the west St. Tammany dialect, and the north Tangipahoa Parish dialect is different from the south Tangipahoa dialect. Sometimes dialects vary just across the street. Of course, you have to figure out how to contextualize it to make a reader appreciate that there is a difference between the way these characters speak. That is challenging, but it can be done. When I first moved to Hammond, I heard an expression in a grocery store when an old woman walked in and said, "How them tomatoes?" The woman behind the counter said, "Oh, they eat real good." I had never heard that before, and I perked up my ears. There's some really primitive dialect around here.

Interviewer: There is a definite difference between the older and younger generations in your work, especially in the novel, in the way they speak and relate to each other.
TG: There is a kind of linguistic evolution in bayou country. People over sixty years old from that region tend to speak with a Cajun accent and use word order left over from French grammar. They often use that reflexive, "I wouldn't do that, me." The younger people are not going to use such accents and patterns as much, except for maybe little echoic devices that they copy from the old people. This is another generation raised listening to television.

Interviewer: Have you done much research on linguistics?
TG: No. It's all from observation. You would be a fool to be a writer living in Louisiana, raised in Louisiana, and not notice the language. Reading Ernest Gaines made me more sensitive to idiom, and also race.

Interviewer: You have previously mentioned the "Frontier" tradition of literature. Why do you feel your writing is more closely related to it than to the notion of "Southern" writing?

TG: I don't like to think of myself as a Southern writer. I'm just a writer who lives in the South. When I was a kid, one of my favorite books was B. A. Botkin's *A Treasury of Mississippi River Folklore*, and, of course, that book had a lot of the Mike Fink yarns in it. Mike Fink was a keel boatman on the Mississippi River before the days of machinery. He was a raftsman. And I read the old Davy Crockett yarns. What those had in common was a kind of energetic hyperbole characteristic of much of America's early campfire storytelling tradition. Mike Fink used to say that he was so fearsome that he could grin the bark off a tree at twenty paces. That type of hyperbole is wonderful, but it's also hard to do. In my story "Died and Gone to Vegas," it's that exaggerated, spontaneous inter-narration of tales that imitates the campfire tradition of two hundred years ago.

Interviewer: That story has been referred to as a Cajun *Canterbury Tales*.

TG: It is, and it emerged mostly subconsciously after I finished the first draft. I said, you know, these people all want to go on some kind of a pilgrimage. It's not Canterbury; it is the secular shrine of Las Vegas. And, of course, that comes from this culture because every old lady in Louisiana wants to go to Las Vegas. If they had a vote on whether or not they should go to Las Vegas or Rome, even if they were Catholic, they'd say, "Well, there are no slot machines in Rome. Why would I want to go there?"

Interviewer: How far back in your memory does storytelling go in your family?

TG: Before television and air-conditioning, and before people were mobile, family members would gather more often. The uncles and aunts would come over. Families were closer in the old days because once a family would generate in a community, it tended to stay in that community. We're talking about the forties and the fifties. There would be lots of talk because there was no television in the house. People would gather together on the front porch because the house was too hot to stay inside until four-thirty or five o'clock in the afternoon. My uncle had a large camp south of New Orleans in Hopedale, and the family would go down there about every weekend— the aunts and the uncles, my mother and father. There were these taverns in Hopedale, and in those days when the parents went to the taverns, they brought the kids with them. The men would drink beer, and the women would gossip. There was always some dancing because there was a jukebox, and the kids would just do whatever kids did—buy firecrackers and mooch money for the slot machines or to buy a Coke. When the kids ran out of things to do, they went over to sit with the adults, who were always telling stories. The men would almost always tell the stories, although the women would sometimes tell them, too, but the women liked to tell elaborate stories about their operations. An operation story could last twenty minutes. The men would tell stories about work. The group I was always around was composed of very old men. To me, they were ancient, but they were in their sixties and seventies. They were retired riverboat men, tugboat pilots, or railroad men. My father was a tugboat captain. They would tell fascinating stories about what they used to do with their trains and their boats. There was a type of structure to the way they would tell their tales. The stories were spontaneous. One man would begin, "Yeah, one time I jumped off the back fantail of the *Johnny Brown* when she got her hawser wrapped around a propeller, and I had to chop it out with a hatchet underwater." He'd tell that story, and the other old guy would say, "Well, that ain't nothing. I was on the Third District Ferry the time the *Sipsey* came between the hulls and cut the pilothouse in half with a smoke stack." Another one would say, "Wait a minute. That tugboat wasn't named *Sipsey*." They would start arguing. There would be this fantastic interweaving of stories because one man would make up facts, and the others would catch him, and their "facts" would throw the story off on a tangent. It was great. These sessions taught me about the spontaneity, the organic structure, and the emotion that is involved in storytelling. Today, I see the short story not primarily as an intellectual endeavor, but as a cultural artifact tightly bound with a necessary narrative structure.

Interviewer: The stories in *Same Place, Same Things* relate to Southern culture in setting and characterization. Did you develop such a tight grasp of the culture from growing up around so much storytelling?

TG: That's a little deceptive because it makes somebody feel that all he has to do is absorb a little bit of culture and he can be a writer. I always liked to write things, and I liked to read things out loud. I was a good reader when I was very young. I liked to tell stories, too. Somebody bought me a little typewriter, a portable typewriter for Christmas, and in the mid-fifties I got a pen pal from Canada. One of my biggest childhood pastimes was coming home and typing single-spaced, two- and three-page letters to this guy in Canada every other day. The letters would cross in the mail we were sending them so often. He would tell me about what things were like in Canada, and I would tell him about things here. After a while, I ran out of things to talk about, so I started making up stuff.

Interviewer: Was that your first experience in fiction writing?
TG: Probably so. Lying to pen pals.

Interviewer: What did you read growing up?
TG: We had the typical small-town library. In it was a series of kid books which were biographies. I read biographies of Jim Bowie, Louisa May Alcott, Thomas Jefferson, and Abraham Lincoln, but they were children's books. I would sometimes just pick a book I didn't know anything about. One time I read a John Hersey novel when I was about ten years old, and I was totally bumfuzzled by it. I would pick out a Steinbeck novel or a Hemingway novel, and I would take it home and read it. I remember reading *The Ox-Bow Incident* and *The Day They Shook the Plum Tree*, which, I think, was a book about railroad robber barons. One of my favorite books was *Great Fires at Sea*, factual accounts of hundreds of bodies burning in oceangoing vessels. I about wore that one out.

Interviewer: Is there a genre of literature you prefer?
TG: I read stuff that people bring to me and say, "Read this." When I go into a bookstore, I choose crap, and I pay twenty-five dollars for it, then I can't stand one chapter. The first two pages look good, the reviews look good, the jacket blurbs look good, and I get it home and get thirty pages into it and go, "Jeez." I seldom buy a book for myself. I'll wait for people to say, "Oh, you've got to read this." Last year somebody gave me a book of Charles Baxter's short stories, and I really enjoyed them. Same thing with *The Shipping News.*

Interviewer: You began as a poet, didn't you?
TG: When I was at Nicholls State University, I took a creative writing class, and the professor asked me to write poetry, so I did. My English professor started entering my poems into student contests, and they did pretty well. That's how I ended up in South Carolina. When I was a senior at Nicholls, I wrote a group of poems and my creative writing teacher at the time, Glenn Swetman, sent them to the Southern Literary Festival student poetry contest, and it won first prize or something like that. Glenn suggested we go up for the Southern Literary Festival meeting, which was being held in

Knoxville, Tennessee. So we drove to Knoxville in 1969, two-lane roads all the way, just about. That trip in itself deserves a novel. We got up there and the main speaker was James Dickey, and he was going through the student pamphlet, a collection of the literature that had won awards at the festival, and he read my poems. He said to Calhoun Winton, his boss, who was with him, "Hunt this boy up and offer him an assistantship." He did, and that's how I got to South Carolina to study under James Dickey.

Interviewer: What was studying under Dickey like?
TG: It was very good. Dickey was a wonderful teacher, very good with his students in class and in conferences. He was very accurate in his assessment of the students' work. Just an all-around good teacher. About as good as you can get.

Interviewer: Do you still write poetry?
TG: I haven't written any poetry since I went to a convention about fifteen years ago where there was a guy on the schedule who was going to read, and he had published, it said, twenty-five hundred poems. I had never heard of him. I leaned over to whomever I was sitting next to and said, "Have you ever heard of this guy?" He said, "No." I thought, if he could get twenty-five hundred poems published and nobody's ever heard of him, then I'm in the wrong business.

Interviewer: Many writers who turn from poetry to prose do so because they feel limited in the form of poetry. In 1977, you took a writing seminar under Walker Percy at Loyola University New Orleans. How did Percy play a role in opening the field of fiction to you?
TG: First of all, when you work under the aura of a great writer, it is always influential. You actually see somebody who is productive and successful and doing something good as a writer. You are very impressed by that. Just being around him was helpful. Percy would focus on very basic things about novel structure: you've got to get the thing off the ground; you can't go on big tangents when you are writing. Teaching creative writing is basically saying the same things over and over. The things that I say to my beginners who have never written a word of fiction are the same things I would say to God if he asked me how to write a short story. It's all the same stuff. There is no magical thing you learn in graduate school. It's all pretty basic. And that's what Percy was saying.

Interviewer: You've said that when you started writing, you wrote many failed novels and crippled short stories. Have you gone back and revised these?

TG: Yes. I have gone back and fixed busted stories because it's a hobby of mine. I believe that writing is rewriting. The only reason I would leave an older piece alone is if it would take too much time. For example, I might be able to write a completely new manuscript in the time that it would take to fix a really messed-up old one. But you know the new one is going to be better, and the old one is always going to be something patched. I might be able to make it wonderful, but I can't make it great if it's seriously flawed to begin with. It's like welding something that is broken. You can always see the seam where the weld is.

Interviewer: Do you feel daunted when you finish a novel then realize it's not working?

TG: You can't let that bother you. Rewrite it or pitch it. I think that is what hampers a lot of writers, an inability to deal with their own bad writing. A lot of us write things we don't want to cut because we feel doing so is like sawing off a little finger. But if a patch of writing is overdone or irrelevant, it needs to come off, like a finger, an eleventh finger.

Interviewer: How attached do you remain to your work after it has been published? Do you take criticism personally?

TG: I've been lucky. So far I haven't had a really bad review. I'm sure if somebody puts a pasting on something I've written it won't be fun to read, but I'll try to learn from those things. Generally, negative comments don't come out of thin air. They are based on something. It might be something small, but still something that maybe needs attention. One reviewer of *Same Place, Same Things* said there was a kind of sameness to the structure of the stories. That sent up a red flag with me. I went back and checked the stories to see if there was some validity to what he said. Naturally, there are similarities in the stories as far as setting is concerned and the social level of the characters, but I really didn't see the validity of his comment. Nevertheless, I do take it seriously and will think about it while I put this next story collection together.

Interviewer: Your upbringing and education were centered around the Catholic Church. Catholicism is integral in much of your work.

TG: In Percy, I saw a writer who was experiencing his divine gift. His novels deal with moral issues, religious issues. That was very influential on me.

Also, being raised a Roman Catholic in a region where Catholicism was a dominant religion has had a very strong influence on me. I guess that is why I don't see fiction that does not have some kind of moral concern as being very interesting. As far as my characters are concerned, if you set characters, particularly middle-aged or older characters, in south Louisiana and they are blue-collar workers, you are going to crash into Catholicism. The scheduling of activities in the region used to revolve around the Mass schedule. When I was going to Nicholls, which is a state college, and a holy day of obligation would roll around, class would be dismissed so students could go to Mass. When I was a kid and I would go into a restaurant and order a Salisbury steak on a Friday, the waitress would ask me if I was Catholic. She was reminding me that I couldn't eat meat on Friday. And that would be a Protestant waitress. You could go into the roughest, toughest, most unbelievably slimy and dangerous honky-tonk in Morgan City on Good Friday and there would be people at the bar drinking beer, but the jukebox would be unplugged. The cord would be hanging over the front because it was considered wrong to listen to music on Good Friday. That's the kind of culture I was raised in. Catholicism permeated everything.

Interviewer: You consider yourself to be a Catholic writer in the tradition of Walker Percy. Do you think you will delve into the philosophical and moral issues that Percy touched on?

TG: Right now, the religious context is tied to cultural context. Even if I were an atheist, I would probably be referring to Catholicism in my Louisiana stories, just to give an accurate portrayal of the culture. The religion would still be there because it's impossible to ignore. As far as this being something that is going to evolve, I think so, because religious questions interest me.

Interviewer: In your writing seminars, you have used an airplane as a metaphor for writing—taking the reader up through an event that changes the character's life. Usually in your stories, this event occurs in the first few sentences.

TG: The purpose of telling a story is to get people involved. Why would you not want to get a reader's attention? If you start to tell a joke, would you start with five sentences of explanation? No. You begin by saying, "A Jew and an Arab got onto a streetcar." There's an immediate conflict there. A joke is the archetype of all human entertainment. Like the joke, the basic story structure is composed of initiation of conflict and then the development of that, called rising action, which leads to either a climax or an epiphany, and last there is a falling action. That structure is not just peculiar to the short story. It is also the structure of a sitcom, a movie, a good football game, of a conversation and a fireside tale. It is a natural organic thing the human mind craves. The people that experiment with the short story often turn out things that are hard to read, and it's because they are experimenting with the wrong thing. They think, well, if I'm going to experiment with something I've got to experiment with the form, and I think that's a big mistake. They can experiment with point of view, with the time period, setting—there are so many other things they can choose to experiment with. But they choose to fool with the one thing that will trip them up and ruin the story, and that is basic narrative structure. They will do something like Washington Irving does in "Rip Van Winkle," start out with eight hundred and fifty words of description of the Hudson River Valley. I've had to beat students with a stick to read "Rip Van Winkle." They say it's boring, and they are absolutely right. That story is put together like a Yugo.

Interviewer: You have taught creative writing at Southeastern Louisiana University for many years. What other courses have you taught?
TG: I've taught modern poetry, English Romantics, technical writing.

Interviewer: What writers did you teach in the poetry courses?
TG: You try to pick out the best of the worst as far as the Romantics are concerned. I'd teach Byron. Nobody teaches Byron, but I taught him because at least he was flamboyant. *Don Juan* has a hundred or so stanzas that are funny, and I could explain what Byron was doing and who Byron was by going through that poem. I'd teach Wordsworth and Coleridge, some Blake. Everybody else is pretty loathsome from that whole period. I really liked the Romantics when I was twenty-one years old. They were accessible. There was a tradition of teaching the Romantics in the South that went back a hundred years. In high school, students had to memorize something by Wordsworth. I thought it was kind of charming and archaic to teach Romantic literature, but ultimately, I realized it's a drag. I don't know. Poetry became too intense for me, I think. I began to get tired of teaching it. I began to get surly when teaching Eliot and Yeats. After a while, I saw students struggling so hard to deal with *The Waste Land*, and I started to think, "Why am I making these people suffer so much?" It was so hard to deal with Eliot's early poems—the theme of which was, basically, life sucks—and my ultimate response was "What was your first clue?" Teaching modern poetry taught me that some intellectuals think too much and they like to strike

poses of darkness and brooding because they think that's what they are supposed to do—you know, if you're educated, you're supposed to be pessimistic. I've become very pessimistic and cynical about pessimists and cynics.
That's one reason I like blue-collar people. With all of their shortcomings
and biases and pent-up angers, most of them understand the value of being
good-natured and having a good time. You'd never catch a welder reading
The Waste Land, thank God.

Interviewer: It is when Paul and Colette leave their families to go to Los
Angeles in *The Next Step in the Dance* that they face their big moral dilemmas.
TG: It comes from being separated from a small community. If Colette's
boss hits on her in Los Angeles, they are living in the middle of ten million
people out there, and she doesn't have any relatives or friends to go to for
help. Nobody is going to care. If her boss in Tiger Island harassed her, her
cousin or her uncle would pay the guy a visit and tell him to lay off. So there
is a kind of familial protection there. When you get away from a town where
everybody knows your business, you gain privacy, but you lose a lot; you are
alone.

Interviewer: In many stories, it is when the characters move away from
home that they discover something about themselves, but in your stories
this discovery occurs when they return home.
TG: That is because sometimes you don't know how you fit into your community until you leave it.

Interviewer: You mentioned earlier that you learned about storytelling by
listening to your father and his friends sit around and tell stories. What role
did your mother play in your development as a storyteller and writer?
TG: A very rich one. The women tended to sit around and gossip and play
cards. They were very colorful in the way they expressed themselves, in their
attitudes, particularly the older women. A lot of these women had husband
who either worked at nautical trades or in the oil fields and they weren't
around for fifteen days out of the month. So most of the women were pretty self-sufficient, and you see this in my characters, particularly the older
women. They are fantastic cooks, and they use cooking as power.

Interviewer: The use of food in the stories, and especially the novel, is very
rich. In the dedication of *Same Place, Same Things*, you say you would have

thanked the National Endowment for the Arts before your wife and sons, but the NEA has never baked you biscuits. In *The Next Step in the Dance*, food is used as a symbol of love and compassion.

TG: Anybody will tell you that food is important in Louisiana culture. Again, it's like religion—an integral part of what you wind up writing about. I work in an English department with several people who have come from many other areas of North American—from California to Canada. They always comment that in the North, in faculty lounges, they talk about ideas, or new books, about the job situation in academics, but down here, everybody always winds up talking about food, what restaurants to go to, how to cook a certain crawfish dish. Food in much of America is still very, very dull. You ever wonder how these supermodels can become anorexic? How they can possibly do without something good to eat? It's because they're not from Louisiana. My wife and I will get in the car and we'll drive two hours to get a good bowl of gumbo somewhere. I don't know if they do that in other states.

Interviewer: There is a strong sense of the prevailing working class in your fiction. Do you feel that the Cajuns, as Faulkner said of people in his Nobel speech, have survived due to their strength, their joy of life, and their resiliency? Your characters are never cynical.

TG: I think I understand Cajun culture, and I am amazed by it. The lack of cynicism—I don't know, maybe it's the Catholicism or the sense of family among Cajuns. Acadian emigrants showed up in Louisiana between 1765 and 1785, and they clumped together and remained an ethnic entity where many other groups lost their identities. South Louisiana was a very strongly Francophone area all the way up until 1945 or so. The same number of French Huguenots settled in Alabama and were absorbed into the general Southern culture. The culture of the French Protestant completely went away. But the Catholic Cajuns tended to be the absorbers of culture. Germans, for example, showed up in Cajun Louisiana and after one generation were speaking French.

Interviewer: In your story "Deputy Sid's Gift," the struggle of racism is ultimately dealt with in the Catholic Church, where the priest is the mediator.

TG: Well, the priest is really the sounding board for the narrator's conscience. The narrator is drawn to show up at the rectory and talk out his guilt. But without the priest, there would be no confession and no story. The whole business of racism is very painful to write about. "Deputy Sid's Gift" is as close as I can come to dealing with it.

Interviewer: What genre of fiction are you more comfortable writing, the novel or the short story?

TG: They are totally different animals, and you've got to realize that from the first sentence. A very inexperienced writer doesn't know the difference, and that is what gets him in trouble. When I'm writing a short story, I realize that every word in it has to be relevant to what the damn thing is about. You cannot waste the reader's time for one millisecond in a short story, just as you can't in telling a joke. A short story is like an automobile engine, and every part is functional and has a purpose. You don't open the hood and see a spark plug taped to the side of the engine with a little note on it that says, "We found this on the factory floor and thought you might like to have it." Everything in that engine has a function, and the short story is the same way. That is what Walker Percy taught me with one or two sentences during a seminar one night. Now, the novel I see as a big, elaborate short story, in that you still can't waste the reader's time. I used to think there was a lot more room for exposition, a lot more room for tangents and description in a novel because it's so big, but that's crazy. Wasting a reader's time is wasting a reader's time. You are going to decrease your tale's effect by boring the hell out of the reader with a big essay on a character's motivations when you can let him know what a character's motivations are with one turn of the head. The novel, as far as line-by-line technique is concerned, has a lot in common with the short story, but I think I know the difference between a short story concept and a novel concept. When I got the idea to write the story "Waiting for the Evening News," about a man who wrecks a train and runs away, I saw that as a tale lasting five days and suitable to be developed into a short story. I saw that the tale was driven more by event than character, which is a tip-off that it was a short story topic, not a novel. A novel I wrote that was never published, *Black Bayou*, concerns a family that discovers a toxic waste dump on their property and all the troubles they go through with state government and the chemical industry to rectify the situation. The old man who owns the property relies on his son, who is a lawn mower salesman in west Louisiana, to come back and help him with his dilemma because he's too sick and old to deal with it. When I first got the idea for *Black Bayou*, I knew this was a novel topic, because it was much too big for six thousand words. It took in the troubles of an entire family, but I knew the novel would be mainly about the lawn mower salesman and his father; the project would be driven mainly by character. Generally, the difference between a story and a novel is that a story is driven by event and a novel by character.

Interviewer: You have a very interesting plan for editing your work. Could you talk about the steps you go through when editing and rewriting?

TG: When I started teaching technical writing and I realized how important a stupid simple mistake was in a memo or a business letter, I became more sensitive to little mistakes in short stories. Let's say there are fifty things wrong with the first draft of a story. I can approach the second draft by attempting to go after all fifty things, or I can focus on one thing, such as sentence structure. So I make a pass going only after sentence structure. I decide which compound sentences should be made into complex sentences, where to bust long sentences into smaller ones. I do just that work, and then I arrive at a level of coherence, flow, and readability. Then, on a second pass, I look for stuff to cut. On a third pass, I go back and look at dialogue and see how true it is. If I put a guy from St. Helena Parish in the story, how does he talk? I go through the story and really look at the dialogue and check the word order and idiom. By that time I've got it fairly clean, but the two things that bother me then are underdeveloped sections and a wrong ending. For that, I've got to show it to somebody else. I show it to my wife, or I'll send it to my agent in New York who sells short stories for me, and I'll ask what they think. Every writer has a blind spot, and he's going to overlook certain obvious things. Other readers catch such mistakes. Endings are the hardest things to get right. That is where experience in poetry writing comes in handy because good endings are often the result of a careful manipulation of the connotative values of images. Sometimes you've got to end with a picture that tells the story. When I get the story back from my readers, I'll go through it again and fix things they've noticed, and it still might not be right. My agent might send it around, and nobody will want it, and I will get it back with a note from an editor that says it's way too long, or there is some other problem with it. Then I have to take it apart and do it over. I wrote a story called "Crazy Music" [published as "The Piano Tuner" in *Harper's*, September 1998] a while ago in which I had this woman piano tuner go out on a tuning call and find this other woman who is depressed. The piano tuner starts feeling sorry for her. It is a story of a nice womanly alliance. I thought maybe I could work some women's themes in there, some contemporary stuff and maybe the *New Yorker* would like that. That was a terrible idea, to go with some kind of market trend. Nobody wanted the story, and then I thought, a woman piano tuner?, give me a break. I changed the character to a man and rewrote the story. What happened is there was this lovely thing—a relationship between a man and a depressed woman, where there could be some kind of sexual attraction, but they have enough self-discipline to realize what an awful idea it would be. The tuner offers her help not based on that psychosexual need that most people write about. Hey, it can happen. Now it's a much better story, but it has taken a great deal of work.

Interviewer: You were saying your wife is often the first person to read your work. What kind of effect does your writing have on her? What type of relationship does your writing allow with your children?

TG: I've taken writing very slowly. I'm fifty years old, and I've got only two books out. Ambition, though, has not been my long suit. I've also understood that the important goal was not to write and be published, but to write well. I've considered myself more of a teacher than a writer all these years, and a husband and a father. I've put twelve million hours in honey-do projects into this marriage, you see. That has always been first. People would ask ten or fifteen years ago how I could find the time to do any writing with two young kids and a marriage and a mortgage. I told them, "I do what I can." That's what you do. You do what you can. I've been very lucky to have some writing success. But you know where that writing success springs from, don't you? It's from building a life with a woman for twenty-six years and raising kids. How could I write the scenes in "The Courtship of Merlin LeBlanc" unless I had kids? How can I write about the relationship between Colette and Paul in *The Next Step in the Dance* without living through normal conflicts that are part of a marriage?

Interviewer: Does it ever come down to writing about what you would like to read?

TG: Who knows where my stories come from? It's amazing what appears on the word processor screen. I've read that a woman is born with all of the eggs she is ever going to produce. I think a story writer is sort of like that. Sometimes, when *a* story is successful and complete, I feel like I've really given birth to something.

Interviewer: This goes back to the stories, where Louisiana is seen as the "other country." In "License to Steal," one character says she wants to move from Louisiana to the United States.

TG: "License to Steal" is a very early story, and it's probably the most negative. I didn't have as much control over what I was doing in that story as I did in the later ones. The only reason I sent it off is that columnist Sheila Stroup, who was one of my students, read it and said, "This guy, Curtis, is really terrible, but I kind of like him." That sympathy, even for an unlikable character, is something I try for. You cannot write about even despicable characters as though they are one-dimensional or entirely evil. There has got to be something that makes the reader see in them something positive or admirable or at least worthy of sympathy. There is nothing so unreal or boring as an entirely evil fictional character.

Interviewer: For the writer, is there a responsibility to show the reader something, as Walker Percy said, that is a verification of what in his reality he has known, but not always known he has known?

TG: Writing provides a certain amount of self-discovery. So much that a writer expresses comes from his subconscious, that realm of the nearly known. He might not ever talk about, for example, the erosion of the institution of marriage, but he might embody the concern in a story or novel. A writer often surprises himself with what is put down on the page. Flannery O'Connor said when she was writing "Good Country People," she didn't know what was going to happen in the story, and she was amazed when it did happen. She was surprising herself, and she knew it was a good story because if she was surprised, certainly the reader was going to be surprised. What she means by being surprised is that the story blossoms and that the blossoming is connected to the previous events of the story. She didn't know that Manley Pointer was going to open a Bible and there was going to be whisky inside the hollowed-out text. When she wrote it, I think I know how she felt. When she wrote it, she probably said, "Yes. This is where this story has been going from the first sentence."

Interviewer: Did you not plot out everything that was going to happen to your characters in *The Next Step in the Dance*?

TG: Yes, I wrote a two-page double-spaced outline which I revised as I wrote. The first draft was out of control because I wrote it in little snippets of spare time, summer and weekends. I have to have a big block of time to work on a 120,000-word manuscript. When a semester would start and I would drop it for a month, I would forget what I was writing about. I'd come back to the manuscript and think, "Who are these people? Why was I so interested in them?" One day Barry Hannah called me and asked if I'd like to be writer-in-residence for one semester at Ole Miss. I asked what I would have to do, and he said nothing, just sit in a house and write and show up once a week to teach a graduate seminar with about ten people in it. I went up there, and I was separated from the ringing phone and the paper grading for about five months. I jumped on that novel, and the characters never got out of my head. I rewrote it, cut it, rearranged it, added to it. I sent it off to New York and very shortly after received a contract offer.

Interviewer: How long did you work on *The Next Step in the Dance*?

TG: Maybe eight years of diddling around with it and not knowing where it was going, then finally having that big block of time. I was writing two novels at the same time, and it took a long time to come up with the first draft of *The Next Step in the Dance*, and it took a tremendous amount of time to come up with the first revision. I sent off an early version of it to New York. With a novel, you get the manuscript together and you send it off, and if you don't have an agent, that baby's gone for five or six months. Then all you get back is a one-paragraph rejection letter with some comment like, "Well, this is wonderful and richly detailed, etc.," but the letter's got "It's broken and we don't want it" written all over it. You send it off again, and it's gone for another half year.

Interviewer: After teaching creative writing all these years, do you find yourself learning more and possibly learning from your students?

TG: Well, I learn from reading other authors. I learn from my experience, and then I teach students what my writing teaches me. The more successful I get, the more I figure I have a handle on what techniques students can use. I don't look for new writing directions, but sometimes they find me. I have some nephews that are Hollywood directors, and they called the other day and said, "Somebody wants us to write a cowboy movie, but we don't have the time because we're tied up on two other projects. We want you to write the script for us." I said, "I've never written a syllable of script in all my life." They said, "You are good with dialogue, and scripts are all dialogue. Just do it." I said, "Okay, what's the project?" They said, "Well, it's a remake of *Henry IV, Part I* in southwest Texas in 1875." So that's what I'm doing now, writing a cowboy movie and learning a lot. Recently, in a lecture, I brought up film writing and its relationship to stories. So I guess I'm still learning, and I'm still sharing.

Interviewer: At some point in your life, you had to make the decision that you wanted to be a writer. How did that decision come about?

TG: It's not like deciding to become a CPA. For me, at least, writing is just something I do, the way other people swim or play canasta. I never took it seriously. I wrote because I enjoyed it. I'd always written, all the way back to when I had a pen pal when I was eleven years old. Now, there was one big moment of departure, and it happened when I sent a story to the *Southern Review* in 1989. They sent me a letter containing lots of compliments saying they didn't have room to publish it. I got a little miffed because I thought this was a story that was really appropriate for the *Southern Review*. It was the first story in which I had control over the language, and I had faith in it. But that faith was based on vanity. The reason they bounced the story was because it wasn't right yet. At any rate, I stuck that story in an envelope the day I got it back from the *Southern Review,* and I sent it to C. Michael Curtis at the *Atlantic Monthly.* He wrote on the rejection slip that the story was okay until the ending, where it turned talky and petered out and that, if I ever tinkered with the ending, he would look again. A little bell went off in my head saying, "They're in a fiction-reading period right now." Six hours after the mailman had delivered the manuscript to my house, I mailed it back with a new and expanded ending. After a long wait, the response from the *Atlantic* came, and it was an acceptance, in more ways than one. I didn't "become a writer" that day, but I did get a signal that maybe I should keep doing what I'd always done, plus try for better endings to better stories.

A Postmodern Southern Moralist and Storyteller: Tim Gautreaux

Julie Kane/2001

From *Voces de América/American Voices* (Aduana Vieja, 2004), 123–45. © 2004. Used with permission of Laura Alonso Gallo and Julie Kane. This interview was conducted on 15 January 2001 in Hammond, Louisiana.

Timothy Martin Gautreaux, who publishes as "Tim Gautreaux," was born on 19 October 1947 in Morgan City, Louisiana. His fictional portrayals of working class characters from southern Louisiana—particularly those of the distinctive "Cajun" ethnic community, descendants of Acadian French settlers who were expelled from British Nova Scotia in the eighteenth century—have earned him acclaim as one of the best contemporary American fiction writers.

After graduating from Nicholls State University in Thibodaux, Louisiana, Gautreaux went on to study for a Ph.D. in Romantic Literature from the University of South Carolina, where he took poetry writing courses from James Dickey. Following his graduation from USC in 1972, Gautreaux began teaching at Southeastern Louisiana University in Hammond, Louisiana—a position that he would maintain until his retirement in 2002. In his fifth year of teaching, Gautreaux took a novel-writing course from Walker Percy at Loyola University in New Orleans, which inspired him to give up poetry in favor of fiction. His early stories were published in "little magazines" such as *Kansas Quarterly* and the *Massachusetts Review*, but in the decade of the 1990s he broke through to national literary recognition.

In 1992, 1997, 1998, 1999, and 2000, Gautreaux had short stories selected for inclusion in the prestigious annual volume *Best American Short Stories*—a feat unmatched by any other writer. During the same time period, his stories also appeared in four volumes of *New Stories from the South:*

53

The Year's Best. The story "Waiting for the Evening News" won the 1995 National Magazine Award for fiction, and another story appeared in *Prize Stories 2000: The O. Henry Awards.* Gautreaux's stories were collected in *Same Place, Same Things* (1996) and *Welding with Children* (1999), both from Picador/St. Martin's. *Kirkus Reviews* called the first book "A terrific debut collection from a Louisiana writer whose stylish, sympathetic understanding of working-class sensibilities and Cajun culture gives his work a flavor and universality unique among contemporary writers." The second collection was named a *New York Times* Notable Book of 1999.

Gautreaux's first novel, *The Next Step in the Dance,* came out in 1998 and told the story of a young Cajun French couple from a small "oilpatch" town in Louisiana, struggling to survive during the oil industry recession years of the 1980s. It won the Southeastern Booksellers Association Novel of the Year Award. Gautreaux's second novel, *The Clearing,* about a shell-shocked World War I veteran adrift in a cypress logging "company town" in rural Louisiana in the early twentieth century, was published in 2003 to superlative reviews. *Publishers Weekly,* for example, stated in its review that Gautreaux was "perhaps the most talented writer to emerge from the South in recent years."

At a time when many contemporary writers have abandoned conventional narrative in favor of postmodern, experimental fiction, Gautreaux continues to entice readers and critics with his storytelling gifts and his memorably drawn characters. Despite his Ph.D. in literature, Gautreaux is the son and grandson of steamboat, railroad, and oil industry workers, and his characters most often make a living with their hands in the Cajun communities of small-town Louisiana. Gautreaux's fiction often depicts characters faced with difficult moral choices—another unusual quality amidst the contemporary American atmosphere of "moral relativism" that is reflected in so much literature. Because of his concern with moral issues, his regionalism, and his Roman Catholicism, Gautreaux is often compared to the late Southern writer Flannery O'Connor. Like O'Connor, as well, Gautreaux writes with a vein of ironic humor, even when his subject matter is violence.

Gautreaux is "rapidly becoming a major American writer," *Kirkus Reviews* asserted in 1998, and the critical reception for *The Clearing* should cement Gautreaux's position in that elite group together with such fellow Southerners as O'Connor, Twain, and Faulkner.

On a drizzly January day in Hammond, Louisiana, I pull up to the handsome, brick, Acadian-style home of fiction writer Tim Gautreaux. The house is surrounded by a cat's-cradle of slender pines. Behind it is a weathered wooden outbuilding hung with iron tools and old railroad station signs: clearly, "workshop" is not just a metaphor to this creative writing teacher.

Tim's wife, Winborne, greets me at the door, concerned about my long trip through bad weather. Petite and blonde, with a soft voice that belies her sharp wit, she teaches American Literature at Southeastern Louisiana University, where Tim is Writer-in-Residence. [Gautreaux retired from SLU in December 2002.]

Winborne settles me in the living area and leaves to make coffee. Waiting for Tim to descend from his upstairs study, I take in the polished wooden floors and soaring ceiling, the comfortably upholstered reading chairs, the piano cluttered with framed family photos, and the "Louisiana Blue Heron" Audubon print hanging above the mantel. At the far end of the room is an enormous metal kennel containing a shaggy, honey-colored dog who thumps his tail with hope that I might let him out of prison.

Tim enters the room. He is slim, of medium height, with dark, smile-crinkled eyes, dark hair, and a thick salt-and-pepper moustache. Soon he is telling me about having driven halfway to Lafayette the day before to go Cajun dancing at a club called Whiskey River Landing. He and Winborne have been two-stepping and Cajun waltzing together for fifteen or twenty years now, ever since one afternoon in Morgan City when, visiting Tim's mother, they found themselves with nothing to do, and Tim opened the local paper and pointed at random down a listing of cultural events.

Winborne returns with a pot of French roast coffee. "The dog's in there because he's wet," she explains.

"Actually, he's triply in the doghouse," Tim qualifies. "He got wet, he got into a fight with the geriatric cat, and he ate a pair of my tennis shoes—but you can't really blame him for the last one, since we'd given him a toy shoe to chew on. How's he supposed to know the difference between a toy shoe and a real one?"

"Did Tim tell you the dog's a Golden Retriever?" asks Winborne. "Ha! Don't listen to him! It's just a ditch dog."

I know, from my research about Tim, that Winborne reads and critiques every word he writes. She "can spot a bad sentence anywhere, anytime," he has written. It is obvious that they function as a superb team. When he takes too grandiose a step, she corrects him, whether on the dance floor, in conversation, or on the page.

Having finished our coffee, Tim and I move upstairs to the two small rooms, linked by a door and lit by dormer windows, that make up his study.

I could just as well be entering a museum of nineteenth-century railroad and steamboat memorabilia. Lined up atop bookshelves filled with crumbling leather repair manuals for now-antique machines are rows of gleaming brass railroad lanterns. "The smaller ones were carried by hand as the conductor walked through the railroad yard," Tim explains. "The larger ones were hung by hooks from the front and back ends of the train." Some of the lanterns have alternating discs of red and blue glass. Suddenly I understand, in a visceral sense, the last two lines of the old blues song *Stormy Monday*: "When that train left the station, there were two lights on behind;/ Well, the red light's for my baby, and the blue light's for my mind."

What at first appeared to be a half-dozen round, brass wall-clocks now reveal themselves to be antique steam-pressure gauges. "My grandfather was a steamboat chief engineer, and my father was a tugboat captain," Tim says to explain his motivation for collecting old steam industry equipment. Under his dormer window are three huge, cylindrical brass sculptures. They are steam whistles that have been salvaged from junked steamboats and locomotives, and Tim owns more than a hundred of them—most of them stored in the attic for lack of display space.

He begins to explain how each rivergoing vessel acquired its own, distinctive "voice." Oceangoing ships, which rarely passed the same ship twice, needed only to warn other ships of their presence, but a riverboat's whistle was its identifying signature. A riverboat would modify its standardized, factory-built whistle so that the sound was unique. Not only that, Tim explains, but steam tugboats on the river developed a kind of "whistle language," where the nuances of their soundings could convey simple messages and navigational instructions to other tugboats.

Striding to his computer, he says, "Listen to the sound effect that tells me when I get a new e-mail!" Not a buzz, not a beep, but the long, mournful bleat of a nineteenth-century steamboat whistle alerts Gautreaux to the arrival of his high-tech mail. "It's an A-major chord," he says, "and I believe it's from the *Gordon C. Green*. I downloaded it from the Net."

Reluctantly, because the interview has thus far been unbounded by the limits of my questions, I take out my tape recorder to begin the interview proper.

J. Kane: You were born in Morgan City, Louisiana. Did you grow up there as well?

T. Gautreaux: Right. I was born in 1947, and lived there until I went to college. And, of course, my mother still lives there—she's ninety-three. We go down and visit her, so we still have connections down there.

J. Kane: In one of your short stories, you portray Morgan City as the kind of rough-and-tumble town where bar patrons hit each other over the head with wrenches and wake up later with tattoos. Are those the kind of images that come to mind when you think of your hometown?

T. Gautreaux: Morgan City was an oil town, and, although it wasn't very large, it had more than its share of barrooms. And the barrooms were filled with single men who wanted to spend as much money as they could—as a matter of fact, it was kind of a sport to see if you could spend your whole paycheck in one night. So some silly things happened with this type of attitude and these types of people having fun, being young and healthy and rambunctious. There were some pretty interesting brawls.

J. Kane: Many of your characters are so familiar with the places they've lived all their lives that they can't even see their surroundings any more. For example, a rusty old pickup truck parked in one character's front yard is described as being "just a thing you don't look at unless you need it," and the title of your first collection, *Same Place, Same Things*, seems to make the same point. Does it take an outsider to be able to see a place clearly?

T. Gautreaux: First of all, I believe that all places are imbued with a type of culture. Even if it's a culture of the mall-rat or the subdivision, it's still a culture. But there are places in America—Latino neighborhoods, Amish neighborhoods, Polish neighborhoods in Chicago, Jewish enclaves here and there, Cajun areas of southwest Louisiana—that are very obviously filled with cultural artifacts of language, folkways, actions. The person who lives in that culture doesn't notice them at all, because he's part of that culture, and nothing of that sort is odd to him. So, if you've had to write fiction within that culture, you've had to figure out a way of not pointing out all of those artifacts, but nevertheless having them occur naturally in the narration, in the movement and speech of the characters. It's a way of using things but not making them at all noticeable, just as the character who is in that culture deals with them, by not really dealing with them overtly. If you just make overt references to nutria and how odd they are and palmettos and how they sound when the wind blows through them, too much, you're writing a type of local color—it's like you're in the business of what Walker Percy used to call "amazing Yankees." And that's one thing you want to try to avoid. So the writer who's dealing with culture has a curious duty of not using cultural details in an obvious manner, but trying to get over to the reader that these are natural in the character's life. What a character does with his cigarette, or his beer, or his rosary, gives you a little window—well, the fact that the character would have a rosary in his pocket, right there that says something about Catholicism that you don't have to overtly state.

J. Kane: You've said in an earlier interview that you grew up listening to retired tugboat captains and oilfield workers trying to top each other with their storytelling. In the story "Died and Gone to Vegas," a college boy working on a steam dredge gets into a storytelling contest with his co-workers over a card game. Is that young oiler, Nick, more autobiographical than your other characters?

T. Gautreaux: That's a good question, and the answer is no. I very seldom put myself in a story. If I think about it, I would imagine that maybe I'm in some of my narrations, but that little guy is not me. He's just a little guy who has kind of a straight vision of the truth and sees through the imagined realities of the storytellers. Even in *The Next Step in the Dance*, Paul Thibodeaux, who is a machinist, who seems to be my alter ego—I've gone through a lot of pains to make him different from me, in many ways. Paul Thibodeaux is muscular and good-looking and young and vibrant and everything—while I'm short and balding. There are many things about Paul that are not like me, but I guess Paul would be the closest to how I feel about certain things. He's a little thick-headed and slow to catch on, and that might be like me. But I'm thinking back through the other stories I've written, and I really tend not to do that.

J. Kane: So all of the characters whose names end in "-eaux" in your stories—Thibodeaux, Simoneaux, Boudreaux—they just reflect the demographics of Cajun country, not any autobiographical impulse?

T. Gautreaux: Right. If you're going to set a story in south Louisiana, you're going to have to have some "-eaux" characters in it. It's sort of unavoidable—just look at the phone book!

J. Kane: Speaking of names, when coming up with proper names for bars and businesses and menu items, you often make sly "Louisiana in-jokes" that would be hard for an outsider to understand without a footnote: a Cajun-funk-salsa band named "Los Head-Suckers," "blackened swordfish" and "bayou lamb" on a California Cajun restaurant menu. Are you conscious of aiming your works at a particular audience?

T. Gautreaux: Well, it's hard to tell what's an inside joke any more. There are so many people who study the culture. There are people who know Amish culture better than the Amish do, and the same thing is true of Acadian culture. I have to confess that probably some of those jokes are inside jokes—the "blackened swordfish" joke, for example, in *The Next Step in the Dance.* Anybody from Louisiana is going to relate to that, and to the Popeye's Cajun this and that they see in Minneapolis, or the Bojangles Cajun ham biscuit that they see in the Carolinas. My stories are kind of parochial in that they're all set in various Louisiana cultures. And a lot of people are not connected to the culture in which they grew up, or just don't realize that they are a part of any type of culture. They can relate to my stories, because the stories give them a kind of window into something they think they don't have. If you are raised in a subdivision and educated at a state university, and you're working as an accountant at a chemical plant in New Jersey, maybe you don't have a feeling that you belong to an enclave. I believe that's why people like southern fiction in general, because so much of it is greatly place-oriented and family-oriented and food-oriented.

J. Kane: In one of your stories, a priest defines hell as being "what someone might deserve," which seems to counterpoint one of Frost's two definitions of "home" in his poem "Death of the Hired Man": that it's "Something you somehow haven't to deserve." In still another story, "Welding with Children," you write of a character that he "walked to the head of the trail the old man had cut and stared to where it turned in the undergrowth." Did Frost influence your work, in addition to the southern fiction writers you've mentioned in other interviews: Mark Twain, Walker Percy, Flannery O'Connor?
T. Gautreaux: Well, I teach the American [literature] survey, and I'm always teaching a lot of Frost, because he's about the only thing the students can understand. And so it's possible that he's an accidental influence. He's a man who gives the image that he is the ultimate authority on northeastern farming or rural ways or whatever, but, of course, he was born and raised in San Francisco and didn't come to the New England lifestyle until he was in his twenties and his grandfather gave him a farm. And, nevertheless, he achieved a great sense of place and culture in his work. I find that really interesting because, when I was seventeen years old, if somebody had asked me, "Are you Cajun?," even though I was born in Louisiana and my father spoke French, I would have said, "What's that?" I didn't know. There was very little awareness or pride among people with Cajun roots in south-central, southwest Louisiana until the great Cajun music revivals of the nineteen-seventies.

J. Kane: Was French-speaking something that young people were embarrassed about?

T. Gautreaux: Oh, yeah, it was considered low class; it was also considered obsolete. My father spoke French to old people who couldn't navigate in English very well. When I would ask him for certain expressions in French, he would say, "You don't really need to know that." That's all he ever said, but implied in that was, "This is something for old people that's dying out, and, when they're dead, it's going to be gone." That was the attitude.

J. Kane: In your short story "Floyd's Girl," a little Cajun girl is kidnapped by her mother's boyfriend and taken to Texas to live. Her Louisiana relatives don't seem to worry about whether he's going to harm her or how much they're going to miss her: they're all too distraught that she's going to grow up without "the okra soul, the crawfish body. . . . the musical rattle of French, her prayers, the head-turning squawk of her uncle's accordion." Without a sense of place, without a regional culture, are we robbed of soul?

T. Gautreaux: Whenever you move away from what you're used to, you wind up with less than what you started with. If you've lived in California, and you're used to clean air and a wonderful climate, and then you move to some meteorological hell-hole like—what's that west Texas town where the wind never stops blowing? Lubbock?—then you realize what you've left behind. You don't realize what you've had until you lose it. In "Floyd's Girl," all of these people that are contemplating the abduction of this young girl suddenly realize what she's going to be losing. They see the food, the religion, the music, the family that she'll be without. And so they grow very intense about this because they understand what is at stake, for maybe even the first time.

J. Kane: In many of your works, a female character—Ada in "Same Place, Same Things," Raynelle in "Died and Gone to Vegas," Colette in *The Next Step in the Dance,* Floyd's ex-wife in "Floyd's Girl," Lucy in "The Courtship of Merlin LeBlanc"—wants more than anything to get out of south Louisiana, while the male lead characters seem to realize that place is central to their identities, and want nothing so much as to stay put. Is the "gendering" of this conflict something rooted in your own personal experience?

T. Gautreaux: I don't know—I think I would have to be psychoanalyzed to figure that one out!

J. Kane: You didn't have a mother who was dying to get out of Louisiana?

T. Gautreaux: No, no. I'm not quite sure what to say about that one, other than that I married a girl from North Carolina and moved her to Louisiana, and of course she's always looking down the road back toward North Carolina. But, of course, if she had been from anywhere else, she'd probably want to go home there, too. But some of the women in my stories are a little rough around the edges, a little hardhearted. And, to tell you the truth, a lot of rural women that I grew up with had to be pretty tough, intellectually and physically and emotionally, to survive the poverty and the rough men they'd married. The women in that bourré game in "Easy Pickings," in the latest book, are resilient old gals, but they're just like the women I grew up around in the nineteen-fifties in Morgan City. They like to smoke, they like to drink, they like to play cards and gamble. They're Louisiana women. They're going to have fun until the day they die.

J. Kane: You got your undergraduate degree from Nicholls State University in Thibodaux, but you also studied under Walker Percy at Loyola University in New Orleans. Was that afterward?

T. Gautreaux: That was in 1977. Walker Percy was offering a novel-writing seminar, and he was hand-picking his students. I believe he chose eight or ten people, and my fellow class members were people like [novelist] Valerie Martin, and Walter Isaacson, the [managing] editor of *Time*, and [Faulkner scholar] Ken Holditch, who's still living in New Orleans and giving those French Quarter tours, and probably a couple of other people I've forgotten who've gone on to do better things.

J. Kane: You have been quoted as saying, "I consider myself to be a Catholic writer in the tradition of Walker Percy. If a story does not deal with a moral question, I don't think it's much of a story." Did your concern with moral issues in fiction predate your period of study under Percy, or did he influence you in that direction?

T. Gautreaux: I'm trying to think what I was writing before Percy. And, of course, that was a long time ago, and I wasn't writing much in the way of fiction before then. But I would have to say that, yes, Percy did—Percy's work did—influence me, simply because it showed me that you could deal with questions of value in contemporary fiction and it would work. Ideals of morals and values, of ethics, whatever you want to call them. And, of course, that dovetails in with my convent-school upbringing, which I survived. What's a story about? Well, a story is a certain narrative chain of events, but what is it about, beneath all that? What are you dealing with? Sometimes I read contemporary fiction and there seems to be nothing underneath the narrative, other than a kind of dark hole of despair, or nothingness, or even a vacuum.

This is the feeling I get when I read *New Yorker* stories: all is doom is gloom and nothing means anything, not even the narrative. You don't have an end with *New Yorker* stories; you just sort of have an "end of track," so to speak, where the train stops and the characters are looking out of the windows saying, "Why are we here?"

J. Kane: A "dying fall"?
T. Gautreaux: Right. A dying fall. But the business about value—what do you do with children, why do you do *anything* in life?—is always behind my fiction.

J. Kane: What was Percy like as a teacher?
T. Gautreaux: Teachers tend not to reveal a whole lot about themselves in the classroom. A good teacher actually lets the students do the work, and he poses questions, and he tries not to be intrusive, because students tend to ignore teachers anyhow. I mean, teachers are there to be ignored because you don't want to do what they say—you don't want to write that story in another gender, because it's too damn much work; you don't want to cut that first chapter, it's absurd—you spent a lot of *time* on that first chapter—but, of course, teachers are always right. Percy was very subtle, very instructive; he was not afraid to talk about basics; everything he said was relevant to what we were doing; he did not bloviate or expand upon certain theoretical approaches to fiction that were not really of any practical help to us—mainly he would ask us a lot of questions. We would workshop a story and he would just ask questions and, of course, in our answering them, we would be instructing ourselves, because the questions were very pointed and purposeful. He was very modest, very unassuming.

J. Kane: You also studied under James Dickey at the University of South Carolina, where you earned your Ph.D. That must have been right around the time that he published *Deliverance*. In contrast to the spirituality of Percy's fiction, did the physicality of Dickey's help encourage the "southern grotesque" streak in your work?
T. Gautreaux: I was a poet when I was studying under Dickey, not a fiction writer, and so Dickey gave me respect for what a line is in a poem. He was very different from Percy as a teacher. He was garrulous and outgoing, and he used to wear coats to class with "POETRY" embroidered on the back, and big cowboy hats, and he'd bring guitars to class and play for us, and he'd brag about how much money a certain contract brought in—which we

thought was fascinating, really a wonderful thing for him to do, because he bugged our eyes out when we learned that he got half a million dollars for *Deliverance* in paperback and movie rights. In 1970, that was an astounding amount of money. But Dickey was a walking encyclopedia of knowledge about poets. It seemed that he knew everybody in the *Norton Anthology* personally. He would say, "Yeah, I remember when I was talking to Randall Jarrell." You half-expected him to say, "Yeah, I had lunch with Gerard Hopkins before he died," because he seemed to know everybody on a first-name basis. And he was very knowledgeable about poetry, and he never said anything about poetry that seemed to be wrongheaded. I have nothing but praise for him as a teacher.

J. Kane: That's probably the longest period of time that you lived outside of Louisiana, when you were in South Carolina. Did you deliberately want to get away for awhile?

T. Gautreaux: No, it was an accident. My creative writing professor entered some of my poems in a Southern Literary Festival contest. Dickey was the main speaker at the festival that year, in Knoxville. My poems happened to win a prize, and they were printed in the festival magazine, and Dickey read them and told his department head to find me and offer me an assistantship to South Carolina, because he wanted me to study under him. And that's how I wound up at South Carolina. It was good because it got me out of Louisiana, and the best thing that happened in regard to that is that I met my wife. She was in the MA program there—not in creative writing, but in American literature.

J. Kane: You published your first book of fiction when you were in your forties. Was your work maturing prior to that, or were editors just idiots?

T. Gautreaux: No, editors weren't idiots—my stuff just wasn't any good until the late eighties, and it took me that long to learn the craft. Also, I was raising two kids and teaching a very heavy load at a state university that had no entrance requirements—that's always taxing. Plus, I was running the usual errands that you have to run when you work in the university: committee work, student contests, recruiting, and things of that nature. I also suffer from that Louisiana disease of limited ambition.

J. Kane: ". . . [Y]ou can't work too steady if you're a Louisiana man"?

T. Gautreaux: I got to lay off a little bit, put some wear on the truck!

J. Kane: You've been a teacher of creative writing for over twenty years now, and I know that you tell your students to base their characters on the people they know. Do your family members and acquaintances claim to find themselves in your fiction, and are they ever correct about it?

T. Gautreaux: Well, that's a question I get asked quite often, and the answer is no, because all of my characters are "vegematized"—you know what the "Vegematic" is? They're just little teeny bits and pieces of various characters that I know. I don't copy anything, because it doesn't interest me to do that. There's a frightening thought embedded here: maybe there's no individual that's interesting enough to be in a short story, so you add all these dimensions to your characters.

J. Kane: The poet Martha Vertreace used to say that poetry begins in real experience, but then you have to "turn the volume up."

T. Gautreaux: Right. I would say that's very accurate about characterization in fiction. Flannery O'Connor used to do that, of course. Somebody once asked her why a character was so grotesque, and she said that, well, for blind people you have to draw big characters.

J. Kane: In many of your stories, you look at English professors, books, and other aspects of academic or intellectual culture from the point of view of working-class Cajuns. A character sees "a bunch of four-eyed English teachers" in a piano bar, or muses that he'd "rather spend eight hours a day with his tongue stuck on a hot pipe than teach in a college," or hears opera music on Public Radio that sounds "like a tomcat hung up in a fan belt." Is this emblematic of your own double-consciousness? Are you both the four-eyed English teacher who listens to Public Radio and Gautreaux from Morgan City who is good with machines?

T. Gautreaux: I think, yes, because you lead kind of a forked existence when you are someone raised in a blue-collar family who gets a Ph.D. in Romantic literature. You always have this two-stage existence and these two ways of looking at things. And then, of course, creative writing teachers are generally a step out of academia. That is, we're not in there with the feminists and the New Historicists and the Derrida people, generally—we're a little separate from it. We're not disapproving of it, or anything, but we're not in there with the critics, and so we have a little bit of distance on that kind of stuff, and you can always imagine what the general public thinks of some of the fringe scholarship that goes on in the academy, and how ludicrous it must appear.

J. Kane: On the flip side of that, do you ever feel any strangeness about basing your fiction on the lives of characters who would never read your fiction, because *GQ* and the *Atlantic* and *Harper's* would be too intimidatingly "high culture" for them?

T. Gautreaux: Well, you know, one reason people don't read short fiction is not because they don't read, but because so little of it is truly readable. I pride myself in writing a "broad-spectrum" fiction, fiction that appeals to both intellectuals and blue-collar types. Many times I've heard stories of people who don't read short stories, or people who have technical jobs, who like my fiction. I have a friend who teaches high school industrial arts in Montana, and he makes his students read some of my stories every year, in a shop class. He wants to show these people something about literature, and something about the machinery of storytelling—an interesting fellow. My nephew, who installs wiring harnesses on oil rigs, was out on one last year, and he saw a man with his legs dangling over the Gulf, reading a paperback, and he walked up to see what he was reading, and it was my first collection of short stories. And I hear tales over and over about blue-collar types sitting around somewhere reading a Tim Gautreaux book. This is the crossover aspect, the broad-spectrum aspect, that I'm talking about, that I like about what I do.

J. Kane: Machines have something of the presence, individuality, and dignity of human characters in your writing; and we know that you grew up around relatives who worked with machines. In a satiric story about a low-rent writers' conference, you have the one decent teacher say that "A novel is a story, and a story is like an airplane. You get the damned thing off the ground as soon as you can." Is a story a machine?

T. Gautreaux: Yes, in the sense of its structure and the way the sentences work on the reader's consciousness. A story has a certain coherence and logic that is very much like the fluid motion of clockwork. The sentences turn like gears against each other, toward a common effect, which is the same motion you see in any type of machine. If you look at any mechanism, there are no redundant parts, and that is the concept of a short story that's been given to us by Hemingway and Fitzgerald and the masters of the thirties and forties, and certainly Flannery O'Connor. A good story is just like an automobile engine. I give this example in class all the time: If you buy a new car and drive it home and lift up the hood, you're not going to find a spark plug Scotch-taped to the side of the block with a note on it that says, "Found this on the floor at the factory, thought you'd like to have it!" Everything under that hood has to be a functional part of the mechanism we call an automobile. You don't have any extraneous junk attached to the mechanism, and I believe that stories operate the same way, which is why, when I revise, I cut so much, or reshape irrelevant things to make them relevant.

J. Kane: If you hadn't been a writer and English professor, what would have been your next choice of occupation?

T. Gautreaux: It's strange how life leads us into directions sort of by accident. If Dickey had not read my poems, maybe I would not have gotten a Ph.D.—maybe I would be a high school teacher somewhere, or maybe I would own a used car lot, or a machine shop that does historical restorations—it's strange. For a long while, I was a piano technician. I was a specialist in rebuilding player pianos. I absolutely loved piano work. I started getting into "reproducing" player pianos, which are designed to interpret classical nuances. But those are really hard to rebuild, and the last time I did one I had fifty-two hundred pieces of mechanism broken apart, and I said, well, I'm going to do this one, but I'm not going to do any more. I started publishing, and that's what killed the piano business—I could either fix pianos, which is not much of a legacy, or I could write stories.

J. Kane: That was my last question. Is there anything else you'd like to add?
T. Gautreaux: Good luck in writing this!

Tape recorder off again, I follow Tim through the door that connects his outer office to his inner writing sanctum. Ringed by an Aztec chieftain's ransom in glittering metal—more steamboat whistles, railroad lanterns, and pressure gauges—is a notebook computer that looks drab and gray in the midst of such resplendent mechanical company. Tim shows me the thick draft of his forthcoming novel, *The Clearing* [titled *Victrola Souls* at the time of the interview], and explains that he's micro-editing it as he would a short story. One of the characters, he explains, likes to listen to "sentimental stuff" on an old Victrola. "To stuff like this," he says, crossing back to the outer room and placing a 78 into the chest-high Victrola in the corner. It is Lester McFarland singing "My Wild Irish Rose." "You'd expect a horn or band section backing this up," Tim continues, "but not in this version. Listen: that's a mandolin. And, if you listen to McFarland's diction, you can hear a little southern accent coming through. Remember, this was way before country music—we're listening to its roots!"

The same character in the novel who likes to listen to Victrola music, Tim explains, also opens a closet, finds an old piano accordion on a shelf, and begins to play it. Having no idea how to play a piano accordion, Tim found one on an Internet auction site for ninety dollars and bought it, "straps and all." He then taught himself to play it before writing the rest of the scene.

Now Tim points to a shelf of books by his favorite contemporary writers: Cormac McCarthy, Susan Dodd, Larry Brown. And Annie Proulx, he adds; he can't understand why some critics didn't like *The Shipping News*, when reading it was like getting "a whole week in Newfoundland for free."

We go back downstairs, where the now-dry dog has been sprung from jail and Winborne is ladling chicken andouille gumbo into bowls of mounded rice. The andouille sausage is from Laplace, Louisiana, Tim explains, and it is the best in the world: you can't eat a whole link of it, because it's too spicy, but it's perfect for seasoning gumbo. Back in Laplace, he continues, they cure the andouille inside tin sheds with padlocks on the doors so nobody can discover the secret recipe. The secret has something to do with banking a pecan wood fire with cane leaves and pouring cane syrup over the fire as the sausage smokes, but that's as much as anybody knows.

The gumbo is, indeed, the best I have eaten in my twenty-five years in Louisiana. As we sip our sweet tea and progress to lemon-iced ginger cookies, Winborne tells the story of how the family acquired their now-eighteen-year-old cat as a bribe to make their eldest son return for his second day of kindergarten. Tim follows with a story about his prankster older brother bringing a pack of grandchildren to the house, then changing into a gorilla suit in the woods to scare them.

Tim says that he's been teaching for twenty-nine years now, and that, lately, he's been having thoughts about retiring to devote more time to his stories. There'd be more time, as well, to putter in the workshop out back where he now works on "household projects and restorations," as he puts it.

". . . only in the opposite order," Winborne says with a rueful smile.

We talk for a little while longer about nineteenth-century Louisiana writer Kate Chopin, admired by both Winborne and Tim; about the new generation of college students who've read almost nothing by the time they reach our classrooms; about the little boy down the street from Winborne and Tim who stares at video games all day long.

"He never goes outside. He never goes beyond his front porch," says Winborne.

"I wonder if anybody ever tells him stories," Tim says sadly.

And that is the line that keeps echoing in my mind as I say my goodbyes and drive past the empty yard of the Nintendo-rapt child, past the moss-stained pink cinderblocks of an abandoned corner grocery store, over the railroad tracks of a thousand country blues songs played on scratchy old Victrolas, and on into the rain and the Interstate highway with its wordless icons for gas, and lodging, and food.

Tim Gautreaux

Pam Kingsbury/2003

From *Inner Voices, Inner Views: Conversations with Southern Writers* (The Enolam Group, 2005), 48-51. © Pam Kingsbury. Used with permission of Tim Gautreaux, the Enolam Group, and Pam Kingsbury. Pam Kingsbury, author of *Inner Voices, Inner Views,* teaches at the University of North Alabama.

Tim Gautreaux's first novel, *The Next Step in the Dance*, won the 1999 Southeastern Booksellers Award. Born and reared in Louisiana, the author recently retired from his position as Writer-in-Residence at Southeastern Louisiana University and has spent the last few months researching his next novel. His work has been selected for inclusion in the *O. Henry* and *Best American Short Story Annuals* and has appeared in *Zoetrope, GQ, Harper's,* and the *Atlantic Monthly.*

Kingsbury: You're from Louisiana . . . .

Gautreaux: I was born in 1947 in Morgan City, a tough oil-patch town in South-Central Louisiana. My father was a tugboat captain, and he wanted me to follow in his footsteps, but the job was too slow for me. After twelve years in a Catholic school and four years in a regional college, I entered an accelerated Ph.D. program at the University of South Carolina where I studied under James Dickey for three years. Ph.D. in hand, I got a job teaching literature and creative writing at Southeastern Louisiana University, taught thirty years, and retired last December.

Kingsbury: What changes have you seen in the state and local culture during your lifetime?

Gautreaux: In South Louisiana, when I was a child, more people spoke French, but the number of French-speakers has declined a great deal in the past thirty years. Cajuns were shy about their culture, suspecting that it was kind of a joke to outlanders, and many didn't pass on the language. I didn't even realize I was a Cajun until I moved out of state to go to graduate school. Nobody talked about being this or that in those days. Nowadays Cajuns are pretty knowledgeable about their history, and though the language has diminished, the music, food, and folkways are thriving here in Louisiana and around the country. Louisiana has developed more of a literary presence also thanks to writers like John Biguenet, James Lee Burke, Walker Percy, Andre Dubus, Shirley Ann Grau, and a dozen others.

Kingsbury: What image or character came to mind first as you were writing *The Clearing*?

Gautreaux: The constable. I imagined his haunted expression as he looked out across the sawmill yard toward the saloon, hearing the yowls of a brawl and knowing that the only way he could save the fighters from themselves was to hurt at least one of them, even though he didn't want to.

Kingsbury: Did you do any research for the historical elements or were they part of local and/or family lore?

Gautreaux: The meaningful details in *The Clearing* came out of my imagination, supported by thousands of bits and pieces of things I heard as a child: a reference to a long-dead relative, an old firearm in the closet purported to have killed someone, an embarrassed turn of the head, a helpless shrug, the way an uncle slowed down his voice when speaking two sentences about what he did in the war.

One thing that makes a child turn into a writer is the ability to understand the importance of remembering everything. And to remember you have to listen and believe that everything you hear is interesting.

When I was a kid, a lot of old relatives were still around and they talked and talked about their jobs, local murders, cops, cancer, lynchings, saw milling, how to repair steam engines, being poisoned by a pork roast, killing pigeons, praying, water-skiing, steamboat navigation, and welding.

I consulted my library of antique machinery manuals and catalogs, read a book or two on saw milling history, but the guts of the story came from shutting up and listening.

Kingsbury: Would you talk about "Writing about the bonds between men without succumbing to sentimentality?"

Gautreaux: Avoiding sentimentality is easy to do. Use not one cliché. Use as little exposition as possible. Focus on action and detail that in a subtle way suggests what you want to say.

Kingsbury: Were you influenced by any particular writers?
Gautreaux: Flannery O'Connor (who hasn't been?), Walker Percy, Jane Austen, Cormac McCarthy, Annie Proulx.

Kingsbury: Would you like to name some writers readers should be reading but might have missed?
Gautreaux: William Gay, Tom Franklin, George Saunders, Jeffrey Lent, and Kent Haruf.

Kingsbury: Does teaching influence your writing in any way?
Gautreaux: Sure. When I teach a room full of students, I teach myself, remind myself. One time a negative review charged that I must listen to my own lectures. I would hope so.

Kingsbury: You've spent the summer promoting the book. What was your impression of the state of bookselling? reading?
Gautreaux: The independent booksellers are the saviors and maintainers of literary fiction. They actually read the books, make recommendations, do each customer a favor by matching that customer's individual taste up with a particular writer, plus they sometimes challenge their customer's laziness and recommend titles that engage the intellect. Again, they read the books and recommend from experience. A chain store clerk can only ask "You want fries with that?"

Kingsbury: What would you still like to be asked?
Gautreaux: "Why is there so damn much machinery in everything you write?"

I'm sure someone will write a master's thesis on that topic, and I don't really understand why myself, fully. I've always been fascinated by any mechanism and love to take lawnmowers and tractors and steam locomotives apart to make them run better.

When I started working on the accordion scene in *The Clearing*, I bought a big accordion for fifty bucks on Ebay, taught myself to play "Lady of Spain" with one finger, figured out the stops and buttons, discovered how the thing smelled, vibrated on my chest, broke my back, wrenched my shoulders, confused my fingers with its left-hand board of 120 identical black chord buttons. Then I took it out to my machine shop and completely dismantled it and figured out how it worked, studied the brass reeds, beeswax, kid-leather check valves, etc.

The thing about a properly designed mechanism is that there are no nonfunctioning parts. Everything has a purpose, every bit and tag, screw and eyelet. Good fiction's the same way.

Tim Gautreaux: Author of *The Clearing* Talks with Robert Birnbaum

Robert Birnbaum/2003

From *identitytheory.com* (1 October 2003). © Robert Birnbaum. Used with permission.

Tim Gautreaux was born and raised in Louisiana and until his recent retirement taught writing at Southeast Louisiana University for thirty years. He has published two story collections, *Same Place, Same Things* and *Welding with Children*, as well as two novels, *The Next Step in the Dance* and recently *The Clearing*. His stories have appeared in *Harper's*, the *Atlantic*, and *Zoetrope* as well as a number of anthologies. Tim Gautreaux lives outside of Hammond, Louisiana, with his family and, given his Catholicism, is assuredly at work on something.

The Clearing takes place in post–Great-War backwater Louisiana with two brothers from Pittsburgh attempting to run their timber mill business against the background of various adversities, including the Sicilians whose business interests—a saloon and whore house—they threaten. Mississippi's Larry Brown sums it up well, "This novel soars in its evocation of a land and people lost to the mists of times. It's a story of men and women bound to a great forest by their destruction of it, and the ties of family and blood and evil and greed and good and human tragedy and human triumph. . . ."

Robert Birnbaum: Is *The Clearing* the best thing you have ever written?
Tim Gautreaux: Probably so. I would say so.

RB: If it were possible to quantify that, by how much of a margin?
TG: It's a step up in project size from short-story writing, which is what I am known for. The short story, of course, is a wonderful form that I love dearly. It is a manageable form. You are in and out in six or seven thousand words.

73

The novel, of course, has to keep going beyond that to one hundred and thirty, one hundred and fifty thousand words, and it's very easy to lose your way. It's a quantum leap from story writing. So it pleased me that I seem to have come out of the woods with this particular one. At least, according to the reviewers, if the reviewers are to be believed.

RB: You said a few things there that caught my attention. Starting with "if the reviewers are to be believed." Isn't it the case that when you put the pen down or hit "save" for the last time on the computer, you say something like, "I've done it"?

TG: No. I don't think so.

[Both laugh]

Not at all. When you finish that first draft you know that you are at the beginning of a long, dark, smoky tunnel. And then, of course, there is second draft. And then you show it to your wife and then you have a third draft resulting from that. And then you send it off to your agent and there's a fourth draft resulting from that. And then he sells it. And then there are fifth, sixth, and seventh drafts that come from that and a couple of final polishes. And even after you cut it loose and you get back the first hard-back copy you are reading somewhere on page six and you say, "Oh I can't believe that I put those two words that close together, etc." So it's never finished. And you never get the feeling like, "This is a grand masterpiece." If it is, you certainly don't know it. At least in my way of thinking. Somebody will tell you if it's great.

RB: Well, is it at least a relief to finish?

TG: I think so. It goes along with automatic writing. The notion behind automatic writing is that things are a little bit out of your control. The language you put on the page is a gift and it comes from somewhere and you are not quite sure where. Very often it is from experience—which means writing a lot over many years and also your own worldly experience that you transmogrify into art. But still you sometimes write a sentence and you ask yourself, "Where did that come from? How did that come out of me?" And that's a wonderful thing about writing or any creative genre—the surprise that you bring upon yourself while you are composing.

RB: You also said that you were pleased to have written this novel, but you have published another novel. Are there other unpublished novels?

TG: There are two or three novels that I have written that are sealed in Tupperware in the attic.

RB: [laughs] That indicates that you are interested in preserving them.
TG: Only from the roaches. I am not sure they will ever see the light of day. Several people I know who are famous writers have two or three rookie novels that wound up in the fireplace because they didn't want anyone finding them. That might be wise.

RB: At this point the publishing industry buzz, for what it's worth, is "breakout novel." You've been at this for quite a while now, haven't you?
TG: I taught creative writing for thirty-one years or better. I'm fifty-five now and I retired in December. And I have always had to write a lot to justify my existence as a creative writing teacher. I started out as a poet and then began to work in the short fiction form in the late '70s at the urging of Walker Percy. It just takes a long time to hit your stride as a writer and teacher. One robs time from the other. But it takes a long time to develop as a writer even if all you do is write. One of the last things I got in the mail before I retired was an anthology of American literature and the last section of the anthology was New American Writers, and I checked the bios on each writer, and the youngest one was born in 1949. Which says something about how long it takes to hit your stride as a writer.

RB: What do you make of the twenty-year-olds that are being published?
TG: They tend to be the exception rather than the rule. These are people with a blinding amount of talent. After all writing a novel is not rocket science, and if you are genius you can do it—but there are damn few of those around.

RB: I've talked to quite a few young writers recently. I wonder where they go from here.
TG: I would rather peak late than early.

RB: Let's talk about the subject at hand, *The Clearing*. Is it a Southern novel or a Louisiana novel or a bayou novel? Or none of the above?
TG: I hope none of the above. Because I am very wary of the label "Southern writer." Of course, I live in Louisiana and I was raised in south central Louisiana, born and raised there. I was raised in every cliché known to man

about the Deep South. Once you allow yourself to be labeled, you begin to believe the label and then when you compose you feel duty bound to include as many of the usual clichés as you possibly can about your region. That's a terrible thing to happen to a writer, and I hope that it doesn't happen to me too much. When people interview me they ask if I consider myself a Southern writer. This seems like an honest question. Well, it is an honest question. But it's a hard one to answer. I prefer to put a little different spin on it—I consider myself a writer first who happens to live in the South. If I had been born in North Dakota I would still be a writer. I would probably have had a similar life. But my people and my settings, my moods, my skies, my waterways would be from North Dakota or South Canada. I would still be writing something.

RB: If you were currently living in Seattle would you be writing about the bay and the ocean, the mountains or about mangrove swamps and alligators and Cajun fisherman?

TG: You'll notice that when I gave the little North Dakota spiel I said, "If I had been born and raised in North Dakota . . ." Wherever you are born and raised tends to have profound effect on your fictional world. I don't know why. Ernest Gaines left Louisiana when he was sixteen. And the only fiction he writes that seems to be really powerful and effective and moving is fiction that is set in Louisiana. And he knows this and he has tried to write about California and San Francisco, where he has lived, by this time probably as much or more than he has lived in Louisiana. And it just doesn't seem to work for him. He has said this himself. One reason he has come back to Louisiana in his later years and is living there at least half the time is so that he can write and get in touch with what matters to him—the rhythms of speech. The music of the language around him and the feel of the weather. It's in his bones. We are talking about a man who really didn't write at all before he left here. He never thought he would be a writer. But everything that has magic to it in Ernest Gaines's writing stems from a period before he was sixteen years old. I think that is the same with me. You really learned everything you need to know about human nature directly or indirectly by the time you are fifteen or sixteen. You know what your family history is, what your structures are, whether you are paying attention to it or not, what their values are. And, of course the language of your region and all that is in your literary bones, so to speak. You know the cadences of the relatives' parlance and you can go somewhere and you can live a long time, and it just doesn't ring true. I used to spend summers with my sister out in California.

In my first novel, *The Next Step in the Dance*, which did really well, I had a long section in Los Angeles, and my editor, who was originally from Los Angeles, said she found it unconvincing, "No, the Louisiana stuff is fine and has heart, but this LA stuff is kind of one dimensional. Let's trim it back." And trim it back. And trim it back. And finally the novel, which was maybe thirty percent in California, was maybe seven percent.

RB: A while back I spoke with Mark Winegardner, and he pointed out that southern readers are extremely loyal to their own. And also that some writers were trying to pass themselves off as Southern. In the past was being called a Southern writer a slur?

TG: I don't think so, but it can be limiting. It's not a big problem. From a marketing point of view, sometimes people see "great southern novel" on the cover of a book, and if you are a Minnesota native you say, "I don't want to read about those nasty people, those sweaty folk down there." So there might be a little market resistance to that. Then conversely, people seek out Southern fiction. People in England are fascinated with it. I have lots of sales from my books in California. For some reason the West Coast is interested in the Deep South and in Southern literature, particularly Louisiana. I don't think it's that big of a problem—but I have forgotten the original question.

RB: Me too. When I was thinking about your book it occurred to me that I loved John Biguenet's *Oyster*. Is he a Cajun? His is a French name.

TG: Parisian French. His family came over in the 1740s. My family are relative newcomers. We came over in 1785.

RB: And I liked John Dufrense's books and James Lee Burke's Dave Robicheaux series. Something about that swamp setting is compelling.

TG: All of us are Catholic. I don't know if that has anything to do with it.

RB: That had not occurred to me. It seems so languidly chaotic. I was talking to Arthur Kempton, who has written a book on black American pop music, and he said he had briefly listened to reggae music but that he was drawn to New Orleans music and he called it American reggae. Though I am certain that it is different from the rest of the state, New Orleans seems to have something special about it.

TG: New Orleans has a wonderful music scene that starts up around ten o' clock and goes and goes and goes. Any big city has this, I imagine, but there'll be thirty or forty bands playing in town on any given night—in small clubs and big clubs and crazy clubs. My favorite is Rock n Bowl, which is an upstairs twelve-lane bowling alley from the 1940s. They changed the locker area into a dance floor and have music nightly—rhythm and blues and Cajun music and Zydeco—just about any kind you want. It is a bizarre gumbo of cultures as you say. The whole place is dedicated to the Blessed Virgin and they have St. Joseph altars there during that time of year for Catholic ceremonies and a big bar serving hard liquor and any kind of beer you want, while all this is going on. It's a wonderful, wonderful place. And you can bowl and dance on the lanes if you want. It typifies New Orleans. It's such a mixture of white music, Afro-American music, Cajun music, and French black Louisiana music. Which is really strange. People still can't get over seeing African Americans playing an accordion and wearing cowboy hats and speaking French. But that's what we have especially in southwest Louisiana. The results of a chemistry even people that live in New Orleans don't understand. And they don't want to understand it, because if you understand something, it loses its magic.

RB: That sounds Catholic.
TG: You're right. Exactly. Three persons in one God. You can't understand it. Well, that's fine. And it's kind of a template for how we live, how New Orleanians live. We don't know why it works but it sure is fun and weird.

RB: Is there a city/country split?
TG: Definitely. Louisiana is three states. Forty percent of it is Cajun country. Although even within that country there are different categories. There are two types of Acadian language spoken down there. Less and less each day. But it is still spoken in some regions. And then there is New Orleans, which is separate, unlike the rest of the state. It's more cosmopolitan. And north of Alexandria and north of Lake Pontchartrain a few miles, it's the Bible belt. Just like Georgia, Alabama, or Mississippi.

RB: *The Clearing* seems like the kind of story that has been gestating or percolating, fermenting for some time. It doesn't strike me as something you just decided to write after you finished with the last thing you wrote.
TG: That's completely on target. It is a novel that has been percolating perhaps twenty or twenty-five years. And started with some tales I heard about lawmen in Louisiana in the 1920s and 1930s. A distant relative was a constable at a sawmill back in the '20s. And my great grandfather was a city marshal in the little town where I grew up. There were other lawmen that

were in the Gautreaux clan on my mother's side too. They came to bad ends at the hands of criminals at the turn of the century. You hear—not stories so much—but mentions at family gatherings, of these older relatives. "You remember Murvie?" "Oh yeah, he was the one that got shot when . . ." And that's it. You would hear one sentence. To a ten-year-old that's magic. That's money in the bank. And you'd ask a question, "Well, why did they shoot him?" "You don't need to know about that." Which makes it even more fascinating for a young child hearing this. Most of my family members were . . . I was the youngest child of a youngest child. So the family members I grew up with were in their seventies or eighties. My mother had me when she was forty-one and she was born in 1907. And she is still alive. She is ninety-six now.

RB: That bodes well for you.
TG: One hopes.

RB: You're going to have a lot of time to fill up.
TG: So the novel has coalesced around an enormous raft of these little one- and two-sentence tidbits that I have absorbed all my life. Starting from the 1950s going back to the '60s and '70s and it all just comes together one day, "Well let's see if I can write a novel about this." And you sit down and that first outline starts to grow like a tomato plant. You start with one fact and then "I'm going to write about this marshal and he's in trouble." "Who's going to help him?" "Maybe he needs a brother?" So you come up with a brother. One thing generates another until finally you've got a structure you can start with and kind of outline. The most important decision I made in *The Clearing*, and this goes back to your original question about the Southern writer, is point of view. I decided in the book early on, even when I was writing the outline, to have the point of view of some outlanders. Some people who were not from the South. So I came up with these two brothers from Pittsburgh. They are the points of view. You see the action of the novel, basically, through their eyes and their sensibilities. And that makes all the difference in the world—instead of this being another Southern novel where the artist has put together a bunch of uneducated deplorable folks and allowed them to self-destruct for four hundred pages.

RB: [laughs]
TG: You have a different chemistry going there. You put the non-Southern reader into the novel with this particular choice that I made. It seems like a

simple choice but it has had a profound effect on how people take the action that goes on in the book. It's not just a bunch of depraved people beating up on each other. It's some sensitive people, some Yankees, my god, who are down there.

RB: There are two women who seem to be unexpectedly powerful. The younger brother's wife who comes down from Pittsburgh. She seemed like she would not do well in this hard scrabble place of a lumber mill in the backwaters of Louisiana. But she thrives. And the black housekeeper who adds some surprising plot twists.
TG: Men don't exist without women. You can't write a novel without having women in it. Let's face it, they are all over the place and they are in every-body's world. So I had to have the women in this novel or it would have been artificial. I have heard feminists complain, with great justification, of how there are some novels particularly western novels, that have no women in them. It's all men. That's just unrealistic.

RB: You could have gotten away with it. This is a very remote place deep in the wilds. Like the Alaska Pipeline. There wouldn't have been any women there.
TG: I guess so. I thought it would be less realistic. These are normal men. They have normal desires and loves. They are going to have their love with them. They can afford to, let's put it that way. Whereas the lumber company employees that are basically single men from east Texas who are there be-cause the east Texas mills have run out of timber. You can expect that work force is pretty much going to be womanless. Which is part of the problem with them. The danger with those characters [you mentioned] is I found them very attractive and interesting and powerful women. The danger was they were going to take over the narrative. So I had to watch myself and limit their influence in the novel somewhat so they didn't take over. The narrative is about the two brothers. The focus is on them. And really, another novel could have been written with the women. They were wonderful. Someone who read the novel thought I gave these women short shrift. If I had devel-oped plot lines for them that were any more elaborate the novel would have been something else. It would have gone off on a tangent.

RB: That sounds like a criticism about the book that you didn't write.
TG: [laughs]

RB: A critic took Tom Franklin [*Hell at the Breech*] to task because the word "nigger" doesn't appear much in his novel, which is set in Alabama in the 1890s. The complaint was that this was not real, a false note. Are you compelled to use vernacular?

TG: If you are going to give an accurate portrayal of a particular time you have to look at the linguistic patterns and idioms of the time. And you have to be honest. It's something a writer thinks about naturally. But I taught *Huckleberry Finn* enough times as a college instructor to understand the purposes of the language in the South, particularly. Some of the positive characters in the novel or at least one of them does use the dreaded "n" word. That's because in 1923 in the Deep South everybody used it and to tell you the truth, a lot of people used it in the North. It's just realism. The main characters don't use it because they are from Pittsburgh and they are educated but that's not the real reason they don't use it. It was considered very impolite and rude.

RB: I understand that some language placed in a character's mouth may ring false. I don't know how telling it is if a character doesn't use certain language.

TG: It's kind of a reverse PC. It's kind of skittery.

RB: Was that the only pejorative term for black people?

TG: There was no lack of them. There were innumerable hideous terms for Jewish people and Italian people. Even Germans. So there is no lack of those for that particular time. There would be a danger of overkill if you just peppered the narrative with dozens of these things. What would be the point? Unless you were trying to deal with a one-dimensional racist character that you were trying to send up. Which I find to be an uninteresting endeavor for a fiction writer to deal with—a one-dimensional character.

RB: It's the kind of thing that Spike Lee did in *Do the Right Thing* and reprised in *The 25th Hour*, where there is a montage of races and religions when a narrator is speaking the most racist, insulting invective. But we digress. *The Clearing* seems to end with a number of narrative possibilities. Why did you end where you ended? Or are you thinking of a sequel?

TG: I had ideas for the novel to go on. I wasn't quite sure how long I could stretch out the tension. The short story writer in me wanted to keep things succinct. I can't give away too much but there is a certain something that happens towards the end of the novel which effectively ends it. I could have not had that happen and extended the novel even unto other sections. For example, I was thinking . . . After the mill was finished cutting that tract of lumber, the family could have gone on to another tract somewhere and then the violence could have followed them. The particular Mob members that were after (that sounds terrible) them could have continued going after them. The novel could have gone into the '40s when the baby grows up and asks questions about its origins. It could have gone through the Second World War and drawn parallels with the First World War and the Civil War, because they figure in this novel. It could have gone on and on and on. I was afraid to lose the focus of the world I had created down there at that lumber mill site. I was dreading the reviews that would go like this, "Well, this was a wonderful novel as long as he stayed in the swamps of Louisiana but the minute he moved back to east Texas . . ."

RB: [laughs]

TG: So I just decided to go for 350 pages or however long the novel is and stop.

RB: Okay, I am still wondering. There is a ripeness about this novel that suggest other tangents and back-stories. May, the housekeeper, is a smart cookie, she seems to be a novel unto herself. Or the one-eyed assassin. Far be it for me to suggest what you should write but a group of inter-connected stories might be the thing.

TG: Believe me I'm thinking about it. As you say, a certain fictional world has been set down as a foundation and it could be something to build on. One hopes that if I do that they won't say I am copying Cormac McCarthy's *Border Trilogy* with a Swamp Trilogy or something. Cormac has done a wonderful thing for El Paso with that first novel and the second kind of built on that success. It would be nice if I could do that. I am thinking along those lines.

RB: I don't think people criticized Faulkner for being stuck in his fictitious county or William Kennedy for the Albany books. Sometimes a locale or family seems to warrant that extended attention. I am surprised that more writers don't do that.

TG: I agree. You can look at Faulkner and what he has done, of course, and other writers as the great archetype for doing that and there is absolutely nothing wrong with it. And some writers have an irrational fear that goes beyond my fear of being labeled solely as a Southern writer. They really want to show breadth, show flexibility and write about Canada and South Africa as well as Vermont, you see. And that's great but it's also great to create a magical and vivid world which you can stay in or stay close to . . . I don't think that's necessarily a bad thing. It's just a different type of writing. Faulkner was a great writer. He stayed in one spot. Shirley Ann Grau is as great a writer and her novels, each one is different from the other.

RB: Where do you live?
TG: Hammond, Louisiana, which is about an hour north of New Orleans. The southeast toe of Louisiana.

RB: When you step off a plane in Boston and you look around besides all the red brick, is there a palpably different feeling?
TG: I was walking around this morning and I thought, "A hundred and fifty years ago there was a lot of money here." You walk around in Louisiana and you say, "A hundred and fifty years ago there were Indians here and trees and no dwellings." New Orleans is an old city but much of the state is . . . the population is half of what New York City is and it's losing people. The feeling is there was money, there was civilization, there was education, and there was good fortune here. When you go down to New Orleans, things are a lot seedier and there is less money and it's just different. You walk down the streets in the older neighborhoods in New Orleans you see a lot of front porches. I noticed that you don't see that up here. That's just dictated by the weather. Up until 1955 you couldn't stay in a house in Louisiana after three o' clock. You had to go out on the front porch because it was too darn hot in the house. And there is a different rhythm of life. If you were a field worker up here, I imagine you could spend the whole day up out in the field working. You can't do that in Louisiana. You would drop dead around eleven thirty. So people got up at four and worked until ten and then knocked off until four and worked until nightfall in the summer. They would get their ten hours of work in but couldn't work between eleven and three.

RB: Sugar was the cash crop?
TG: Mainly sugar cane in the southern regions and there was some cotton. Cotton has always been a poor man's crop. Without getting into a six-hour lecture, the agricultural entities up here and in the Midwest were controlled by individuals. In the South they were controlled by, in the beginning, plantation owners and after slavery the plantation owners and the bankers and

the local storeowner. The whole economy was controlled by that. It has always been a poor man's economy, the agricultural part of it. That changed in the '40s and '50s but not until then.

RB: Was Huey Long a symptom or a result of change?
TG: Long was a demagogue who took advantage of the times. People praise Huey Long in Louisiana for building bridges and roads but the truth is in the 1930s all the states were building bridges and roads. The technology for developing concrete or asphalt highways and bridges had come to the point where it was time for the Deep South to be paved. And it was happening all over. Huey Long didn't do that for Louisiana. It was the same thing that was happening in Alabama and Arkansas and Georgia.

RB: And Louisiana State University?
TG: It was only by accident. He wanted a big football team that he could brag about. Like most politicians he cared not a whit about education.

RB: To return to what may be enveloping you, the warm fuzzy feeling of having written a well-received book. You are going to spend some period of time going out and talking about it and then what?
TG: Life after the book tour? I guess you go home and start writing another one.

RB: You recently retired. Are you spending more time on the front porch?
TG: I mentioned before I was Catholic and that comes with a suitable amount of guilt. I heard the parable of the talents where terrible things happen to you if you don't take advantage of what has been given to you. I have often said this, "If you are a talented singer or dancer you would somehow feel it was wrong not to sing or dance." I think a literary artist is the same way. If you decide I have enough money, I have all the fame I can handle, so let me do something else. You can do that. That's fine. It would make me feel guilty as if I was not giving what I should be giving.

RB: And is there a parallel drive to get your stories down on paper?
TG: You have to use your talent whatever it is. And that's what you do when you sit down in front of the word processor. If you didn't you would feel bad. [laughs] Also I can remember when I was a child and there was this woman in the neighborhood that had a gorgeous singing voice. She would come over and have coffee sometimes and she would, if there were enough

people around, someone would say, "Well Georgia why don't you sing us a song?" and she would stand up and sing something, some old show tune or whatever. She had a marvelous voice. I thought, "This woman is not in the entertainment business at all. She could just go through her life and not sing a note except in the bathtub but she chooses to share her voice with others." I saw that as the right thing to do.

RB: How clear is your sense of what you are going to do next?

TG: I feel really good about whatever it is I am going to do next. [both laugh] I enjoy writing once I can get into it. It's just that I have so many other interests. It's hard for me to get started again sometimes. So I have to rely on a sense of duty. I am looking forward to my next project. I have two or three short stories down—I am thinking maybe the basis of another collection. And there is one busted novel that possibly could be resurrected and rewritten.

RB: You are going to unseal the Tupperware?

TG: [laughs] Those are also sealed in gorilla glue and way in the corner of the attic. This is a novel set in Louisiana about the chemical industry. Believe it or not. It's got some bad things in it. I was reading too much James Lee Burke when I wrote it so there are some Taiwanese assassins that have to be removed. But it might be able to be salvaged.

RB: Given your confessed religious predilections, are you self motivated to publish every few years?

TG: As soon as I can. I think once I can actually sit down . . . my computer committed suicide about six weeks ago. A totally useless piece of machinery. And I have thrown it away and I have ordered a new whiz bang computer with all the bells and whistles and big plasma screen and I expect that to have some effect on me. I'll feel guilty about not writing with this expensive machine in my office.

RB: This book strikes me as much as anything I have read, maybe more so, as the foundation for a terrific movie. Anything happening on that front?

TG: I have a film agent, of course, sending out copies of the book. I tend to think in cinematic terms. I like to craft words so that they have a strong visual effect on the reader. Not just a glimpse but a glimpse occurring within a larger construct. Which is one reason why I was afraid of moving the novel past the main setting of Nimbus, Louisiana, this sawmill town. I spent so much time placing the reader in this world. One review out in Los Angeles said, "Finishing the novel was like coming out of matinee into the sunlight and thinking that world that you had just emerged into is not the real one but the one in the theater is the real one." That was a great compliment. But it's something that I worked very hard to achieve. And I want to continue that in any next work. When you mention trilogy (I mention trilogy) I thought it would be nice if somehow I could continue that. I wandered away from the question . . .

RB: Whether there is real interest in making *The Clearing* a movie?
TG: My stories have been optioned over and over for various movie projects. None of which, except some excellent student films, have been made. People do write me for movie rights every now and then and if you know anything about the Hollywood crowd, they are always reading fiction and calling up the house and saying, "I really like this as a movie project. Would you be interested?" I say, "Sure," and then I never hear from them again. But at least people are thinking about the cinematic possibilities of even the short stories.

RB: Well, good. Thank you so much.
TG: Thank you.

Tim Gautreaux: A Conversation with Darlene Meyering

Darlene Meyering/2004

This interview was conducted by Darlene Meyering before a live audience as part of Calvin College's Festival of Faith and Writing on 22 April 2004. Used with permission of the Festival of Faith and Writing, Darlene Meyering, and Tim Gautreaux. The interview was transcribed by Lowell Wyse and edited by L. Lamar Nisly. While some informal elements have been regularized, the conversational component of the occasion is maintained in this written version.

DM: Good afternoon and welcome to this time of interview with Tim Gautreaux. My name is Darlene Meyering, and I serve as executive associate to the president of Calvin College. I've always been an avid reader, a lover of words and books, bookstores and book discussions, and have been in a couples' book club with my husband for over fourteen years. So today we will converse as reader to writer with Tim Gautreaux, and hopefully will have time for your questions as well. Tim Gautreaux was born and raised in Louisiana and until his retirement served for thirty years as professor of creative writing at Southeastern Louisiana University. His first collection of short stories, *Same Place, Same Things*, was published in 1996 by Picador, after first appearing in an impressive list of magazines, like the *Atlantic Monthly*, *GQ*, and *Harper's* among others. The second collection, *Welding with Children*, recognized twice by the *New York Times* in their annual one hundred noteworthy books list, was published in 1996, adding journals like *Story*, *Fiction*, and *Zoetrope* to his credits. His first novel, *The Next Step in the Dance*, was published in 1998, and his most recent novel, *The Clearing* in 2003 by Knopf. Tim Gautreaux was the John and Renee Grisham Southern Writer in Residence at the University of Mississippi, and has received both a National Endowment for the Arts fellowship and the National Magazine Award for Fiction.

Critics and reviewers call his stories exquisite windows into the lives of ordinary, hardworking, blue-collar Louisiana Cajuns. In the style of Faulkner, his characters survive due to their strength and resiliency. They are realistic and they endure. Although I've been to most of the states in the U.S., somehow I've never made it to or through Louisiana—until this past year when I was introduced to the work of Tim Gautreaux. I've still never stepped on the earth in the state, but I have felt the heat and humidity. I've smelled the gumbo and beans. I've tasted the refreshing, cold beers. I've seen the claptrap gulf towns, the abandoned cars and trucks in the yards, the wash on the line, and the oily rusting steam engines left in the deserted factory yards. I've tapped my feet to the lively dance music and the Cajun accordions. I've seen the deep faith of the people and have heard the click of the rosary beads as they've waited for a shrimp boat caught in a storm.

One cannot introduce the work of Tim Gautreaux without noting his uncanny ability to master the use of similes. I'll pick up a few. The first, from the short story "Waiting for the Evening News," serves as an example. This is a description of a nondescript backwater town, and it goes like this: "One of a few asbestos siding and tin communities strung along the railroad like ticks on a dog's backbone." Or, from *The Next Step in the Dance*: "Colette, you've got a tongue on you like a fillet knife!" Or, "words lodged in her open lips like an undelivered kiss."

If you have not yet read the books of Tim Gautreaux, I hope this small taste today will have you lined up at the bookstore to buy all four.

DM: Your first published collection of stories was released in 1996, after about twenty years in teaching. I've worked in the academic environment for twenty-one years, and I know that time for writing must be found. What was it like for you to balance your urge and need to write yourself with the rigors of teaching writing, especially the grading of papers and student stories?

TG: First of all, one reason I became a short story writer early on is because the short story form can be created in the little interstices of available time to professors. Those of you who write and are academics know that you might have a day, an afternoon, or maybe a weekend, several late nights available for you to put some sort of fictional world together, and the short story form lends itself to that type of development. You're only dealing with 7,000 or 8,000 words—you can handle it. The problem for teachers is the larger projects. That's why I sort of came to novels and longer works late. The first novel was *The Next Step in the Dance*, and I had sent it through a couple versions and it wasn't coming together very well. Then a friend of mine, Barry Hannah, who was writer in residence at Ole Miss called me up one day and said, "You know, Tim, we need a writer in residence for a while up here at Ole Miss. Why don't you come up here and work for us. And I said, "Well, what do I have to do?" and he said, "Well, just sit in a house across the street from Faulkner's place and write." I said, "Well, sign me up!" While I was there, every day the novel stayed in my mind. In other words, when you're writing a long manuscript and you have to stop for two weeks to make out midterm exams and grade exams you come back to the manuscript two or three weeks later, fire up the computer and stare at the screen and say to yourself, "who are these people and why was I interested in them to begin with?" But, if you have a big block of time—three, four, five, six months—the characters stay in your head and you can deal with them every day. Even if you only write a half hour a day or an hour a day, they're there; you don't lose them. I believe it was Hemingway who said that when he was writing a novel he would stop on a Tuesday and on a Wednesday he would take it up again, and he would have to scan the entire manuscript up to the point where he'd stopped to try to remember what he was doing.

DM: You show a very deep love of family, faith, community, and Cajun culture in your writing, yet most of your characters have little education. As an educator, what have these people taught you?
TG: Well, I'm basically a blue-collar kid. My folks were not well educated; they basically had a high school education. Of course I went to college in the sixties when in America there was an astounding upsurge in college attendance, so I'm just part of the normal demographic of that era. But I grew up around a lot of uneducated, blue-collar type folk in a region of the area known for its poverty—a region of the United States really known for the rural nature of the swamps and things. You write what you know about, and these are the types of people that I know about. Somebody asked me one time, "Why don't you write a story about an accountant?" I wasn't raised around accountants. You know, I didn't come from an accountant factory, or whatever.

DM: You've been quoted as saying, "No story is interesting unless it deals with matters of values." Does that principle play out any differently in your short stories than in your novels?

TG: I don't think so. You know, if you're interested in questions of good and evil, right and wrong, having the guy with the white hat at least achieve some sort of Pyrrhic victory in your fiction—this is just part of your nature as a creator, as a writer, as an inventor of narrative structures. Fiction that's completely negative just doesn't interest me. I find it one-dimensional. Teachers of creative writing face this dilemma a lot. It's sort of fashionable among young intellectuals to be totally dark in their outlook. To be a card-carrying intellectual you have to be an atheist or something like that—I never did of course subscribe to that. I thought it was just kind of a stage. Maybe if Nietzsche had lived to be a lot older he would have converted to Episcopalianism or something.

DM: Music is integral to so many of your stories—the lively dance tunes of *The Next Step in the Dance*, the sentimental ballads in *The Clearing*, the healing, smoky tunes of Michelle on the rebuilt satin-black Steinway in the Lafayette motel bar. What is your musical training, and why is music so important in your stories?
TG: You know some people have said that writers write to create things that they don't have. And one thing I've always wanted to have is a good musical ability—which I don't. My motto as a pianist is "never let the right hand know what the left hand is doing."

DM: Well, my piano teacher told me, "My dear, your talents lie in other areas."
TG: But music of course fascinates me. Mechanisms interest me—the logical behavior of motors and machines, steam engines, windmills just sort of fascinate me—it's just a genetic defect. And I tend to see narrative structures like stories or poems or novels in kind of a mechanistic way. Especially in the part that a mechanism like a lawnmower or an automobile engine doesn't have any extraneous parts, and neither should a good narrative or story. You know, we call them tangents or irrelevancies, but if you really think of a good story—a tightly woven story—as a mechanism, it's easy for you to clip what should not be in the story. And sometimes the quality of a story depends not so much on what's there, but what's been left out. What was the original question? We've wandered off.

DM: Music.
TG: Music. Right. You know when I started teaching, as a professor, my salary—I had a Ph.D. in hand—my salary was $10,000 a year. That was in

1971 or '72, whenever I started teaching. But you can't do much on that. Most academics did other things—they were music teachers or mechanics. I had a good friend who was a Ph.D. in American literature who used to work as a cook off-shore on an oil rig just to make enough money to support his family. In those days the salaries for academics were incredibly bad. (They're a little better today.) But I started tuning pianos—because you don't have to be able play to tune, and the mechanism interested me. I started getting more and more involved in pianos. I was a tuner. I began to rebuild player pianos, and then I graduated from regular upright players to reproducing grands, and I was kind of a specialist—player grand pianos, the old pneumatic types, Ampicos and Duo-Arts. And I was able to make some money to help support the family that way.

DM: I had not heard of George Steck pianos before I read your book, but they're mentioned a couple of times. Is that a typical old Southern upright?
TG: Yeah, Steck was a tough old piano. They were marketed a lot in the South because they could take a lot of moving, a lot of humidity.

DM: A lot of your stories involve children—especially the second generation—who are a disappointment to their parents, like Bruton's four daughters in "Welding with Children" or Merlin LeBlanc's daughter in "The Courtship of Merlin LeBlanc." Frequently the parents start to parent that generation, and they're better parents to them than they were to their own children. And they become better people. Where in your experience do these repeated themes come from?
TG: Well, it's no secret to anybody that there are a lot of grandparents raising children—young children, grandchildren—and it cuts across all levels of society and economic condition. I would notice as a teacher of a survey course in a fairly rural university—and a sophomore survey course has thirty, forty people in it—I started noticing that I would get a lot of excuses from women. Well, the shortened version is I had a lot of single mothers in these classes. And the excuses would be, "Well, my grandparents couldn't take care of my kids today, so that's why I can't come to class." You know, I get a phone call. Or, "My grandparents can't keep the kids today. Can I bring them to class with me?" So I taught many, many lectures on W. B. Yeats and sexual dysfunction, or something like that, with five-year-olds coloring in the front row. No, I never really said that much about Yeats's sexual dysfunction—kind of an English teacher's joke. But I did cover some tough topics. You know we'd be talking about maybe racism if I was teaching *Huckleberry*

Finn, and there would be these babies there. And this was once or twice a month for thirty years.

DM: Your stories are mostly all based in a small area of southern Louisiana. The names you mention often are Lake Pontchartrain, Grand Crapaud, Tiger Island—these places become so vivid to us and real to us as we read. They offer a richness of characters and sights that don't grow dull to us, and they certainly don't grow dull to you. How can one small geographical area be so full of story? Tell us a little bit about the geography of your birth and the richness that you find in it personally.

TG: Well, first of all, every place is fascinating. As a creative writing teacher what you have to do is turn your students on to wherever their territory is, and explain to them, "Where were you raised?" "I was raised in a subdivision on the outskirts of Atlanta," and you have to explain to them, "Well, that's your God-given territory." You have to tell them that that subdivision is not like any other subdivision.

I did this with a student one time who was despairing of coming up with anything original to write about. She says, "I'm a mall-rat; I'm a subdivision kid. There's nothing interesting happening. Where I live is just like every other place in the world," which is of course not true. And I was familiar with the subdivisions in the region, so I said, "Then your subdivision is just like Beaux Chenes, which is a mile away from yours." And she said, "Oh, no; those are rich snobs." I said, "Oh, well, it's just like Oak Glen then." And she said, "Oh, no; those people are, like, one step up from trailer trash, don't compare us to those." And I named several other subdivisions and she said, "No, no. We're different from those people, you know, those people are all technocrats. Our fathers are all store managers." And I said, "Well, you see, what you've done is kind of illustrated to yourself, I hope, that your subdivision is—if you look at it in the right way, study it close enough—just as exotic as a Tibetan mountain encampment. I mean think about it—bring some Sherpas down to Atlanta and put them in a subdivision and see how amazed they are at what they see. It's just a point of view thing." So I find every place can be interesting, whether it's Minneapolis, Pittsburgh, Saskatchewan, God knows. And people think the Deep South is interesting, and it's some kind of foreign country or whatever, but I think that's a myth perpetuated by a lot of tourist commissions (and also some bad southern writers).

DM: What comes first in your fiction—the character, or the story itself?

TG: Well, short stories are propelled by narrative, by story structure. Novels are propelled more by character. And in different proportions. That's kind of a simple rule of thumb. I was at a loss for a new story project one time, and my wife said, "Why don't you write a story about a drunken priest, a priest that likes to drink too much?" And I thought boy, this is just a natural, automatic story here. Any way you want to start that story it's going to be a winner because you've got this natural tension here of a religious person who has a little drinking problem. And it was a very successful story for me. It's called "Good for the Soul." I believe it's in *Welding with Children*. But all she had to give me was a little narrative thread, and I could generate an 8,000 word construct out of it. But you can't do that with a novel. A novel's a lot more demanding. You're dealing not only with story—it's got to have a good story, of course—but you've also got to have a kind of intense and complex development of character, because that's ultimately what's going to keep you reading. You ever start a novel and you just don't like the characters and you put it down? Or do what I do—throw it against the wall? I keep waiting sometimes for some kind of redeeming quality to come into this character's being and it never happens. I just get fed up with it. Who wants to read about these people?

DM: I didn't realize that you had been a piano tuner, and you have a story about a piano tuner in *Welding with Children*. Did you ever have a woman come on to you like that when you were a piano tuner?
TG: Alas, no.

DM: Now that you're retired from teaching—an early retirement, by the way (he's a young retiree)—how do you spend your time as a writer? Are you disciplined? Do you have a daily writing goal? And what's your process then to bring a book to completion?
TG: No, if I were disciplined I would be rich and famous. It's a good question. I write much less than I should. I have a lot of other things that I'm interested in—writing's not the only thing. Writing is hard work. It's painful work, and it's not fun. It's maybe enlightening or whatever, and it's certainly rewarding in many ways. When I think about writing I think about what one of my characters said (I believe in "Welding with Children")—"Everything that's worth doing hurts like hell." And that's everything. If it doesn't hurt, it's probably illegal. So at any rate, it's painful to sit down and start a monstrous project and know you're going to have to go on a book tour if it ever gets published or something.

You know, I got a fat retirement and the house is paid off, and the kids—

one's a lawyer and one's an electrical engineer—and I'm all set. I could not do anything—just ready to fade off into the sunset. I could do tours like this and just be satisfied with that, except for one thing, and that is a Catholic education.

DM: You mean guilt is good.
TG: Yeah, guilt.

DM: You know, Calvinist education does the same thing.
TG: I'll bet, yeah. But especially, you know, I remember those Bible stories we were read in maybe third grade or something like that. Especially the Parable of the Talents—you know that one, right? You know what happened to the guy who didn't invest his talents wisely, right? So, I don't want anything to do with the weeping and gnashing of teeth.

DM: A good place to stay away from.
TG: Yeah, that's got to be the outline of a new novel.

DM: We talked a moment ago about characters, and you said that you need characters who go through both the dark and the light. Where did you find Jesse McNeil and the toxic train disaster? Where did that come from in "Waiting for the Evening News?"
TG: Jesse McNeil in "Waiting for the Evening News" is just an engineer who's more or less doing his job and his train derails.

DM: Well, he does have an alcohol problem.
TG: Well, he drinks a half a pint of liquor before he goes on—it's his birthday and he wants to do something different. So he hides behind the engine house and drinks a half a pint of whiskey. It's on his train. And his train comes apart and wrecks. But as he points out himself (and the narrator, too) the same accident would have happened if he had been sober as a judge; it was just a mechanical malfunction. But he realizes he's schnockered and his train is blowing up behind him, so he runs off. Which has a lot of precedent for it—engineers who have been responsible for great disasters have run off before. "Waiting for the Evening News" is based on a story that's true. About seventeen miles from where I live, the Rolling Bomb (which is the Baton Rouge chemical train) passes. And it fell apart one day and blew up. And we're talking about 125 tankers of vinyl chloride and phosphine gas—

DM: So all that stuff that was mentioned in your story really happened—

TG: Yeah, all of that stuff just went on the ground and caught fire and burned. They were scared to put it out because the tankers kept blowing up and the streets were running three feet deep with Barsol and toluene and everything else. (It's a nasty train that goes through Hammond, from the Baton Rouge direction anyway.) And it burned for two or three weeks. So they just let it burn out; then they went in and dug up the whole town and threw it in the trash. They literally did. It was fantastically expensive; half the town burned down.

So, you know, the strange thing about that—you hear about truth being stranger than fiction. Actually the fact that Jesse McNeil was drunk and ran away is a vast simplification of what happened. The real engineer of the train got real drunk, and he was riding in the locomotive. He had deadheading with him a female clerk. She was riding back to Hammond from Baton Rouge in the engine cab (which of course is illegal). And right before the big wreck he said, "Hey, honey, you ever drive a train?" So he put her in the engineer seat, and she was blowing the whistle going down the track at 45 miles an hour. Just then a rack came off a log truck right in front of a big tanker of propane and punctured the propane tank. It blew up, and then all of the trailing cars crashed into each other in a big pile. It was sort of like a big campfire of tanker cars lined up and burning—you could see it from outer space. But if I had written that people would have said, "Oh, no, this is not believable at all. Give me a break—female clerk, you know, running the train—"

DM: And how did you come up with naming the priest—who brought Jesse, really, to a point of redemption—Lambrusco?

TG: Isn't that a wine?

DM: Yes it is.

TG: No, there's a lot of Sicilian priests in Louisiana.

DM: So it was nothing to do with Jesse's drinking then.

TG: No, I just chose that off the top of my head.

DM: Faith—we talked a little bit about that. Biblical images, stories, priests, prayers, miracles, nagging doubts—all those things are honestly and unashamedly evident in your books, yet none seems overly pious or pedantic, or even sentimental. How do you strike that balance as a Christian writer?

TG: It comes from just living in Louisiana in the 1950s. Louisiana is one of those places that has a very strong spiritual presence, even though it's a place where people like to drink and fight, and they're kind of coarse in some levels of society. (That's a vast oversimplification here.) But when I was a kid if you walked into a restaurant and you were maybe fifteen years old and ordered a hamburger, even a Protestant waitress would ask you, "Well, do you remember that it's Friday?" They'd look out for you—you weren't supposed to eat meat on Friday in those days, you see.

I went to a public university in Thibodaux, Louisiana, for four years, and there are, I believe six or eight Catholic holy days of obligation where you have to attend mass that's not on a Sunday, like All Soul's Day for example which is November first, August 15 the Feast of the Assumption, I believe. Well, the school would be dismissed so the Catholics could go to mass. No Louisiana college had class on November first because everybody was cut loose to go to mass. Or at least they would cut loose at a certain time.

DM: Did they go to mass?
TG: I went to mass, yeah. We go to mass drunk—you had to go to mass.

DM: Although your books are not racy, sex and relationships are central topics in many ways—sex, desire, lost dreams, secrets, innocence, loss of innocence—the stuff of love. What are your personal boundaries when writing about love, sex, and relationships?
TG: Well, I'm never graphic. There are some intimate occurrences maybe, but I'm never graphic. If you want graphic sex fiction, go buy a *Playboy* or something. I've been pious about this point before and said stuff like, "I'm not fond of building whorehouses out of words." But it's true, you know, I just don't see the point of being *nasty* in fiction. There are times I guess when an erotic approach will be right in fiction. Anything can be justified and right in a piece of fiction, particularly if a writer considers his duties to realism. But I don't go out of my way to titillate or arouse or anything. I figure that's Hugh Hefner's job, or Larry Flynt's.

DM: A lot of names recur in your books. Minos was your father's name. That character is in your books several times, or Etienne or Octave, and Thibodeaux, or Boudreaux. Do these names come only from your memory, or are the characters developed from the people sometimes?
TG: Oh, I don't use family members that much in fiction. Nothing that I

write in the way of a character is a copy or an approximation. Everything goes through the big creative veg-o-matic in my mind and really is a composite of many, many different characters. In *The Clearing* there is a sawmill constable named Merville. No, he's a town marshal for a sawmill town.

DM: And your grandfather was a town marshal?

TG: And my great-grandfather was a town marshal, but he died in 1931. Nobody knows a syllable of anything about him, so he's a complete fabrication. In other words, I never had a great-grandfather, so I invented this guy sort of as a family member, but I had no idea what he was really like or anything about him. Except a couple stories where he did have to break up fights with a shotgun.

DM: Well, that happened a lot in *The Clearing*, that's for sure.

TG: Yeah, I did some research on law enforcement in those days, and policemen in the 1930s were poor physical specimens. They were political appointees. Very often they were small people, sometimes they were old, and they were paid hardly anything—they had almost no fiscal budgets—and they were asked to do things like turn out at two o'clock in the morning and go into a kerosene-lit saloon and break up a razorblade and pistol fight between thirty lumberjacks. And if they didn't do it they would be fired. The reason they would be fired is not because they hadn't maintained the law; it was because several workers would be cut up and the business owners—the lumber mill owners for example—would be very angry that they had lost members of their work force. It would slow down their lumber production for a day or two. So that's the kind of relationship that the lawman had with the community. Basically he had to do anything to stop the fight—generally it was walk in the room and shoot the first guy that was handy, particularly if he wasn't a local.

DM: The character Colette in *The Next Step in the Dance* is so unhappy and ashamed of her life, I guess you might say, or community or family. She longs for more, and she goes all the way to California to find it, to seek her dreams, only to return home again. But still it takes years of change and tragedy and all sorts of experiences to wake her up or to mature her or to settle her down. Colette and Paul are certainly engaged in one of the most complicated dances of life ever possible. What makes it so hard for Colette to wake up and find contentment in family and community?

TG: Well, because she's human like the rest of us. You know, my wife tells me every day, "You really ought to get busy on this next novel. You know you could make a bazillion dollars." I say, "Yeah, yeah, right."

DM: But does she have a tongue a fillet knife?
TG: No, no, not at all. But it's slow for people to turn around. In other words people don't follow advice very easily. That's just our human nature. The last thing we want people to do is to tell us what to do, even if it's the right thing.

Walker Percy was looking at a manuscript of mine in 1977. It was the beginning of a novel that I had started to write. It was about two state policemen. And he said, "Well, this is all well-written and everything, but state policemen really don't think like this, they don't behave like this. Think about what you're doing here as far as logic and realism are concerned." And my reaction was, "Yeah, right, you know, this old guy is trying to tell—" This is *Walker Percy* giving me some literary advice out of the goodness of his soul, and I'm saying, "Yeah, what does he know." National Book Award winner . . .

And I was a creative writing teacher; I knew that it was important to listen, and I didn't. That novel was finished, and it's sealed in Tupperware in my attic right now.

DM: Will it ever come out?
TG: No!

DM: Families are strong in your books. Relationships are deeply rooted generations back. But many of the families have been deeply fractured. Yet the people move past the hurt often and take risks for each other. You credit your own family in most of all your acknowledgments in the front of your books. How did your own family shape your personal faith and values?
TG: Well, that's a good one. My father was always a very honorable man. You know, it's hard for me to explain what that means. He was a tugboat captain. He always tried to do the right thing. He was always very kind and good to me. But the sense of values probably that I have I couldn't even attribute. Because you grow up and you absorb these things like a plant and you don't really ask where these values come from or what they are. They're very complex, and it takes years long for them to develop. I was taught by Marianite nuns, which was a teaching order based in New Orleans—a very excellent group of nuns. A lot of Catholics I talk to talk about the nuns, how they used to beat them and stuff like that. But that was not the Marianites. And if they did whack you, you deserved it. What's the problem?

So they were very good religious teachers, too. And they gave me a good basis in values very early. You know you don't give somebody values when they're fourteen or fifteen or sixteen—you give them when they're two and three and four. Then when they're seven, and they reach the age of reason you have to hit them real hard. These people would say, "Well, I'm going to let my kids—when they grow up and they're twenty-one, they can decide whether or not they'll believe in God." I think they're taking a gigantic risk. I don't particularly believe in that.

DM: You just talked about honorable people and people who are not honorable. In "The Pine Oil Writers' Conference" you have two budding authors rooming together at this conference, and one is not very honorable while the other is trying to do the right thing. What's that story about? Any personal stuff in there?

TG: Oh, yeah, yeah. "The Pine Oil Writers' Conference" is basically about one of these writers' colony type things where the writers go and they have intensive meetings with published writers. They try to figure out the "answer," you know, what they can do to make them famous and world-renowned. There is no "answer." And it's about their trying to find this easy route. These couple of guys, they're trying to find the easy route to whatever makes excellent literature. And it's based on a couple of writing conferences that I went to in the early 1970s.

I went to one—I'm not going to say where it was or anything—but I asked my roommate, "What do you write?" And he says, "Well, I like stories." And I said, "What do you write? Have you ever written a story?" "No, I've never written anything." And I said, "Well, how many of these conferences have you been to?" And he says, "Oh I go to these a couple, three times a year. I really like coming to these things." And I said, "But you're not writing anything." And he says, "Well, no, but I'd like to."

So that got me curious. I started asking other people. And there were people in their fifties and sixties who had like written one short story or a quarter of a novel or whatever. And I realized that these people just liked hanging out at writing conferences; they never really did any writing. Basically they showed up because they wanted to go to a bunch of new restaurants (and maybe get laid). A couple years later I went to another writing conference about three states over and the same people were there. They were just riding the circuit, you know. This is what they liked to do.

Now there are some writing conferences at which a lot of work gets done, a lot of helpful information is picked up by young writers. Then there are some writing conferences that are just not very productive. You have to, I guess, get recommendations or talk to people who have actually been to them before you send in your money.

DM: Let's move now to *The Clearing* which is your latest book and probably has gained the most popularity. It's quite different from your other books. Same region, although it's historically much earlier, and it's a lot of the same names, the same light and dark ideas, but much darker than the others. So it's same in flavor, and the geography is the same (although it's wooded, not as swampy). What gave you the idea to write about your region, first of all, three generations back in history?

TG: I was a history minor in college, so history interests me. There are a lot of us working now who are really amateur historians. I was talking to Annie Proulx the other day who wrote *The Shipping News*, and she basically studied to take a Ph.D. in history. She made me realize that a lot of us are interested. We do a lot of reading of biography and historical works.

As far as why I set a novel in 1923, a lot of it is personal family history that's kind of woven into it. I was the youngest child of a youngest child. My mother was born in 1907. So my uncles were from that era or older. My uncles were born and my aunts were born in the 1880s and 90s. And then when they would get together and talk you can imagine what they talked about—it was really old stuff. And so really I grew up having a much better feel for the 1930s than I did for the 1960s, because I'd listen to these generations of old relatives recounting their experiences and telling stories about growing up in the Depression and working on steam locomotives in the 1920s. So that's one reason why I chose that era. There was just so much that I'd heard about it, so much I knew about it. There's a lot of research about that era available. And also there's not much written about that time. People think the 1920s in the South, for example, was the modern age. And it's not. In the rural South we were behind the West. The West was more or less "civilized" in 1910 or something like that with railroads, telegraphs. You could build highways pretty easily over those deserts. But in the Deep South and the timber breaks and swamps there were lots of areas that were not reached by civilization until the early 1940s. Rural electrification didn't come to many areas of the Deep South until the early to mid-1950s. So you get kind of a *Heart of Darkness* effect in the novel. Since the point of view characters are from Pittsburgh actually, there's a descent from the Northeast and the paved roads and the telephones into areas where the infrastructure is weaker and more rickety and then nonexistent and then unheard of when you wind up in this sawmill at the Gulf of Mexico level of geography. And you're very disconnected from all of this. It's not like you're in America in 1923 at all. It's like you're in maybe Bogota, Colombia, in 1894 or something. It's really primitive.

DM: Were any of your relatives psychologically damaged in the first World War as Byron was?

TG: Oh, yeah. I had an uncle who was born in 1897 who was in all eight major American engagements—Château-Thierry, Meuse- Argonne—all of them. And he was shot up and gassed with mustard gas. He was alive until the 1980s, and he was always around the neighborhood, a visitor in our home. And so I saw what shellshock and being in the middle of that type of conflict could produce on a veteran. He was just absolutely ruined and devastated by it. But you have to realize that it was just an astounding meat grinder. You cannot imagine anything as bad as WWI was. And you think of things like that first big battle which lasted a good while when the British went in and lost their entire regular army, Ypres, and then the Battle of Verdun, where there were 435,000 men killed.

DM: *The Clearing* is really about as dark and muddy as the waters of the Chieftain that it's about. What accounted for your change of tone in this novel? It's so different from the love story of *The Next Step in the Dance*.

TG: Well, I always respond to criticism, being a good Catholic boy. Several critics thought that *The Next Step in the Dance* was fairly unambitious thematically. So I asked myself, well, what did they want? And I listen to every criticism. I involved myself with some more sophisticated themes with *The Clearing*—darkened the literature a little bit. Because some southern writers will tend to drift into a kind of amusing and anecdotal style and they get into the business of what Walker Percy called "amazing Yankees." "Let's people our little village with oddities and odd folk and have them do all sorts of depraved and amusing things that people in Minneapolis can condescend to while they read." "Oh, glad I don't live down there." I mean that's a danger because I think you turn out a fairly low-grade fiction if you set too many of your novels in beauty parlors. So I wanted to get away from that, branch out a little bit. It's one reason why I chose, as my point of view and my main characters, northerners. Because it added a whole new perspective on the narrative. The people in Minneapolis could be amazed with what was going on down there along with the two brothers from Pittsburgh. Whereas if I had just peopled it with a usual southern cast, nobody from out of the region, it would have been, I think, soundly labeled merely "southern fiction" and "here's a bunch of weirdos; let's see how they self-destruct."

DM: It seems like you could follow those characters in *The Clearing* and go beyond to yet more story. Have you thought about that? Is that in the works?
TG: No, but that's a good question, because in the outline for the novel I did go beyond where it ended. But there was a problem. I had created such a powerful presence with Nimbus, the mill town, that if the novel would go into East Texas or another section it would really lose a lot of steam. Just think of something like *All the Pretty Horses* finishing up in St. Paul. It just doesn't seem right, does it?

DM: Where did the incongruous name of Nimbus come from for this dreary and desolate ugly place?
TG: Well, lumbermen tended to be rather capricious with the way they named their camps. Nimbus just means cloud. And like a cloud that forms and then dissipates most of these lumber towns, particularly the isolated ones, just formed and disappeared. If you were a lumberman, what you did is you bought a 20,000-acre tract, and you built a railroad into the middle of the wilderness. Then you built houses enough for your workforce of 500 or 700 men; you built the mill; and you went into business. You cut the entire tract down to the last tree. And you had a town of 500 or 600 people out in the middle of the wilderness. You would then dismantle it. And within a month it was all gone.

DM: I had a lot more questions, but I'm just going to ask one more and then open it up to the people out here. The title *The Clearing* really has a lot more layers of meaning than just that lumber, that stand of lumber. That's the obvious one—that's certainly cleared—but there is so much that is cleared in many ways: the town conflicts, the racial conflicts, Byron's mind in some ways, the family tensions, marital relationships. Was it truly thought about that this has all of these layers of meaning, and is that part of the concentric circles of clearing the stand of lumber? There was just a lot of clearing going on.
TG: Yeah, a whole lot of clearing going on. Well, I didn't think about it all that much—you know titles don't mean much to me.

DM: Well, I'm so . . . I'm devastated!
TG: I mean, the book is kind of more important than the title.

DM: Well, yes it was!
TG: You know, my editor came up with that title.

DM: After he read it?
TG: Yeah.

DM: I'm, I'm crushed.
TG: He's a lot smarter than I am.

DM: The blind horse was smarter than the characters, too.
TG: Yeah, that's true. That's right. Everybody wonders about the symbolism of the blind horse, you know, and the symbolism of the Victrola and all that. And I don't deal in symbols too much.

DM: Well, we were finding them, weren't we?
TG: Well, you know, once an author turns a work loose on an audience it belongs to the audience, and if there are symbols in there, go for them!

DM Let's have some questions from you.
Q: In *The Clearing* there is one scene where Merville comes into the kitchen with Randolph. The baby is there with May. May walks out, and Merville takes the baby's hand and looks at the palm. Randolph says, "What are you doing?" And I want to know, too.
TG: There are several references in there like that. What Merville is looking for, of course, is how dark the child is. This predicts his future in the South. If the child has a certain skin tone he can be whatever he wants. If the child is just the tiniest shade wrong people will always wonder if he's of mixed blood, and in the South of course in the 1920s that was important. He's trying to figure out whose child it is. People were very color conscious in the Deep South in the 1920s—even African Americans were very color conscious. When African Americans would choose a mate—particularly in New Orleans—they would try to choose one that was the same color as they were. And light-skinned women did not associate with dark-skinned men, even from the same class. So it was not only white people that were interested in this question. The question of skin tone was always there in the Deep South. If someone's too red, we wonder if he's got some Indian in him, and if someone's too swarthy, we try to figure out the mix of Italian, and Spanish, and Indian. Nowadays it doesn't make any difference, but back in those days it did.

Q: Do you work from an outline? Do you always have one?

TG: I don't outline a story necessarily. I might jot down a few sentences to remind my fifty-six-year old brain what I'm doing. But a novel has to be outlined, in my view, because if you don't—and lots of novelists disagree with this—but if you make a mistake in structure in a novel, it can cost you just absolutely months of time. For example if you go off on a tangent. You don't outline the thing, you're writing along, and you develop this character named Nellie Bell. Then you spend six months working on her and produce 20,000 words of really good manuscript. Then you go on another 40,000 words, and you tell yourself, "You know what? This character Nellie Bell doesn't have anything to do with anything." So you've wasted all this time and all this energy, and she has to be cut out and thrown away. If you write an outline it will tend to keep you on track. Now an outline can change—it doesn't mean that you have to end the novel the way your outline suggests— but it's an arrow pointing you in a certain direction and keeping you on track. And I can't tell you how many of my friends who are novelists tell me these horror stories about getting hung up in an 1,100-page manuscript or a 750-page manuscript, saying, "I can't end this thing." And I think part of their problem is they didn't really outline, they didn't have a notion from the beginning of what might be extraneous.

Q: Did you grow up speaking French, Acadian French?

TG: My father spoke French, and we played at it around the house a little bit. But the older people didn't teach the kids French because they thought that it was obsolete by the 1940s. Also, in Louisiana speaking French meant that you were low class. If you spoke French you belonged to the class of *petits habitants*, the little people, the little residents, which is what some Cajuns were called. And of course, up until the 1950s if you spoke French in the public school on the playgrounds you were whipped by the English teacher. Basically the language is an eighteenth-century or seventeenth-century French that came down from Nova Scotia. For those of you who don't know what Cajuns are, they were exiles from Nova Scotia—the British kicked the Nova Scotians out in 1755, and a lot of them relocated in Louisiana.

Q: I'm a creative writing teacher. What do you think as a teacher was some of the best advice for writing students?

TG: One thing I stress is what a plot is. And the fact that plot is not some invention of a Republican congressman forty years ago. It's not peculiar to short story, and it's not even a literary device. Plot is what interests humans in any type of endeavor. By plot I mean the entanglement of two conflicts, the development of those conflicts up to a climactic moment. And then maybe some falling action, two or three sentences so that the reader's elbow doesn't fall off the table when he finishes the story. "And then the boiler blew up and killed everybody." We need a few more sentences to tie up some loose ends.

But that's the structure of a football game—the entanglement, the rising action, the climactic touchdown. It's the structure of a joke; it's the structure of a TV sitcom, of Shakespeare's plays. It's the structure of anything that engages human attention. So it's not peculiar to stories. And any time you violate the notion of plot—"I'm going to write this story backwards, start with the end"—you're just lying to yourself. You're not writing well. You're just trying to come up with some kind of weirdness that will gather somebody's attention. But nothing will gather somebody's attention like the entanglement of two conflicting forces. And that's one thing I really stress.

Also I tell students to let down their bucket where they are, into their own wells. Look at family history, talk to the old people, pay attention to the old people in their family, even the cantankerous ones that don't like them. Because every time an old person dies, a library burns down, and we lose all of this. As I was saying earlier about making students look upon their own territory as a special place and *their* territory, and very often their territory alone—that's important. It's hard to get young people to see that, but that's what I try to do.

DM: You also said last night when we spoke that you use the mechanism of an engine often as a mechanism for teaching students because nothing is unnecessary. Talk about that a little bit.

TG: Yeah, if you ever buy a new car and you go out in the driveway and you open the hood, do you see a sparkplug scotch taped to the side of the block, with a note on it saying, "found this on the floor at the factory. Thought you'd like to have it"? No! Everything under the hood has a purpose. There's nothing extraneous—"isn't this neat! Here it is." It's doing something; and a good story is the same way.

DM: I'm just going to read one thing before we close. If your appetite has not been whetted by this conversation maybe this quote will do it—but you have no excuse, really. "*The Clearing* itself gets bigger as it goes along, the prose, dense as anything Faulkner ever wrote, swelling and overflowing from the page. The beauty of his words caught me up short at least once every dozen pages, and caused me to slow down, savoring the novel bit by bit, phrase by phrase." Tim Gautreaux, thank you for doing such wonderful work.

TG: Thank you very much. Thank you.

DM: We're waiting for more.

Tim Gautreaux

Christopher Scanlan/2004

From *Creative Loafing, Charlotte* (16 June 2004). © 2003 Creative Loafing Charlotte, Inc. Used with permission of Creative Loafing (Charlotte) and Christopher Scanlan.

In his first ten years of writing fiction, Tim Gautreaux collected enough rejection slips to paper the four walls, ceiling, and filing cabinets in his office at Southeastern Louisiana University, where he taught creative writing for thirty years. His breakthrough came in 1990 when the *Atlantic Monthly* published one of his stories. He's since published two collections, and the novels, *The Next Step in the Dance*, which won the 1999 Southeastern Booksellers Association Award, and *The Clearing*, winner of the 2003 Mid-South Independent Booksellers Association Award. The son of a tugboat captain, Gautreaux, fifty-six, has crafted an unforgettable fictional territory in gritty oil-patch towns, like his native Morgan City, and a turn-of-the-century cypress mill, populated by the modern-day descendants of French-speaking Cajun exiles who settled southern Louisiana in the eighteenth century. Married and the father of grown children, he lives north of Lake Pontchartrain in Hammond, Louisiana.

Scanlan: Why did you become a writer?
Gautreaux: When I was a kid, somebody gave me a new typewriter and I figured I ought to use it. I started to write to pen pals from around the country, but very quickly I ran out of things to say, so I started to make things up, to lie to these people about my life—how I was hunting alligators and things like that. It was just fun to tell stories. But it wasn't until many years later, when I took a novel-writing course under Walker Percy, that I understood that fiction writing was something for me to take seriously. Also, if I hadn't become a creative writing teacher, I wouldn't have developed into a writer of any quality. In the classroom, the writing teacher has to justify his author-

ity, and the only way to do that is to get published himself. Teaching helped me understand the process of becoming a writer and that it doesn't happen in four-and-a-half months, which is a semester's length, or even a year. For most writers, ability is something that evolves slowly and is helped along by their day-to-day experiences of living. I understood after about fifteen years of teaching that the events of my life, my children, my marriage, my spiritual life, my hobbies, my work life—all that gave me the raw material that I could feed into the machine of my creativity. What came out was a story.

Scanlan: Why don't you have to be Southern to appreciate Southern writers?

Gautreaux: You would think that there would be a regional bias. Somebody in Minneapolis would pick up a book by Kaye Gibbons and say, "Oh, this is another one of those Southern women stories, I can't relate to this." But, indeed, they do relate to it. Why? Beats me, but if you go to Ohio, you don't find many people from the Deep South touring around. But if you come to New Orleans or Lafayette, the Cajun capital, you see all sorts of folks from New England and the Midwest just wandering around looking at stuff. What are they looking for?

Scanlan: You've said you're leery of the label "Southern writer." Does that mean you'd rather not be considered one?

Gautreaux: Not calling myself a Southern writer is a trick I play on myself. If people tell you you're a Southern writer and you believe it, you put yourself in a little claustrophobic room, you restrict the way you look at the world and when you go to write, you say to yourself, "Let's see, I've got to have some alligators in here and some French accordion music and a sheriff with mirrored sunglasses." In other words, you start thinking in clichés. You can't let yourself think like that or else you'll be, as Walker Percy once stated, in the business of amazing Yankees. So I'm not a Southern writer. I'm just a writer who lives in the South.

Scanlan: Why do you write about your people?

Gautreaux: Wherever you're born, that's your territory, a place with a culture just as complex as the culture of a Tibetan yak herder. You might live in a subdivision and think it's not an exotic place, but if you brought a Tibetan yak herder over and camped him in your back yard, he'd think you and your culture were plenty damned exotic. If you're not curious and amazed about your own territory—your family, your neighborhood— you're not a writer.

Scanlan: You once said, "No story is interesting unless it deals with matters of values." Why is that?

Gautreaux: There's no substance. What is this about if it's not about a question of right and wrong or good and evil or somebody making a right or wrong decision?

Scanlan: Why is the South such fertile ground for fiction?

Gautreaux: The Southern writer loves where he's from, warts and all. When I think of the history of my family, I think of how hard it was for people to work and survive and how much my family members suffered living in a tough climate and tougher poverty. Sometimes I recall one of my father's first jobs, which was cutting down cypress trees that were five feet through the middle. He had to stand in waist-deep water, fighting snakes and leeches, and work with a crosscut saw in 95-degree heat. When a man paddled out from town in a skiff and hired him as a tugboat deckhand, he felt lucky just to be above the water for a change. Sometimes I remember that my grandfather worked under the thumb of a stingy plantation owner for sixty-five cents a day. You look back on all that history and all that misery and you almost feel like a traitor if you don't respect the people you came from and the place they made. In one way or another, you have to tell their story.

Scanlan: What are you in the business of?

Gautreaux: People ask me, what do you do? I tell them the truth: I'm a retired schoolteacher.

Scanlan: Why don't you tell them a writer?

Gautreaux: That strikes me as being pretentious. Mostly I'm not a writer. I've only had four books published, and right now I'm not really working hard on anything. I've got one cooking in my mind, though. It's about the Mississippi River in the '20s and '30s, and the thing that's driving me to write it is basically religious guilt. If you have a talent, it's wrong not to exercise it.

Scanlan: What is your novel *The Next Step in the Dance* about?

Gautreaux: It's about the moral decision you make when you abandon your roots, your class, when you think you're better than your raising. But it's more than that. It's about bailing out of a marriage that could be fixed, and about what it means to be in a relationship for the long haul. Every marriage is broken when it starts. When young people get married, they have no idea what marriage is about. They think they do, but I can tell you as a veteran of thirty-two years, I learn something new about marriage almost every day.

An Interview with Tim Gautreaux

Maria Hebert-Leiter/2004

From the *Carolina Quarterly* 57.2 (Summer 2005), 66-74. © 2005 the *Carolina Quarterly*. Used with permission of the *Carolina Quarterly*.

Tim Gautreaux is the author of the short story collections *Same Place, Same Things* (1996) and *Welding with Children* (1999), and of the novels *The Next Step in the Dance* (1998) and *The Clearing* (2003). Born and raised in Morgan City, Louisiana, he grew up among blue-collar Cajuns. From this past experience, Gautreaux creates a fictional world that relates the everyday lives and cultural ways of south Louisiana Cajuns. In 1972, he received his Ph.D. from the University of South Carolina, Columbia, where he wrote his creative dissertation under the direction of James Dickey. He taught at Southeastern Louisiana University for thirty years before retiring in 2002. On October 15, 2004, I interviewed Tim Gautreaux by phone. We discussed his literary influences, his Cajun identity, and his motivation for writing.

MHL: Like Faulkner and Gaines, you write about your postage stamp of land, which you call Tiger Island and which Louisianans recognize as Morgan City. How much have these two authors influenced your work?
TG: Ernest Gaines, of course, is a great influence particularly in the way he treats language. Gaines has an excellent ear, and when I was attending a conference one time, Gaines gave a reading. It was the first time I had heard him. It was many years ago. And in his reading I could hear that he was working with the cadences and the grammar of individual speakers in such a way as to really give a vivid and accurate representation of their language. Now you don't pick that up exactly or as much when you're at home reading his books, something like *A Gathering of Old Men* or *A Lesson Before Dying*. But what that reading did for me is make me go back and read all of Gaines again and to see what he was doing with dialogue. And how important that

was to a feeling of authenticity for the readers. And so when I began to work on my own dialogue, I always kept what Gaines was doing in the back of my mind.

A sense of place was always very important to me. Gaines created his entire fictional universe out of a single gravel lane in Point Coupée Parish, but a place he moved away from when he was about sixteen. He lived a very long time in other places and would try to create a fiction out of these non-Louisiana locales, but it just didn't work very well for him. However, whenever he set something in Louisiana in an imaginary landscape that was similar to where he grew up, well, he was very successful. And that of course told me something that is pretty obvious from the beginning of any writer's career—that is that a writer . . . owns a certain literary territory. It's the place of his birth, where he grew up, the language that he listened to, the values that were implied, and the everyday commerce of his life. And this is something that the writer has to remember and pay attention to.

Even though Gaines's origins are very humble and he grew up with what you might consider unimportant people, he made great literature out of it. And that was kind of an archetype for me. You can say what Gaines does forms a pattern that I noted when I started to write fiction.

MHL: Interesting because I did hear Gaines read *A Lesson Before Dying* twice, and it is a very different feel when he reads it to you than when you read it in your head. There is very much an oral quality in his writing that I do think you are picking up on in your own. And that these Cajuns are talking in your fiction.

TG: You have to pay attention while reading Gaines . . . the one thing I learned from Gaines and other sources, too, [is] how important it was to listen to the people around you and to remember as accurately as you can how people spoke when you were younger.

MHL: So Gaines obviously has had a strong influence on your work. I think that any Louisiana writer today couldn't ignore him. Who else has most influenced your work?

TG: Probably Walker Percy from the standpoint of ideas. . . . What was interesting to Percy is not that people did things but why people did things. That carried over to his teaching of fiction. He would lead us in class to think not how we wrote, but why we wrote. There was always this moral foundation to whatever he wrote. And he was never didactic or preachy. He was always asking us, his readers, to think about why we did things. And when he taught me (a novel writing course in 1977, at Loyola), he was not very opinionated as to what we should write about, but he was very adamant in letting us know that we're all on some kind of a quest. The writer is always looking for something, the characters are always looking for something. It's an exploration. An exploration of what? Well, for Percy, it was, at least in part, always spiritual.

We are looking for what makes us happy, and the characters are looking for what makes them happy. And for Percy it wasn't money, and it wasn't fame. So what was it? Well, he never really told us, but you could guess.

MHL: How did you come to take that class? I read that you were one of the students in I think it was Patrick Samway's biography of Walker Percy.
TG: The fact that the class was going to be taught was actually in the paper, I believe. And people were invited, writers were invited to submit samples of their work. That's how we got in to the class, based on samples of our writing. And there were ten of us chosen, as I remember. And one of them was Valerie Martin, who is a successful novelist. Another one was Walter Isaacson . . . . And so, it was an interesting class.

MHL: Is there anyone else, besides Percy and Gaines, or are those your biggest influences?
TG: Well, naturally an influence on just about everybody writing in the South was Flannery O'Connor. She's probably the country's premier short story writer. If you analyze her stories you see she was working with tragedy, and humor, and irony. And putting all of these elements together in a technically perfect way, and that was because she really took to heart what the instructors at Iowa gave her in the way of how to put a story together. She was *very* expert in the way she assembled her story structure. Also, you know, she was Catholic, and I can relate to that because I'm Catholic.

MHL: So you obviously have Louisiana literary ancestors with Gaines. Do you recognize yourself as a Louisiana writer? And do you recognize yourself as a Cajun writer?
TG: Well, the short answer is no. Because if you think of yourself as a particular kind of writer, you limit yourself and you also lead others to define everything you do by some labels. And I think that's a bad thing. And also you tend to begin to rely on stereotypes and clichés if you think of yourself as a Midwestern writer, or an Indian writer, or an Amish writer, if there is one, or a Polish writer. You limit yourself, I think, by doing that. I just prefer to think of myself as a writer who just happens to live in the South.

You know, I sometimes ask myself what I would be writing if I were raised in Chicago. I would be writing about that city, using the same technique, and the same type of wit, and the same structure that I use now. The stories would just be about a different part of the country. Sometimes I meet writers who identify strongly with a region, they might call themselves an Alabama writer, or they might call themselves a western writer, and they sometimes get trapped in this notion that they have to use details from their region that people from other regions expect. And that's dangerous for a fiction writer. A writer shouldn't write what others expect of him. Now if I use a character named Boudreaux and he's eating a plate of crawfish étoufée in a restaurant, it's because I was . . . that's my territory. I was born and raised in a place where people ate heavy stews every day. But I'm not using such details because people *expect* it of me. There's a difference between paying attention to details of a region for the sake of authenticity, and using details for some cornball notion of being entertaining.

MHL: When did you know you wanted to be a writer?
TG: Well, writing is something like singing or tap-dancing, it's a born talent. If somebody has a good singing voice, he'll sing in the choir, he'll sing in the shower. Even if he's not commercial about it, he'll utilize his talent in some fashion. So it's something I always fiddled around with. This business about when did you know you were going to be a writer, it's something that happens over an entire lifetime. It's not as though a light bulb comes on at any one moment when you say, "oh, boy, I can be a writer." I don't even consider myself a writer. I'm just a retired school teacher.

A better question might be, "*Why* did you write?" And one reason for that was to give myself credibility in the classroom. If I was going to teach three and four sections of creative writing during the year, I had to have some justification for my competence. So I always wanted to be published in good places, in order to tell students, "See, this is how it's done."

MHL: If Cajun still, to some degree, means a somewhat rural person with somewhat limited outside experience, can Cajuns write about educated Cajuns while still capturing Cajun culture in their fiction or is it just in writing about more rural Cajuns who have not gone very far from home that represents a true, more complex picture of Cajun life?
TG: Someone asked me one time, "Well why don't you write about doctors and lawyers?" [I do not write about them] because they're not very interesting, culturally at least. Someday I might write about doctors and lawyers, Cajun doctors and lawyers. [It goes] back to my raising again, and my ter-

ritory, because the people I knew were blue-collar people. They were rural people. They were fisherman. They were mechanics. They were dredge-boat operators and tugboat captains and railroad engineers. They weren't doctors and lawyers. So that's probably the main reason I deal with those types of people. That's my territory.

And, like Gaines, very often when I stray out of that territory I don't do as well. In my first novel, *The Next Step in the Dance*, people tell me that the California section is by far the least interesting part. I do have some experience in California. I used to spend summers out there with my sister who lived in Los Angeles. And I still couldn't put into it anything that was really first rate, that is writing about California. When I got back to the territory that I was raised in, I could do a lot better.

MHL: Do you think that education removes Cajuns from a traditional way of Cajun life in such a way that perhaps that's why doctors and lawyers don't make as interesting characters?

TG: Yeah, I think so. Because, and that's the way with just about anybody who is raised [among] the lower-middle class or blue-collar people and becomes educated, begins making money, begins to prosper, begins to move in the popular culture. [You] begin to feel that your plainer beginnings are something you should leave behind. And I think that's sad. You begin to lose all sense of history and all sense of the past, and then you lose the sense of the importance of present things. For example, when I was a kid, I was the one who was always sent out to paint the family graves on All Saints' Day, actually on All Souls' Day is when we used to do it. And that was a very important thing, to maintain the memory of your ancestors. And over the years, especially the three years I was not living in Morgan City, I sort of lost track of that, the importance of maintaining the family tradition of painting the graves. And now I'm even further away from it. I mean I'm closer to the traditions of south Louisiana in some ways, but in that way, I'm not. And it's kind of sad because nobody maintains the graves now. Sometimes they get in sad shape. Maybe some day I'll go down and do it again in my older age.

MHL: Is that why in *The Next Step in the Dance*, when Colette's parents die, you have a passage where Abadie says that when somebody dies, the younger generation turns on the television set. Does that passage come from your own experience?

TG: The more you get caught up in making money and in a busier, modern, non-rural lifestyle, the more you are insulated from the things that count. And that's true not only in Cajun culture, but in any culture.

MHL: How has your education affected your Cajun identification and your writing of Cajun culture in fiction?

TG: I try not to think about it too much. You see things have changed a lot [over the last fifty years]. I was born in '47, however old that makes me, and people from my age bracket didn't think about being Cajuns when we were growing up in the fifties. It just didn't occur to us. If you would have asked me when I was twelve years old, "Are you a Cajun?" I would say, "I don't know." It was when I moved away to South Carolina when I was maybe twenty-one, twenty-two years old (for graduate school), that I found myself in a different culture at that point, and realized how different Louisiana was, south Louisiana in particular, from the rest of the country. When I moved to South Carolina, the food was totally different, and the religion was different, the politics was different, everything was different. Attitudes were different. At that point it began to be clear to me what being Cajun was. And it had to do with attitudes, the value of food, the value of religion, and things of that nature. And it's sort of an attitude about life. The attitude that though people think they're better than you, you know different.

MHL: I guess it was kind of a generational thing. Now it has become this academic study.

TG: Yeah. I think a lot of it started in the 1960s and '70s. In Lafayette there were several people [who] realized that this traditional Cajun accordion music was sort of passing away from the scene. So they began to put together Festival Acadienne, for example, and several other festivals in Lafayette that showcased local music. Well, people from far away started to come to those festivals, and certain record companies started to put out CDs, well they didn't have CDs in those days, but tapes of Nathan Abshire, who was at that point a watchman in a garbage dump, but he was recorded. And they began to tape the Balfa brothers and other musicians, and Cajun music began to be kind of a regional thing. It began to spread out of the area, of southwest Louisiana. And by the early '80s, you start to hear a little Cajun music even in New Orleans, for God's sake. Now, you never heard accordion music east of the Atchafalaya River. It just didn't exist. Starting in the '70s and '80s, you began to see more and more Cajun music in barrooms, in nightclubs, in dancehalls, and also in restaurants in New Orleans. It began to be more and more popular. People began to understand that it was . . . was eminently danceable. [This interest in Cajun music] led to a heightened interest in Cajun food.

You couldn't get a lot of Cajun food in New Orleans until, oh, the 1980s. It was all French cuisine or just standard New Orleans Creole fare, like Shrimp

Creole and stuff like that. But as far as a lot of gumbo, particularly *étoufées* and stews, or white beans or anything of that nature, you never saw that in New Orleans till the '80s. So the Cajun influence sort of followed the music out of Acadiana. And then, there were a couple of bad movies made. [. . .] And several companies started exporting Cajun spices and Cajun hot sauce. . . . There's Paul Prudhomme and the blackened fish stuff, and Justin Wilson, all these cooks had nationally syndicated cooking shows and would mention Cajun foods and derivations of Cajun foods. And all of this made local people think better about the culture. To grow up in the '80s as a Cajun was a thing to be proud of.

My father spoke French, but I guess I thought everybody's father spoke French in the United States. And my favorite thing to eat would be, you know, shrimp okra gumbo, and I thought shrimp okra gumbo was served in every restaurant in the United States until I left and found out otherwise.

MHL: You can now find it, though, in most states if you look hard enough. It's been that exported. And now there are even international bands. There are bands in Australia and Great Britain who play Cajun music.
TG: Cajun bands tour, too.

MHL: Times have changed. So, what do you think of the state of contemporary Cajun culture?
TG: It's hard to generalize. It's hard to put your finger on it. But, you know the music is still going strong, and the food will always be there. And, as far as people speaking French, that's dying off because it's hard when there's no practical application for a language, it's hard to utilize it daily. There are school programs. The CODOFIL program [Council for the Development of French in Louisiana] down here in southwest Louisiana. And there are some young French bands, [made up] of very young people, who are singing songs in French and even learning French. They speak better French than the old people. So there's a limited maintenance, I guess you might call it, of French speaking that is still going on in the Lafayette region.

A lot of Cajun culture flies below radar. And if you want to experience Cajun culture you have to go to Breaux Bridge, St. Martinville, Henderson, or Whiskey River Landing and dance on Sunday afternoon. It's not in books. Well, it's not in many books. And I tried in *The Next Step in the Dance* to record the culture as it was in the 1980s. There are also elements of the '70s, and '60s, and '50s in that story, particularly all the fist-fighting scenes. Because I found that if I didn't nobody else would. There aren't many people down there writing "literary" fiction about blue-collar Cajun culture.

MHL: It seems that Cajun literature is trying to deal with tensions we've been feeling between identifying yourself as American and taking pride in Cajun culture and its differences. I do recognize this tension in your Cajun characters. Especially among your women who leave their husbands. For instance, Colette who goes to Los Angeles because she wants something more or better. How do you feel about this tension? Do you feel it yourself? Why is it especially your women who embody this tension in your fiction?

TG: Someone told me one time that they thought Colette was kind of mean. Women I was raised around were just like Colette. I'm not quite sure why Colette is the way she is. I'm going to go at [the topic of women's lives] from a south Louisiana perspective. Life then was very hard for women in the 1950s, in that Louisiana was a poor state. It's always been a very poor state, and very often women had to work at jobs in addition to raising a family. Particularly if you were a fisherman's wife or a trapper's wife, you helped. And even if you were the wife of a sugarcane farmer, you sewed, you raised chickens, or you worked as a secretary in town. And this is true of many cultures, I guess, where the common denominator is poverty. But Louisiana and Mississippi have always been the poorest states in the union. The women had to be very tough, and they also had to assert their dominance in the family. . . . The Cajun mother was very influential and strong. She had to keep her husband in line. . . . And if she was a push over, she had a miserable life. So she had to run the finances, so to speak, of the family and keep her husband in line. She couldn't be a sweetcakes, you know. Sometimes she had to be pretty rough with her husband to get him to behave. This attitude, I think, was passed on to the daughters, because I remember even on the playground the girls were pretty darn mean. They would throw rocks at you. If some girl was especially interested in you, she would throw a big rock at you.

MHL: So what do you think about films like *The Big Easy* and *The Waterboy*.

TG: [. . .] Hollywood is very superficial. So unless you're watching a documentary, you're not going to get any type of serious treatment of culture out of Hollywood. They just don't understand culture. And the directors and the studios in Hollywood more or less believe that every place in the United States is like every other place. If there's a Burger King and a record store in a town in northern Alabama, it's just like New York. . . . Well, [they think] it's all the same. They actually believe that popular culture has totally conquered everything in the way of culture in this world and in this country. And really nothing could be further from the truth. There's still a lot of ethnic diversity in this country. It tends to stay regional, and media moguls tend not to think much about it. . . . Hollywood just doesn't seem to know how to make use of Mexican polka festivals, for example.

MHL: Do you find yourself writing in response to the Hollywood depictions?

TG: No. Hollywood is not on my radar screen.

MHL: Ken Wells defines Cajun sayings and gives pronunciation keys in a glossary at the end of each of his novels. You do not define your characters' Cajun French when they do speak it. For instance, I know in *The Next Step in the Dance*, you don't. I find it interesting that you do not because of Cajun loss of Cajun French usage. Why don't you translate your Cajuns' French phrases?

TG: Well, for one, in context, you ought to be able to figure out what they're saying. [. . .] Two, . . . you know, I don't believe that a reader should be made to understand every molecule of what's going on in the story. I might mention a certain type of wrench, and you might not know what that wrench looks like. Well, do I have to sit there and explain it to get an effect? No, that would be tedious. What do I do, not mention it? Well then that robs the story of a certain authenticity and texture. If I mention a certain machine, you don't know what it looks like. But does that mean I shouldn't write about it? If you actually look through an average novel, there's lots of stuff you don't understand. That doesn't mean [the author] has to explain what it is or anything. . . . This is . . . a complaint that people make against Cormac McCarthy, that he uses Spanish phrases in his novels. But you can figure out from the context what the phrases mean. . . . And even if you don't understand one speck of Spanish, you're not going to miss anything in the novel. So Spanish is put in there for authenticity, for texture. . . . I think it's insulting to a reader's intelligence, turning a fictional work into a manual.

MHL: Marcia Gaudet wrote in 1989 that "there has not yet been an accurate portrayal of Cajun culture by a major American literary figure." And this statement is part of a larger argument that Cajun literary representation is more a misrepresentation than anything else. I believe that you answer her call for accuracy. How do you feel about her statement, and have you ever consciously written in response to such statements?

TG: I think that she's right. It's really almost impossible to understand a culture unless you live in it. And literature can, I think, go a long way towards letting you know what a culture is like, but you still won't totally understand it unless you live among the people. Unless you see and smell where they live. Literature can only do so much. Now, of course, Marcia's statement that it's not been well represented is true, and that's why I wrote *The Next Step in the Dance*. Some people read the novel and ask, "Well, what's the point?" And I think they don't see it as an archetype, a tribute to a culture that could be imitated.

MHL: That completely answers my question, because that's how I feel whenever I read it. It's certainly more accurate and more sincere. It's very much . . .
TG: [People who] read it and say what's the point, those are people who don't think there is any type of culture in America at all. That it's just a mall rat culture. That there's nothing else. . . . They just don't understand how intense and cherished many different cultures in the United States are.

MHL: So you wrote it to celebrate this Cajun culture or these cultural ways that don't just disappear when a Dillard's moves into your neighborhood?
TG: That's right. Recently, I was in a little town in Michigan and they were having a Dutch festival, and people demonstrating Dutch folk dancing. . . . That kind of stuff goes on all over the United States, and most Americans don't know about it.

MHL: What is your next project?
TG: I'm working on a novel set in the same period as *The Clearing*. It begins in Louisiana, in New Orleans, and takes place on a boat on the Mississippi River. I'm in the early stages of writing it, so we'll see where it goes. It might wind up in Chicago!

A Catholic Who Happens to Write: An Interview with Tim Gautreaux

L. Lamar Nisly/2005

From *Interdisciplinary Literary Studies* 8.2 (Spring 2007), 92-99. © *Interdisciplinary Literary Studies*, 2006. Used with permission of *Interdisciplinary Literary Studies*.

Although Tim Gautreaux has made his mark as a fiction writer, he began his writing career as a poet, writing a volume of poetry for his dissertation at the University of South Carolina. He began teaching creative writing at Southeastern Louisiana University in 1972 and was later named writer in residence, positions he held until his early retirement in 2002. Instrumental for Gautreaux's career was a 1977 writing seminar, taught by Walker Percy, which led Gautreaux to turn to fiction writing. Two novels that Gautreaux wrote in the 1980s were not published, but he began to receive notice for his short stories, with "Same Place, Same Things" accepted in the *Atlantic Monthly* in 1991 and included in *Best American Stories of 1992*. The years following these successes included an array of stories published in prestigious journals and magazines, such as *Harper's*, *GQ*, *Story*, and *Virginia Quarterly Review*, with Gautreaux winning numerous awards as well. In quick succession, two short story collections, *Same Place, Same Things* (1996) and *Welding with Children* (1999), were published by St. Martin's Picador USA Press to considerable critical acclaim. The stories tend to feature blue-collar characters in southern Louisiana, showing them with humor but also considerable warmth and care. Gautreaux found increased time to focus on his writing when he was named the John and Renée Grisham Southern Writer-in-Residence at the University of Mississippi in the fall of 1996, leading to his first published novel, *The Next Step in the Dance* (Picador, 1998). This novel, which won the 1999 Southeastern Booksellers Award, examines the lives and off-and-on marriage of Paul and Colette Thibodeaux as they struggle to learn together and survive the economic downturn of the oil bust 1980s. His latest novel, *The Clearing* (Knopf 2003), which examines the brutal world of a Louisiana sawmill in the 1920s, has been highly praised, with *USA Today* including it in the ten best books list and Mid-South Bookseller's Association naming it the best novel of 2003.

This interview was conducted by email in late 2005 and early 2006.

LN: You have indicated that the label of "Southern" writer does not seem particularly helpful in identifying you or others. However, I'm curious if you find yourself feeling any affinity with other writers or groups of writers. Would you align your own work with that of any other writers?

TG: I enjoy reading writers who know how to take language seriously, who aren't afraid of technical details of, for example, how a windmill works, or how to break a horse, who aren't afraid of describing either a rural driveway or a mountain range, who see metaphor as a tool and not as interior decoration for sentences. I always look forward to reading anything by Annie Proulx or Cormac McCarthy. I enjoy the rare book that combines wit and some comment on values, so this is why I like George Saunders. Authentic sense of place? Richard Russo and William Gay. I don't know of many writers of literary fiction who consider themselves part of a "school." That depressing word reminds me of the dozen big goldfish one sees in the fiberglass pond outside of a Chinese restaurant. That's a school. They're all alike and I'd wager they all wish they were somewhere else.

LN: Since almost all of your writing is set in Louisiana, how do you manage both to dwell deeply in that place while also connecting with broader, more universal themes?

TG: I've learned that every little neighborhood contains all the universal themes any writer needs.

LN: I understand that you attended Catholic school as a child. Can you describe your experience of Catholicism as you were growing up? For instance, how important were Catholic traditions and rituals in your family? Was everyone around you Catholic?

TG: Yes, I attended a Catholic parochial school for twelve years. In Louisiana the Catholic school system was huge and had been in place for many decades, so I never felt I was a part of something "small" or marginalized. Nearly every classroom was in the charge of a Marianite sister, and the Marianites were well-trained educators who of course taught the traditions of the church while at the same time doing a fine job in science, history, and English. I guess they realized that a well-educated Catholic was better than one that was devout but dumb. My mother made sure I observed all church rules regarding abstinence and fasting, and church attendance, and at school the student body attended special masses, confession, Lenten observances such as the Way of the Cross, and for Holy Week we were in church every day. The month of May brought special devotions to the Blessed Virgin. Our church was a tall neo-Gothic structure full of elaborate stained glass windows and life-sized stone statues of saints. It was a physical metaphor benefiting those who missed the point of words. Mass was in Latin, and school Masses were sung by the school girls' choir, usually a well-trained group of altos and sopranos singing the Mass in shifting harmonies. The singing was really quite beautiful. There were quiet, meditative times imposed on our unruly selves in church, and sometimes the church was hot, and sometimes the rituals seemed to go on for too long, but looking back on it now I see that the music and the meditation were seeds that grew me out of my crude and tactless youth. It was a time and place that probably can't be duplicated. The town was mostly Catholic in population in those days, and certainly mostly Catholic in sentiment. This was a place where a local waitress, raising her order pad and pulling a pencil from behind an ear, might habitually remind customers who had ordered a dish containing meat that it was Friday.

LN: Did you tend to have much contact with people from other religious traditions?
TG: Well, I married a practicing Methodist.

LN: In the course of your lifetime, the Catholic Church has changed significantly, particularly with the alterations of the Second Vatican Council. Do you think the changes in worship practices or the new emphasis on ecumenical relations of Vatican II have affected your sense of Catholicism or of "being Catholic"?
TG: The short answer is no, personally. It's still the same church, after all. If there is a difference for Catholics younger than myself, if people are less observant or devout, it's not because of popular culture so much, or liberal theologians, or the lack of priests, or the pressure of being religious in an overcrowded affluent urban area. It's the lack of nuns as teachers. For some reason, nuns disappeared in the 1970s. There used to be rafts of them in their habits traveling the streets, Dominicans, Little Sisters of the Poor, Carmelites. You couldn't turn around in New Orleans without running into

a nun, in habit, somewhere. The nuns were positive examples for us, especially the teaching nuns. They lived the religion they taught, owning nothing, rising before dawn to pray and prepare lessons plans.

LN: How do you respond to the idea of being identified as a "Catholic writer"? Is such a designation helpful or limiting?

TG: Instead of adopting the tag "Southern Writer" I prefer to think of myself as "A writer who happens to live in the South," so by extension I prefer to be "A Catholic who happens to write."

LN: In another interview, when you were speaking of the chemistry created among people from the intermingled cultures in southwest Louisiana and New Orleans, you said, "they don't want to understand it, because if you understand something, it loses its magic." In a broader sense, could you say more about the importance of living with a sense of mystery, of magic? How do we retain a sense that there is something beyond what we can rationally understand?

TG: The question itself begs for the destruction of mystical qualities in our lives. It assumes we can figure everything out. I can't explain the unexplainable. I can only say that I feel sorry for people who profess with certainty that science is the answer to everything. They only succeed in making of science a religion in itself. And remember, for scientists, aspirin is a mystical element because they can't figure out how it works.

LN: In a couple of your stories, such as "Navigators of Thought" and "Dancing with the One-Armed Gal," you focus on academics, but that theme is not prominent in your writing even though you taught at the college level for thirty years. Why do you tend to focus on settings other than universities with less educated characters?

TG: One reason is that it's hard to make academic narratives and characters engaging. Maybe most readers prefer not to read stories about schoolteachers, I guess because of certain preconceived notions of university professors being condescending, their parlance always laced with trivia, insider wit, and sarcasm. Come to think of it, I've been guilty of those errors. The main reason I often focus on less educated small town or rural characters is that they don't always use standard English. People of limited vocabulary and knowledge of grammar are infinitely creative in the way they express themselves, because they're constantly making up the deficit with home-made metaphors or inventing new grammar. An educated shopper might look at a stack of ripe tomatoes and say "Those look like they'd be delicious." A rural type might say "I bet they eat real good." Which is more interesting language?

LN: Many of your stories end with a suggestion of hope, perhaps even a moment of grace. Do you plan those movements before you begin the story? Are you often surprised at the end of the story?
TG: No, hope and grace, if either is there in the ending, does not grow out of forethought or planning. It might grow out of the types of characters I choose to create, to mimic. Yes, my endings surprise me. They'd better. If they don't surprise me they won't surprise a reader.

LN: What motivated your writing *The Next Step in the Dance*? Did any image or moment in the novel serve as a catalyst for the whole story?
TG: That novel is a tribute to a certain time in a certain culture combined with a love story. The book is image-rich, and I can't recall one of the many that might have been a seed for the whole. Maybe it's Colette and the irony of her great beauty coexisting with her abrasive spirit.

LN: In a number of stories and in your first novel, older people, especially grandparents, figure prominently in the writing. Why are older generations so important in your stories?
TG: Something I noticed when I was a university teacher was that nearly every class contained single parents, mostly women. Their parents and sometimes their grandparents kept their kids and sometimes everybody lived with the grandparents/parents. I would find out the details when the students would explain why they were absent or why they brought their children to lecture. It's a stressful social phenomenon that I find interesting, so that's why there are teams of old people interacting with children in my stories. Another reason is that I was around lots of old relatives when I was a child. I was the youngest child of a youngest child. My mother was born in 1907.

LN: In some of your stories—I think, for instance, of "Sorry Blood"—the tone is more foreboding than in a more rollicking story such as "Welding with Children." Yet even with this handful of more somber stories, *The Clearing* still quite clearly seems to be a departure from your earlier stories and novel. Could you describe why you decided to write this darker novel?
TG: I don't know, exactly. I believe, of course, that a writer should not feel

obligated to stick in one mode throughout his career. For *The Clearing* I just happened to deal with some regional history that was pretty dark. I wanted the reader to consider with dead seriousness what I was writing, so I made do with as little overt humor as I could.

LN: Some reviewers have linked *The Clearing* with Joseph Conrad's writing, particularly in the moral wrestling and ambiguity that are present. How do you think about the moral role of fiction? Why can the novel's main characters, Randolph and Byron, never find clear answers of right and wrong?

TG: I think readers found some echoes of Conrad because *The Clearing* deals with a man's separation from civilization and with the results of that separation. As for the moral role of fiction, I think that if a story or novel doesn't touch on a question of right and wrong, of good and evil, of indolence or personal striving, for example, it really isn't a complete tale. As for Byron and Randolph finding clear answers of right and wrong, all I can say is that life is not science and certainly religion is not science. The brothers understand that it is wrong to kill people. They also understand that morally they are allowed to preserve their lives and the lives of others, even if they have to kill someone in the process. Living with such contradictory notions gives them cosmic pain and keeps them thinking at all times about the consequences of their actions.

LN: *The Clearing* contains many violent episodes and quite gory descriptions, yet the novel, it seems to me, most certainly does not glory in the violence. Can you talk about the challenges of writing a violent novel that seems, at least on one level, to be an argument against violence offering any satisfying resolutions?

TG: Much violence in movies is presented in such a way that the anguish of those who love the victim is invisible or far in the background. The anguish of the person causing the violence likewise seldom figures in the plot. The violence just happens with the significance and effect of a summer fireworks show. If violence is to be justified in a literary work, it has to have a purpose beyond the spectacular display, and one way for a writer to make violence purposeful is to show the effects or lack thereof on both sides of the act itself.

LN: Can you give us any updates on any movie versions of your novels? Do you ever think in terms of a movie—scenes, dialogue—when you're writing?

TG: I listen to my characters as they speak to make sure they make their pronouncements in a realistic way that is loyal to education, place, and culture. While I'm writing, I don't imagine my fiction being made into a movie, but like any writer who grew up watching movies, I am aware of movie technique, for example the need to show significant things to the reader/viewer in a coherent fashion. *The Clearing* is currently under a third film option, and someone is writing a script, but who knows if it will ever be made?

LN: Can you tell us anything about your current writing project? Is your sense of guilt adequately driving you to keep writing?!
TG: I don't really have to write, but I do feel that I'm wasting time if I don't write or at least think about writing. At the moment I'm working on a novel that begins in 1918, and it's about the kidnapping of the daughter of a couple who work as musicians on a Mississippi River excursion steamer.

LN: Do you think that you'll keep writing short stories as well as novels? Do stories offer you a kind of change of pace between longer projects?
TG: The short story is a great form and I find it nice to work in this medium because it allows such control. I can micromanage each sentence. If I damage the structure of the plot, it's easy for me to straighten out 7,000 words instead of 150,000. I can take greater risks in the story form because a story is so fixable whereas a novel is not.

LN: How do you balance the need to continue to find fresh directions for your work with building on the fictional landscape you've already developed?
TG: It's pretty simple. I just keep my duty to the reader in mind: the reader expects me to write what nobody else can write, and he expects me to surprise him.

LN: You've received considerable recognition for your writing, with *The Clearing* in particular gaining a lot of attention. How does that attention affect your ongoing work? Are the book tours, conferences, requests for interviews (!) distractions from your work? Do they in some way spur you on to keep writing?
TG: Yes, the public aspect of being an author is time consuming and tiring, but on the other hand, the activity keeps me intellectually engaged and puts me in touch with some delightful people. But does recognition or duty to audience make me write? I don't think so. Writing literary fiction is hard work. Coming up with a great plot is like designing a space vehicle. Making

and remaking those sentences is as tedious as stone carving. However, when the writing's going really well, I figure I'm doing what I was meant to do, and there's no better feeling than that.

An Interview with Tim Gautreaux: "Cartographer of Louisiana Back Roads"

Margaret D. Bauer/2008

From *Southern Spaces* (May 2009) http://www.southernspaces.org/2009/interview-tim-gautreaux-cartographer-louisiana-back-roads. © Margaret D. Bauer. Used with permission.

In his 1983 book, *The People Called Cajuns*, James Dorman observes that Cajuns "rarely speak for themselves" in the various sources that refer to them—historical, biographical, or literary—but that same year Louisiana's Tim Gautreaux published his first short story, "A Sacrifice of Doves," in the *Kansas Quarterly*.[1] In the more than quarter-century since, he has published two short story collections and three novels, most recently *The Missing* (Knopf, 2009). Gautreaux's name reveals his ethnicity, and in his fiction readers find his Cajun perspective. He is a descendent of the French Acadians who settled in south Louisiana after the British drove them out of Nova Scotia in the eighteenth century.

In spite of Gautreaux's importance in adding a seldom-heard voice to literature, he resists such labels as southern or Cajun writer. And certainly his fiction is not limited to the perspective of Acadian descendents—or southerners. The two main characters of his second novel, *The Clearing*, are from Pennsylvania. While the main characters of his other two novels, *The Next Step in the Dance* and *The Missing*, are Acadians, the characters in his short stories are more likely to have working class backgrounds than to be identified as Cajun. His protagonists are predominantly white, blue-collar, south Louisiana men, their ages ranging from the twenty-somethings of his novels to the numerous grandfathers in his stories. It is the Louisiana white working man's story that Gautreaux tells—or rather, the various stories of blue-collar workers, a voice fairly new to southern literature, offered by other writers of Gautreaux's generation (such as Mississippi's Larry Brown and South Carolina's Dorothy Allison), countering or deconstructing poor white and "white trash" literary stereotypes.

Born in 1947, in Morgan City, Louisiana, Timothy Martin Gautreaux is the son of a tugboat captain and the grandson of a steamboat chief engineer. Other men in his family worked for the railroad and offshore on oil rigs, and many of them enjoyed storytelling.

After attending parochial elementary and secondary schools, Gautreaux went to Nicholls State University in Thibodaux, Louisiana, graduating in 1969 as an English major. One of his professors entered poems Gautreaux had written in a Southern Literary Festival contest held in Knoxville. Keynote speaker James Dickey read the winning poems, among them Gautreaux's, and invited him into the Ph.D. program at the University of South Carolina. Gautreaux's Ph.D. dissertation was a volume of poetry called *Night-Wide River* (1972).

Gautreaux returned to Louisiana in 1972 to teach at Southeastern Louisiana University in Hammond, east of Baton Rouge and about sixty miles northwest of New Orleans. He brought with him his new wife, Winborne Howell, a North Carolina native he had met in graduate school. Five years after moving back to Louisiana, he applied for a seat in a fiction writing class taught by Walker Percy at Loyola University in New Orleans. Percy selected Gautreaux, along with other writers who would go on to have successful careers, such as future novelist Valerie Martin and future *Time* magazine managing editor Walter Isaacson. From this experience on, Gautreaux wrote fiction.

Due to the heavy teaching load of a small state institution, along with raising two sons (Robert and Thomas), and maintaining interests beyond academia, it took Gautreaux into his forties to surface on readers' radars. After a couple of early publications in literary magazines, Gautreaux's stories were accepted by such venues as the *Atlantic Monthly*, *Harper's*, and *GQ*, and selected for the anthologies *Best American Short Stories*, *New Stories from the South: The Year's Best*, and *The O. Henry Awards' Prize Stories*. His stories also attracted the attention of Barry Hannah, who invited Gautreaux to be the 1996 John and Renée Grisham Southern Writer-in-Residence at the University of Mississippi, allowing him to finish his first published novel.

Gautreaux's first book, a collection of twelve stories, was published by St. Martin's Press in 1996, a year before the writer's fiftieth birthday. *Same Place, Same Things* was blurbed by fellow Louisiana writers James Lee Burke,

Robert Olen Butler, Andre Dubus, and Shirley Ann Grau and reviewed by the *New York Times*. Calling it "[a] terrific debut collection," *Kirkus Reviews* noted the writer's "sympathetic understanding of working-class sensibilities" and compared Gautreaux to Flannery O'Connor. The Catholic magazine *Commonweal* praised the collection's stories for providing a "welcome relief from the blandness of McWorld; they bring reassuring evidence of the continuing existence of places away from the big place where, increasingly, we all live." And the reviewer for the *North American Review* remarked that Gautreaux "knows how to get out of a story's way and just let the characters do what they need to do. . . . These characters move through the world compelled by important motive. The characterizations are swift and precise, rooted in gesture, speech, and action."[2]

Gautreaux's second book, the novel *The Next Step in the Dance* (Picador, 1998), was also reviewed in the *Times*, with the reviewer, Andy Solomon, remarking upon the author's "poetic mix of colorful detail and rapid-paced suspense," as well as "his keen ear for Cajun dialect." The *Missouri Review* also admired Gautreaux's "unmatched ear for the speech of rural Louisiana," as well as the writer's talent for writing about machines: "Here is a writer who can make the refitting of an engine as compelling as another author's love or death scene." This reviewer, however, found that the novel "suffers from a lack of urgency and momentum" and "overstays its welcome." By contrast, the *New Orleans Times-Picayune* argued for the importance of *The Next Step in the Dance*: that the 1980s, "a time of great trauma for this state[,] . . . certainly deserved a literary piece to memorialize it."[3]

In 1999, St. Martin's published a second volume of Gautreaux's stories, *Welding with Children*, which the *Times* again selected for a lengthy and positive review, praising the author for his "cartograph[y in] mapping with affectionate but unflinching accuracy both the back roads of Louisiana . . . and the distance between parents and children." Reviewing this collection for the *Hudson Review*, Susan Balée called Gautreaux "[t]he master of the Cajun short story," as well as one of the three "best short story writers in America today"—praise that would please a writer who resists regional labels. Reviewer Alan Heathcock lauded Gautreaux's "invention of clever, out of the ordinary conflicts" and "his ability to render true the voice of his Louisiana working-class characters." Heathcock sums up the collection: "The stories are all about people who want to be good, who want to help others and end up helping themselves in the process. They are about redemption, with a tender sense of humor, as seen through the kind eyes of their author."[4]

Next, Gautreaux tackled an historical novel set in the 1920s, dealing with a World War I veteran suffering Post-traumatic Stress Disorder, perhaps prompting *USA Today*'s comparison of *The Clearing* (Knopf, 2003) to Charles Frazier's *Cold Mountain*. The *New Yorker* responded to *The Clearing* by calling Gautreaux a "Bayou Conrad," and several reviewers began to compare (and contrast) the author to Cormac McCarthy. *Publishers Weekly* suggested that *The Clearing* confirms the opinion that "Gautreaux is perhaps the most talented writer to come out of the South in recent years."[5] His growing reputation is reflected in the larger number of reviews of this novel in a broader spectrum of venues, from local papers to the *Christian Science Monitor* and the UK's *Guardian*. This happened as well for *The Missing*, another post–World War I novel, promptly reviewed in the *New York Times Book Review* and the *Washington Post*, as well as by several UK publications. For both historical novels, the author did his homework—researching details that would allow him to realistically depict life in the 1920s in a Louisiana lumber mill town in *The Clearing* and on a Mississippi River entertainment steamboat in *The Missing*.

After drafting a volume on Tim Gautreaux for the "Understanding Contemporary American Writers" series published by the University of South Carolina Press,[6] I drove to the author's new home in western North Carolina to fill in some biographical blanks and test some theories about his work. Having read every interview I could find, my own interview did not cover the usual ground.[7] It was the first interview I'd conducted—though as a journal editor, I've certainly read and helped shape my share of interviews.

Gautreaux is very easy to talk to, a natural raconteur (which will surprise no one who has read his fiction), but some of my questions, while not receiving blank stares, were not responded to with the assurance that I was on track with my readings. Rather, Gautreaux occasionally seemed surprised—an interested, intrigued surprise, but still surprise—by my interpretations. And suddenly, in the middle of it all, I understood that of course he would be. If he had intentionally set out to accomplish what I was asking him about, his work would not be as good as it is. Rather, he is just telling his stories, crafting his stories, polishing his stories. I'm the literary critic who then analyzes what he's done within those stories—while he goes on to the next one.

With this realization occurring as I sat on his living room couch, I wondered why I was wasting the man's time with an interview—why we ever ask writers these questions about their work, questions that suggest that the writer sets out with some agenda besides telling the story, when it is probably the case that the writer with a predetermined agenda is usually not the writer we bother interviewing.

Since he knows I am working on a book about his writing, at least I could reassure him during the interview that I appreciate his writing and know it very well—better, perhaps, than he does, he later admitted. And so we continued to talk, not just about his own work but about literature in general and about our common home, south Louisiana, for the rest of the evening, long into the night, and the next day—though after the "formal" ninety minutes of "interviewing," we stopped recording and just talked. Gautreaux's wife, Winborne, another lover of literature, joined us as we shared our favorite novels and writers and figured out who we know in common, having grown up in small towns just about twenty miles apart. After a stimulating visit, I traveled back home to eastern North Carolina with most of the answers I had been looking for and much more, including a bittersweet homesickness for the music of the voices, the celebration of fine food, and the family and friends I've left behind in Louisiana.

This interview took place July 9, 2008. It has been edited for clarity by Tim Gautreaux and me, and to avoid the distraction of brackets and ellipses, such minor changes are not noted in the text below. I thank Tim and Winborne Gautreaux for their hospitality during my visit to their western North Carolina home. Thanks as well to an East Carolina University Faculty Senate Research/Creative Activity Grant funded by the University's Division of Research and Graduate Studies, which provided a summer stipend to complete a draft of my Gautreaux book, travel money to interview the author, and a graduate student stipend to transcribe the interview—for which I also thank Elizabeth Howland for her quick and accurate transcription.

Biography

Bauer: Let's start with some biographical information. I've found the basics in interviews and the *DLB* article on you, but I noticed the date 1969 for your Nicholls degree and then 1972 for your Ph.D. So is the 1969 date a bachelor's degree? And you went straight from that to a Ph.D.? No master's degree?
Gautreaux: That was because the University of South Carolina offered an accelerated program for the Ph.D. where you bypassed the master's. It was ultimately an academic mistake for an institution to do that because the

program wound up generating so many Ph.D.s that it contributed to the Ph.D. glut of three or four years after that. So you don't find many colleges— or any colleges—offering that type of program anymore.

Bauer: I've read the story of James Dickey discovering your poetry and inviting you into the South Carolina graduate program, but would you talk about your decision to go to college, coming from a family of blue-collar, working men? And what was their reaction to your going to college? How did you end up going to college?
Gautreaux: Well, no one really said much about it. I did well in high school, and that summer after high school graduation it occurred to me that I had to do something. So, a friend of mine was going to college and he said, "Why don't you go to college with me?" and I said, "Okay." College was so incredibly cheap in Louisiana in those days. A summer's semester tuition was twenty-five dollars, and I had received a little scholarship as a senior in high school. I think it was a reduction of fifteen dollars off of that twenty-five dollars, so basically my first semester in college cost ten dollars tuition. So it really wasn't any giant financial decision. I went down the road thirty miles to Nicholls State University and began studying English there.

Bauer: Do you have any brothers or sisters?
Gautreaux: I have one sister. She's about fifteen or sixteen years older than I am, and she's a housewife. And then I have a brother who's eleven years older than I am, and he's in the oil business.

Bauer: So you're the first in your family to go to college?
Gautreaux: Of the immediate family, yes.

Bauer: And you say your sons both went to college?
Gautreaux: Yes. One's an electrical engineer and one's a lawyer.

Bauer: I'm also wondering about the focus of your Ph.D. program on Romantic literature. Why did you choose that period in particular?
Gautreaux: Well it's hard to say. I think that the answer would be in undergraduate school I had a really good professor who taught English Romantics. The English Romantics are very accessible. It was a time in literary history that I found more interesting than eighteenth century, more interesting than Victorian.

Bauer: And you were focused on poetry at the time?

Gautreaux: At the time, right. I found, in particular, Byron's long narratives to be interesting. They were witty, they were gossipy, and I probably liked them for the same reasons that people who read them in the early nineteenth century liked them.

Bauer: I've noted that several of the stories in your first collection had been published in pretty major venues and selected for the various *Best Stories* anthologies. Prior to that, did you publish in the usual literary magazines before breaking into the big time? You published early on in the *Atlantic Monthly*, *GQ*, and *Harper's*. Are there some other stories, in other words, that I might not have read yet? I did find two stories that are not in the first collection, one called "A Sacrifice of Doves," that appeared in *Kansas Quarterly* and another story, "Just Turn Like a Gear," in *Massachusetts Review*. Any others?

Gautreaux: No, I never wrote many stories. Every story that I wrote got published. I just write them with the idea that I'm putting them together in the best way that I can. I guess I'm kind of a perfectionist when it comes to short fiction, and also I didn't really see the point of writing dozens of stories for very small venues that really wouldn't do much either for my career or for my finances. So I always aimed high.

Bauer: You didn't start publishing until you were in your forties—do you think this accounts for the absence of the typical autobiographical first novel among your books—or is there such a novel in your attic?

Gautreaux: I really don't have much of an interesting life to write a biography about. I got out of undergraduate school very young. I had a Ph.D. by the time I was twenty-three or twenty-four, and then I got married and started teaching full-time at Southeastern Louisiana University. I was teaching writing, and I figured that if I was going to teach it, I should have some credibility. And that's one reason—or maybe the main reason—I always tried to become a good writer and to get published in major venues. After I began publishing I could mention this in class and students' ears would perk up and they would say, "Oh, well, he's got some success himself." Because there are a lot creative writing teachers who really don't have any publishing record, and it's kind of rough sledding for them in class because the student always has in the back of his mind, "Okay, you're teaching me how to write artistically; you're teaching me to write, presumably, a publishable type of literature. What have you done?" So that's one reason why I tried so hard, I guess. But then, I've always liked to write. In other interviews it's come out that as a child I had pen pals all over the place and would write voluminously to these people every week.

Bauer: You have mentioned in other interviews too that there are a couple of novels that you wrote and didn't get published. One you said you drew on for the scene in the boiler in *The Next Step in the Dance*. Is one of them the autobiographical novel that the beginning writer often writes?

Gautreaux: No, no interest whatsoever in ever doing anything autobiographical. There are more interesting stories to tell.

The last book I got as an academic—the last free book that a publisher sent me—was an anthology of American short fiction. It was a huge book, and there was a section in the back of the index called "Most Recent American Writers" or "Young American Writers," something like that. And the youngest writer in that group—and there were twenty of them maybe—was born in 1949. So when you mentioned that I only started publishing in major venues in my forties, well, most people do that. It takes twenty years for you to develop the language skills, the intellectual filters in your brain that tell you what to put on the page and what to leave off the page. It takes an incredibly long time to develop these skills.

Bauer: Yea, but a lot of people in the meantime, send out to small magazines, and with the self-publishing, a lot of people don't wait. They just want to get it published.

Gautreaux: But where are these twenty-year-olds being published? Unless you're a truly rare talent, generally you're not going to sell a book to a decent house or in a major publication until you're along the line a ways.

Cajun Identity

Bauer: I found the Marcia Gaudet essay on the depiction of Cajuns in literature that is alluded to in one of your interviews.[8] At the time she published that in 1989, she was able to point out that there were no Cajuns *written* by Cajuns. She talks about Longfellow's Cajuns in *Evangeline*, noting that Longfellow had never been to Louisiana, then traces other depictions through Ernest Gaines's fiction. Certainly Gaines has firsthand knowledge of Cajuns, but still is not Cajun himself, and the role of Cajuns in his fiction is pretty negative. Now I know that you're "writing what you know" and not consciously answering some call for a previously absent voice, but would you talk about your contribution of this missing voice in light of more stereotypical depictions of Cajuns that preceded in fiction and film?

Gautreaux: I don't really think about it. I know that's probably not what you want to hear. I don't think of myself as any particular type of writer. I am what I am. I was born in a certain area of the country, and the people around me happen to speak a certain way and have a certain set of values, and pursue a certain type of lifestyle, and that's all I know. That's where I draw my characters; that's where I draw my dialogue, my sense of timing, my values. If I were raised in some other area, naturally, I would be drawing on some other set of characters and culture. So I don't think that I have to ennoble or expose a particular type of culture. I don't feel a particular duty to region. I just weave narrative out of where I'm from. I think it's bad for a writer to think that way—that "okay, I'm Polish, I have to do this tribute to my area of Chicago" or wherever my little group is—because that's what forces a writer into using clichés. He figures, "Well, okay, I'm going to write a Polish story, so I've got to have some cabbage rolls in it or some kielbasa or something like that." While that's part of the fabric of that particular culture—just as étouffée or boiled crawfish is part of the fabric of Louisiana—you don't consciously sprinkle details like that throughout your writing like salt and pepper. If they happen, they happen, but you don't consciously plant them with the idea of "amazing" readers who are not of your culture.

Bauer: Now, I know you resist the label "southern writer," and I agree with all the reasons that you give in the various interviews I've read—especially the fact that everyone is a regional writer, but also the danger then of being self-consciously southern à la Rebecca Wells. That said, your identity as a Cajun writer is so important, since you're filling in a previously unheard voice. How do you feel about this label?

Gautreaux: I'm not interested in labels; I'm interested in storytelling. And nobody even knows what a Cajun is. I put a redneck character in one of my stories in *Welding with Children*, and a lot of people have called him a Cajun, and he's from Alexandria, which is the most un-Cajun place on the face of the earth. And he's not Catholic, and he doesn't have an Acadian surname. Anybody from the region understands who that fellow is, but people out of the region will read other things into it. I just can't worry about that.

Bauer: What about when you see Cajuns in film? I hear a voice that is more authentic coming out of your fiction than in the film *The Big Easy*.

Gautreaux: *The Big Easy* was a very popular movie. It painted New Orleans as being a Cajun town, which is absurd. It didn't worry me at all because a long time ago I understood that Hollywood never gets anything right as far as culture is concerned. Not for one nanosecond, anywhere, in any way, shape, or form, will Hollywood get it right. And the only thing Hollywood is concerned about is bucks. They're not interested in culture.

Bauer: I notice that you do not resist the label of Catholic writer. You're more inclined to talk about that in various interviews, your Catholicism and how it influences your writing. Why is that label less problematic for you?

Gautreaux: Cajuns are in Louisiana; Catholics are all over the planet. None of us knew we were Cajuns until all the hoopla in the mid-1970s when a sort of Cajun Renaissance started and brought out of the closet, as it was, Cajun music and food. I really don't consider myself some kind of dyed-in-the-wool southern cultural phenom.

In south-central Louisiana, I never really ran across many people that considered themselves southerners in the sense that Georgians or Mississippians consider themselves southerners. And I don't consider myself to be any kind of alligator-eating Cajun type. As I said, that's kind of superficial. But I've always been a Roman Catholic, since baptism, since birth.

Bauer: In one interview you talk about the inspiration for *The Next Step in the Dance*—wanting to capture the oil bust of 1980s Louisiana. First, I want to ask you why that period in particular was so attractive to you.

Gautreaux: It's something I lived through. I was born and raised in Morgan City, Louisiana, which is an oilfield town. And the entire oil industry in Louisiana crashed and burned during the eighties. I saw the effects first-hand: the out-migration of white-collar people and skilled workers, the idle boats and oil rigs, and so many people out of jobs, houses that were worth two hundred thousand dollars going down to ninety thousand dollars in value overnight, just about. I could see it happening around me, and nobody else was writing stories about the oil bust. I'm sure people who experienced the Dust Bowl in the thirties had the same feeling: is anyone going to write about this? I felt that if I didn't produce literature out of this, maybe nobody else would. There are lots of events in American history that are ignored and unknown because nobody wrote anything about them. And I had the feeling that this was going to happen. People talk about the oil bust as an economic phenomenon, but *The Next Step in the Dance* shows it as something that affects people in a very painful and personal way. It's one thing to say that twenty thousand jobs were lost; it's another thing to put a reader inside the house of one of those people who lost his job.

Influence of War

Bauer: Now, would you talk about the inspiration for each of the other two novels? What has drawn you twice now to the period just after World War I? To the lumber mill in *The Clearing*, the excursion steamboat in *The Missing*?
Gautreaux: Many of the uncles in my family were in World War I, and they all came back with their stories, and I heard a lot of them. *The Clearing*, of course, is about this damaged veteran who returns shell-shocked. I had an uncle that was in all eight major American engagements and endured some horrible things. And I knew what it was that he endured through family stories and through talking with him because he lived to be quite old. I knew him many, many years. Of course he was very unlike the character in *The Clearing*, but nevertheless I could draw on the psychological damage that I witnessed in him to develop the Byron character in that novel.

Bauer: Is it significant that you've been writing postwar novels during the two Gulf wars? Do you feel like you're inspired by what's going on now?
Gautreaux: No, I don't think about the present conflicts much. It just happens that everybody that gets involved in the business of shooting people with rifles winds up damaged and changed. When someone writes a novel thirty or forty years from now, there's going to be a war going on somewhere and the same question is going to be asked: "Are you thinking about this present war?" There's always a present war, it seems. The fact that it's going on while I'm writing a novel about psychologically damaged warriors, that's just the way it happens. In a way, all wars are the same war. The other novel, *The Missing*—really, the novels can be analyzed side by side because in one, we have a protagonist severely damaged by his experiences in World War I, and in the second we have a protagonist who arrives in France on the day the armistice is signed and doesn't get to shoot anybody at all. Even though he is briefly involved in the aftermath, the cleanup of the battlefield, he's not affected by the carnage, and really, even while he's over there, he understands this. Then we follow him through the rest of his experiences in *The Missing*, and we see that he behaves differently from Byron in *The Clearing*, has a different life, a different outlook. The novel is negative definition: Sam, the main character in *The Missing*, is defined by what he does not do. If I had had him show up two months earlier on that troop ship, while the killing

was still going on, it would have been a different novel. I think the whole narration is propelled by the fact that he did not have to shoot anybody in France, that he showed up by an incredible stroke of luck on the day the armistice was signed.

Bauer: And I did read that you have another uncle that that happened to?[9]
Gautreaux: Nobody knew anything about battlefield disposal. There were so many millions of tons of unexploded ordinance left all over Europe buried in the mud that farmers are still plowing it up to this day. One uncle was sent out right after he got there; it was just like in the novel. They gave him a bunch of clips of ammunition and a rifle and said, "Go here, and shoot at this ordinance; we've got to get rid of it somehow." He went out for a day or two, but it didn't work; it was an absolute screw-up. Most of that in the novel is imagined, of course, but I could sort of put two and two together from what he'd told me. His squad didn't do that more than a couple days. The officers immediately realized that it wasn't working, that it was dangerous, that it was going to hurt more people than it was going to help.

Bauer: Were you in Vietnam?
Gautreaux: I was going to join the Air Force, but they had that draft lottery, and I drew number 361. Number one went, and the further away you were from number one the less likely you were to go. When I drew the number, I had already taken my physical and everything; I was headed to boot camp, but I hadn't signed the enlistment papers yet. So I guess I was lucky.

Bauer: Going back to *The Clearing*, why did you choose to leave Randolph and Lillian childless at the end? Byron and his wife are expecting a baby, and they have Walter by then. The nice clean, bows-all-tied ending would have been to give Randolph and Lillian a child, too, but I am curious if it was a conscious choice not to do so, if there was something in that?
Gautreaux: It was a conscious choice: to show how much Randolph loves his brother. It was a big sacrifice to give up that child. I think the fact that they remain childless through the end of the novel is to demonstrate how big a sacrifice giving up Walter really was.

Outlander Perspectives

Bauer: In various interviews, you have talked about the value of capturing the voices of home, and you have been praised by interviewers and reviewers for the authenticity of your dialogue. So it must have felt like a risk to choose for the central perspective of *The Clearing* two Yankees. Would you talk about that choice in light of what you have said about writing about Louisiana?

Gautreaux: The point of view characters are the two outlanders from Pennsylvania. That was done to open up the novel to all readers so that we wouldn't have so much a hermetically sealed, southern novel with southerners looking at southerners. We have a novel in which these northerners are looking at the culture and the people down here, and the readers in Minnesota or Oregon or Canada look at things through the main characters' eyes. The non-southern point of view makes *The Clearing* less of a southern novel, and I think improves it, broadens it.

Bauer: Well actually, if you think about the nineteenth-century southern literary tradition of bringing the northerner in to see that the South is not so bad, it actually is an old tradition of an outsider looking in. What Byron and Randolph see is completely out of their experience. Randolph doesn't know what to do with it. Byron says, rather, "This is what I've seen of the world; this place is no different."

Gautreaux: They come down, and the stereotypical notion is that they're going to condescend or hate the place. But they don't. The anonymity and isolation are what Byron wants. Randolph finds himself empowered by coming south. He's really, for the first time, in charge of things. When he goes back to civilization he finds it to be inconsequential. Swamp life is a tough existence, but then again it's an intense one. It's one that he grows used to.

Bauer: You have also mentioned that you ended up cutting the California section of *The Next Step in the Dance* down significantly in order to bring your characters back to more familiar territory.

Gautreaux: For two reasons: one, because I don't know California culture that well; two, readers seem not to be interested in that. They don't want to read about California.

Bauer: The best scene in California is when Paul eats in the Cajun restaurant.[10] I have always connected Cajun tourism to the oil bust—"we have to make some money, and we're not going to make it in oil now; let's build a Cajun village tourist site"— but you were saying before that it was earlier, in the 1970s.

Gautreaux: I think the people associated with USL (now UL) got the public in touch with Cajun culture, and then Vermilionville and Cajun Village and the promotion of Cajun culture and all that stuff came out of that earlier "renaissance."[11] The oil bust didn't do anything except make everybody poor.

Bauer: What I was thinking was that they started hyping up tourism to try to replace the oil business, but maybe that was just New Orleans.

Gautreaux: The hyping of tourism is in western and south-central Louisiana, too, but I don't think it was because people were looking for stuff to do. Really, there was an out-migration of a quarter-million skilled workers in the eighties; geologists, the best welders and machinists, they just left the state. They didn't start up some Cajun enterprise.

Voice, Violence and Steamboats

Bauer: Do you have something in mind for what's next after *The Missing*?

Gautreaux: I'm starting to think about it, but I don't have anything sketched out yet. I don't know what the next one will be. I've got this old cranky guy in my imagination, and I might give him a book. I've never written a book in first person and it might be time to try that. I had good luck with "Welding with Children"; the voice in that story was really good. It's easier to write in first person than third person. It doesn't take the same discipline. So I might start playing around with that.

Bauer: Although in *The Missing*, right when we are getting worried about the little girl, Lily, you have a chapter in which we find out that the scoundrels who kidnapped her are not abusing her. So third person allows this information, which is kind of a relief to the reader, who can go on with Sam's adventures, knowing that Lily is at least physically okay, especially when we learn about the boy who was adopted and then sexually abused— which brings me to the violence in the new novel. But first, backing up a bit, throughout the novel, Sam keeps meeting himself—in the German girl, in Lily and August—until he finally meets the Cloats and deals with his past. Now there's a scene! Leading up to Sam's own experience with the Cloats we hear Constable Soner's story about them—he alludes to a dog involved but doesn't ever get specific—just says that whatever his wife witnessed, she couldn't get over. Again, then, the violence occurs offstage.

Gautreaux: It was hard to rein that one in. You have to know when to stop because you can ruin things for the reader. You can give him a piece of graphic violence that will just overpower the rest of the narrative for him because he can't think of anything else for the rest of the story except some horrible scene that you've detailed for him, which you don't need to do anyway because whatever's in the reader's imagination is worse than anything you could paint for him. Even in the scarier parts of a Cormac McCarthy novel, I can see his restraint where he doesn't want to cross that line into ghoulishness. Then I remember the books that I've read where authors have gone into ghoulishness, and it's just like a trip down the meat counter at Piggly Wiggly—sensory overload. A writer just has to know when to hold back.

Bauer: Thinking about taking Sam up and down the Mississippi in *The Missing*: it's very *Huck Finn*; you have this Mark Twainian thing happening. Can you talk about Mark Twain?

Gautreaux: Yes and no. I enjoy Mark Twain. I enjoy *Adventures of Huckleberry Finn* immensely, and of course when I was a kid I read *Life on the Mississippi*. But where I get my knowledge of the Mississippi River is the fact that my father was a tugboat captain. He ran up and down the Mississippi River, and I used to ride with him sometimes. And my grandfather was the chief engineer on a steamboat. I was born in 1947. I can just barely remember some of the old steam-powered craft in the New Orleans harbor. When I was a kid the Jackson Avenue Ferry and the Esplanade Avenue Ferry were reciprocating, steam, paddle-wheel boats and I used to ride them just to watch the engines work. I liked to listen to the machinery and the whistles and smell the hot boilers. There were still a few old sternwheel boats running in those days—the government inspection steamer, *Mississippi*, and *John Newton*, and a couple of others: in New Orleans we'd see the *Delta Queen* or the *Gordon C. Green*. My father knew the people who worked on these boats, and we'd go through the engine room and talk to the engineer. And when I was a kid I used to ride on the old, side-wheeled steamer *President* down in New Orleans, which was steam-powered all the way until 1980. And I'd be down in the engine room listening to how engineers answered the old bell system of communication rung by the pilot upstairs. I'd go up on the roof and watch the pilot in the wheelhouse blow the big whistle. So a lot of what is in *The Missing* is from firsthand experience, and then of course I've done all my reading, taken passage on the *Delta Queen*, ridden the *Belle of Louisville*, and whenever I'm around any kind of old, nautical, reciprocating machinery, I make a point to photograph it, visit it, talk with the docents that take care of it.

Bauer: You talk about the different steamboat whistles in the novel—the pilot knows who is coming by the different whistles. This has not been captured in fiction since Mark Twain, and these things are gone. But in your new novel we get on that steamboat and ride up and down the river during that time.

Gautreaux: It's sort of like writing about the oil bust: nobody has really written any fiction that included the world of excursion boats. From say 1910 to 1940 the excursion boats were a big deal all throughout the South and the Midwest. These big steamers would run on the Mississippi from New Orleans all the way up to Minneapolis, on the Ohio all the way up to Pittsburgh. They'd stop at towns along the route and show up with a great jazz band and huge dance floor and entertain a community, clean up, and move on to the next one. There were probably forty or fifty boats that operated in that trade in the thirty-year period we're talking about.

Bauer: It does also echo *Huck Finn*—as Huck and Jim go up and down the river, they meet all these different people. It reminds us that every community has a different voice. Twain was apparently a linguist who captured all the different dialects. One of the things I like about your Louisiana stories is that you recognize that not every Louisianan sounds the same. Different main characters have different voices. Linguists in Louisiana could probably put them where they're from, whether it's Morgan City or Lake Charles or Alexandria.

I feel like that's in both novels. In *The Clearing*, you've given the main point of view to the outsiders, but all the different voices are still there—the Cajuns and the Creoles and the African Americans.

Gautreaux: It's important for a writer to pay attention to accents and grammar. If you walk around this area of North Carolina, you'll hear retirees from Florida who are originally from New Jersey; you'll hear Mexicans. The priest at the local church is from Vietnam. And then there are mountain people here that I have trouble understanding sometimes. The locals here are very friendly and open people—some of them say *thar* for *there*—I mean a deep *thar*. I might say to someone, "Well I think I'll go up to West Jefferson," and he'll respond, "I wouldn't go thar this afternoon. Up thar they's a-workin' on the highway." Their speech rhythms are also wonderful. One might assume that a region's accents are homogenous, but that is never true anywhere— especially in the South.

Bauer: There are a lot of Souths, and speaking of the South, you mention in one interview that "Deputy Sid's Gift" is the closest you come to dealing with race, acknowledging the painfulness and thus the difficulty of this topic. That interview was before *The Clearing*, because you do deal with race in that novel with May and Walter, and you also deal with race with the musicians in *The Missing*. Would you talk about race and why you don't write about it, even as a writer of southern literature? Your reviewers don't find the subject missing, by the way—I've found no one noting the subject as missing in your work. But you are from Louisiana, as I am, and I know race is still an issue there.

Gautreaux: I don't even think about it, not for a nanosecond. I don't write about race. I write about people. I included black characters in *The Missing* because the best musicians on the dance boats were African American. The new jazz music was money in the bank for a big dance boat. The white bands couldn't play like that, not at first, so the boats hired the African American, New Orleans musicians, not because they were black—it wasn't a racial issue—it was because only they had the sound, the good dance sound, and these were dance boats. The second decks were three hundred-foot-long, waxed dance floors, and the boats were after young people generally, who wanted to hear the latest hot music. The best jazz was African American. To put a white band on a New Orleans-based boat would not have been realism. Let me tell you why nothing big in the way of racial stuff happens: always stick to the narrative. The story of *The Missing* is driven by Sam's character, and his character involves him in this rescue search, and that's what the whole novel is going to be about. The minute a writer says, "I'm going to write about race" instead of "I'm going to write a story about people" he has already failed.

Place, Character, and Intervention in Short Stories

Bauer: Do you think you'll write any North Carolina-set stories, now that you're living here part-time?

Gautreaux: I won't know until I set pen to paper. But I find myself testing the waters outside of Louisiana. For example the story that I was working on this morning is set in north Mississippi. I've got a feel for north Mississippi because I was up at Oxford for a semester as writer-in-residence, and one of my sons went to Oxford, so we were always up there visiting him. And I have relatives in Memphis; I've got some kind of a feel for the lay of the land, so we'll see how that comes out. It's possible that I could write something set in North Carolina. I'd be among good company.

Bauer: And speaking of North Carolina writers, Jill McCorkle has actually told me she prefers writing short stories—I was so glad to hear that because after devouring each of her collections, I've looked forward to the next one. What about you? Which do you prefer to write, or do you have a preference?

Gautreaux: The short story; it's controllable, and it's—how can I put this?—you can work on a short story sentence by sentence almost the way you work on a poem. And you can micromanage it. You can go back over it many times and make everything line up. You can make sure that the logic of the first sentence ties in with the logic of the very last. You can't do that with novels; they're just too large. I guess you could if you were a genius or something, but I don't fall into that category. I think the short story is more of an art form, really, than the novel. I'm sure a lot of people would disagree with me on that.

The short story is a very important genre. Think of the major American writers who are known more for their short stories than their novels. That statement goes back to Hawthorne and Poe and applies to contemporary writers like Joyce Carol Oates. If Joyce Carol Oates had never written two short stories, "Where Are you Going, Where Have you Been?" and the other one with the long funny title, "How I Contemplated the World from the Detroit House of Corrections, and Began My Life Over Again," which are anthologized in everybody's phonebook even, you wonder how many people would know who Joyce Carol Oates is. But those two stories are in every university anthology known to man, and so she's taught all over the world and students go on to her longer works after they read those two, or to her story collections. The college anthologies are like wonderful advertisements for short story writers. Similarly, if a twenty-one-year-old college student knows Faulkner, it's probably through an anthologized short story like "A Rose for Emily," not because he read *Absalom, Absalom!*. You can go through indexes of American literature texts and look at the important stories and see how much they've done for the reputations of major American fiction writers.

Bauer: Well you mentioned "A Rose for Emily," so I have to ask—in my book on William Faulkner, I included a chapter on your story "The Piano Tuner" and "A Rose for Emily."[12] I resisted, while I was writing it, asking you, so now that it's already done I have to ask, did you by chance have Faulkner's "A Rose for Emily" in mind when you were writing "The Piano Tuner"?

Gautreaux: I had in mind instead the archetype of the spinster lady left with the family house, which happens not only in the South but all over the place. You don't see it so much anymore because families now are composed of two kids. But say in the 1920s, a man would have a large house, and he would have six kids, and four of them would get married, one of them would get killed in a car accident or something, and then it seems like there was always one daughter that was left over; she never married, and she would wind up living in the father's house. And the father's house of course had eight bedrooms in it, and she couldn't afford to heat all of that, so she would close them off one at a time over the years.

She would take in boarders, and then she got too old to manage boarders. Then there was this old woman living in one or two rooms of this house built in 1900. Such spinsters were all over the place. I knew several women like this, a lot of old women, and I even have a couple of them in my family. So that's where the archetype for that story came from. And that's probably the archetype that Faulkner drew on to write "A Rose for Emily."

Bauer: Well, the difference is that Emily's dead when the story starts. She's lived to the old age that you're talking about. The town is mourning her passing—or at least the story's "We" narrator is. But they wait until she's dead to go see her. Even when she bought the poison to kill Homer Baron there's the telling line, "So the next day we all said, 'She will kill herself'; and we said it would be the best thing."[13] But nobody tries to help her. In your story the piano tuner gets involved. And this is what attracts me to your stories: these men who say, "What can I do? I have nothing to do with this, but I could do something." Faulkner's prototypical Quentin Compson feels really bad about the oppression he witnesses but Hamlet-like just worries and doesn't do anything. You're sending in these guys who are not sons of the aristocracy but they're doing something about it. I'm curious if this is your reaction to Faulkner—if you're responding to these sons of the aristocracy. Ernest Gaines has said, "Faulkner wrote about Dilsey in his kitchen; I wrote about Miss Jane in her kitchen."[14] Are you also responding to Faulkner?
Gautreaux: There are several of my stories that you could call intervention stories, where somebody's in a bad way, and a character takes that step to help, breaks through the mirror, to go to the other side. There's no story unless somebody does something like that. You see, if the piano tuner had come out and tuned her piano and then went home, never went back, and then she died of old age or something, there wouldn't be much of a story. What propels the story is his decision to help.

It's like what Rust Hills, the old *Esquire* editor, used to say: there's fixed action and moving action. Fixed action is the stuff that you expect to happen and happens every day—it is kind of a pattern. You go to the mailbox every day to check your mail; you stick your hand way down in the mailbox, if it's one of those old post-mounted ones on your porch, and you look for the stuff, and you pay your bills. This is all fixed action: every day you do the same thing. One day you go out on the front porch, stick your hand in the mailbox, and feel something kind of crawling, and you pull it out and it's a big chicken snake, and you're scared to death, and you holler and you drop it. Then you hear laughter, and across the street your neighbor is just doubling up because he's put that big, harmless chicken snake in your mailbox as a trick. Well that's moving action—that doesn't happen every day. A pattern has been broken, and it's going to generate other action. The reader already sees what's going to happen: he's going to play a trick on the guy across the street.

The same thing when the piano tuner decides to help out the woman by getting her a job. The pattern of fixed action is broken, and we're now in moving action: we're in a type of thing where we don't know what's going to happen; we can't predict what's going to happen; we're in a series of events now that's new for both characters. That's what interventions do. But all of that comes from being raised Catholic where we have been taught to help people who are less fortunate than we are, not just by praying for them but by actually going out and fixing their busted air conditioners and stuff. And it also comes from my blue-collar raising. My father never made a lot of money and the people that were his friends never made a lot of money, and when their cars broke down the one of them that was best at fixing cars would go over there and fix it, and when my father's air conditioner broke down the guy in the neighborhood that was best at fixing air conditioners would come over and fix it and it was sort of a *quid pro quo* relationship among blue-collar workers that way and that's true all over. It's another form of this intervention mentality where you help people for no real reason. Intervention in a purer form occurs in stories like "The Piano Tuner" and in "Resistance" where the old guy helps the little girl with her science project. It's kind of a distilled form of altruism, and there is a point in many of my stories where the character feels put upon by fate because he says, "I gotta make this decision: I can turn around and I can walk away—or I can help." And when he makes that decision, then the story is rolling.

Bauer: That's what I like—they make the decision not to turn around and walk away.
Gautreaux: Well, if they walked away there would be no story or there would be the usual "life has no meaning" story.

Bauer: Yes. As I tell my students when they complain about reading what they consider one negative story after another, "No conflict, no story."
I do find it interesting that there are so many very specific details that are

the same between your story and Faulkner's—there's so much we read that's out there, that's in our heads—for example, the fathers in both stories ran all the suitors away.

Gautreaux: That's coincidence—just another part of the archetype; that's why the old lady wound up by herself. It was common for the father of the family, the patriarch, to run the suitors away for several reasons: they weren't good enough, rich enough, but you wonder if he really wanted that daughter to stay around to take care of him, to take care of his wife. He didn't want her to get married and move away. He'd lose a nurse.

Bauer: And the mothers often died after having so many children, so he wanted someone to take care of his house.

Responsibility and Compassion

Bauer: Another pattern I've seen in your stories is the grandfathers. I'm fascinated with my father's enjoyment of his grandchildren. He truly plays with them when he babysits (or when they Poppysit for him, as he puts it). His generation of fathers did not participate in childcare the way my generation of fathers does, and I think they realize now, watching their sons and sons-in-law, how much they missed. You have several stories with grandfathers stepping in to take care of their grandchildren—"Welding with Children" and "The Courtship of Merlin LeBlanc," for example. Would you talk about the men in these stories? What is your inspiration for this particular focus on grandfathers becoming involved in raising their grandchildren?

Gautreaux: Grandfathers in the stories come from two sources. One, I never knew either of my grandfathers because they died before I was born. One thing a fiction writer does is he makes things that he doesn't have, so I make grandfathers for myself while I write. Another thing is that in teaching survey courses with thirty-seven students in them, I always had a number of single mothers who had child care problems. And I always got a lot of excuses, like "Oh my mother or father couldn't take care of my kids so I couldn't come to class." Or, "My kids are sick and my mother and father can't take care of them because they're scared they'll catch the flu themselves, so I have to stay home." Or they show up with the kids. They bring the kids to lecture, so sometimes I've had two, three, five kids in this classroom. So that's kind of where this interest in grandparents comes from—there are a lot of grandparents and great-grandparents out there taking care of little kids. It's because the girl has gotten pregnant once or twice, and she has no husband and no job. Sometimes the student's mother doesn't live close by or she's disappeared or something, or her mother never had a husband maybe. And so the kids' great-grandma and grandpa, who are these 1940s relics, who grew up, did right, got married once, and worked forty years down at the mill and lived the straight life, they're left to deal with the mess.

Bauer: This is tied into your theme of taking responsibility—like the bug man who comes in to spray. It's not his responsibility to help the woman; he could just spray and leave. Or the grandfather—it's not really his responsibility, but it is his grandchild, and he did raise the mother who had this child out of wedlock. You see this theme of responsibility again and again in your fiction. Is this part of the Catholic background, too?

Gautreaux: It's not anything I really thought about much; if it's there it's there. I can honestly say I don't think, "Well let me only write about responsible people" or anything like that.

Bauer: It's a worldview that is in your fiction—the choice to take responsibility.

Gautreaux: I don't know what to say about that, but let me start talking about something that maybe I do know something about, and that's the notion of hopelessness or despair that I see in a lot of contemporary fiction. I seem to run across two types of stories that worry me. One is the *New Yorker* type tale where everything is a joke and the reader can't really take anything, including death and disease, seriously. The reader feels he's not supposed to have intense emotions about anything because that's silly and bourgeois. And the other type of story I run across is a truly dark narrative about vicious people who don't learn anything from what they do and are not punished in any way and never get their comeuppance. Sometimes that's realism. And such stories belong in the canon. But the mistake a writer of those types of stories makes, I think, is to write *all* of his stories like that because then, cumulatively, the author gets away from realism.

Now what do I mean by that? It's unrealistic to ignore compassion and the ability people have to cope and even triumph over their problems. You can write a story about how horrible it is to die from a certain type of cancer. That's realistic. Yet I run across many people who have coped with their cancer and are in fairly good shape the night they die. I've known people like this. Where is their literature? I read this student's story about a woman who was molested, was totally ruined emotionally, and eventually committed suicide. I've known many male and female students who were sexually abused, and most have coped in various ways. Some of them even write about it, which is disturbing to read, but nevertheless—maybe it's therapy—they're able to do it. Somehow people who suffer in this way or that are able to triumph over what they're going through. Where are the short stories about the small successes that people have dealing with their problems? Well, they're not out there because they're hard as hell to write without making them seem simple-minded or clichéd or insipid or sentimental. The most frightening thing in the world to an intelligent writer is sentimentality. He doesn't want a molecule of it in his fiction. But I think if you read enough and you understand how to blend humor and irony and the right tone in with the bad stuff, you can write a story that carries an emotional load yet is not sentimental in the least. If anybody wants to know how to deal with this type of thing, he can read my stories. I'm not exactly sure how I do it myself, but it's a conscious mixing of comedy and tragedy, of irony and straight non-ironic storytelling. A lot of it's like tap dancing or jitterbugging or singing: either you got it or you ain't.

Notes

1. James H. Dorman, *The People Called Cajuns: An Introduction to an Ethnohistory* (Lafayette: Center for Louisiana Studies, 1983), 36.

2. Suzanne Berne, "Swamped," *New York Times Book Review* (22 Sept. 1996): 16. *Kirkus Reviews* 11 (Sept. 1996): 991; Rand Richards Cooper, "Local Color," *Commonweal* 8 (November 1996): 25; Perry Glasser, "True Dirt," *North American Review* (March.-April 1997): 45.

3. Andy Solomon, "Books in Brief: Fiction," *New York Times Book Review* (14 June 1998): 21; John Tait, rev. of *The Next Step in the Dance* by Tim Gautreaux, *Missouri Review* 21.2 (1998): 212; Susan Larson, "The Writer Next Door," *New Orleans Times-Picayune* (15 Mar. 1998): E1.

4. Liam Callanan, "La. Stories," *New York Times Book Review* (3 Oct. 1999): 31; Susan Balée, "Maximalist Fiction," *Hudson Review* 53.3 (2000): 520, 519, emphasis added; Alan Heathcock, "Book Reviews," *Mid-American Review* 20 (2000): 249-50.

5. Bob Minzesheimer, "Clearing Is a Cut Above," *USA Today* (31 July 2003); "The Critics: Briefly Noted," *New Yorker* (30 June 2003): 101; "PW Forecasts: Fiction," *Publishers Weekly* (26 May 2003): 49.

6. Portions of my introduction are adapted from Chapter 1 of *Understanding Tim Gautreaux* (Columbia: University of South Carolina Press, forthcoming).

7. See the Recommended Resources, in which I list all of the interviews with Gautreaux that I have found.

8. Marcia Gaudet, "The Image of the Cajun in Literature," *Journal of Popular Culture* 23.1 (1989): 77-88.

9. See Gautreaux's essay "Left-Handed Love," in *A Few Thousand Words about Love*, ed. Mickey Pearlman (New York: St. Martin's, 1998), 139.

10. In California to try to mend his relationship with his estranged wife, Louisiana native Paul Thibodeaux orders the only thing he recognizes on the menu, gumbo, and the waiter brings him "a small cauldron of bitter juice so hot with Tabasco that after the third spoonful, Paul broke into a sweat." When asked how it tastes, Paul remarks that was too hot and is told, "It takes time to develop a true Cajun palate," to which Paul responds, "it sure don't take much time to ruin one" (*The Next Step in the Dance* [New York: Picador, 1998], 81).

11. The University of Southwestern Louisiana (USL) is now the University of Louisiana at Lafayette. Vermilionville is a "Cajun/Creole heritage and folklife park [that recreates life in the Acadiana area between 1765 and 1890" (http://www.vermilionville.org) and Cajun Village is comprised of "[h]istoric Acadian buildings, restored to house unique specialty shops" (http://www.thecajunvillage.com).

12. See Chapter 7, "Don't Just Sit There; Do Something: Frustration with Faulkner from Glasgow to Gautreaux," in William Faulkner's Legacy: "what shadow, what stain, what mark" (Gainesville: UP of Florida, 2005).

13. *Collected Stories of William Faulkner* (New York: Vintage, 1977), 126.

14. Gaines made this remark when guest-speaking at a class I took at the University of Southwestern Louisiana (now the University of Louisiana at Lafayette) in the spring of 1986. Gaines also refers to a similar, if not the same, episode in an interview with John Lowe: "Someone asked me when I wrote *The Autobiography of Miss Jane Pittman*, was I thinking about Dilsey in Faulkner's novel *The Sound and the Fury*. And I said, 'No, I did not have Dilsey in mind.' And by the way, the difference between Dilsey and Miss Jane Pittman is that Faulkner gets Dilsey talking her story from his kitchen; the young schoolteacher in my book gets Miss Jane's story from Miss Jane's kitchen. And it makes a difference" (John Lowe, "An Interview with Ernest Gaines," *Conversations with Ernest Gaines*, ed. Lowe, Literary Conversations Series [Jackson: UP of Mississippi, 1995], 313).

A Conversation with Tim Gautreaux

Dayne Sherman/2009

From *Image* 63 (Fall 2009), 43–53. © Dayne Sherman. Used with permission.

Tim Gautreaux was born in Morgan City, Louisiana, in 1947. He attended Nicholls State University and the University of South Carolina, where he earned a Ph.D. in English literature. In 1972 he began teaching creative writing at Southeastern Louisiana University, where he directed the creative writing program until his retirement in 2003. His books include the story collections *Same Place, Same Things* (St. Martins) and the *New York Times* notable *Welding with Children* (Picador) as well as the novels *The Next Step in the Dance* (Picador), *The Clearing*, and *The Missing* (both from Knopf). *The Clearing* made several top-ten lists, including the *USA Today* ten best of 2003, and Annie Proulx called it "the finest American novel in a long, long time." His stories have appeared in the *New Yorker, Atlantic Monthly, Harpers, GQ*, and many other magazines, as well as in *Best American Short Stories, New Stories from the South*, and *O. Henry Prize Stories*, and in several university literature textbooks. His essays have appeared in *Oxford American* and *Preservation Magazine*. Among his awards are a National Magazine Award, Southeastern Booksellers Award for best novel, Mid-South Booksellers Award, Heasley Prize, John Dos Passos Prize, and an NEA creative writing fellowship. He has served as editor of *Louisiana Literature* and was the John Grisham visiting writer-in-residence at the University of Mississippi. Presently he is professor emeritus and writer-in-residence at Southeastern Louisiana University. He is married to Winborne Howell and has two sons, Robert and Tom, and a grandchild, Lily. He was interviewed in Hammond, Louisiana, by his former student Dayne Sherman.

Image: How did growing up in Morgan City and spending your adult life in Hammond influence your writing?

Tim Gautreaux: Morgan City in the 1950s was an oil-patch town with kind of a Wild West flavor to it. There were maybe twenty churches and forty bar-rooms. The place was an odd mix of locals and outlanders brought in by the oil industry. In my earliest years, the town was about ninety percent Catho-lic, and in at least one restaurant if I forgot what day it was and ordered a hamburger on a Friday, the waitress (who knew my family) would remind me that Catholics don't eat meat on Friday. Our neighbors were Cuban and African American and Tennessee hillbillies, and across the street were French-speaking Creole black ladies. Down the street a bit were some rich Italians. There was no segregation, and most neighborhoods were jumbled up like this.

I think most little towns in America present a mixture of all sorts of cul-tures, and this makes me suspicious of stereotypes based on the assumption that a certain region is peopled by one type of person. Back in the 1950s I thought Texas was all cowboys and oil men listening to Hank Williams or Bob Wills, yet traveling by train through Texas with my transistor ra-dio I picked up Mexican polka music played on German accordions. This marriage of musical cultures introduced me to the idea that no region is one thing only. A writer has to keep this in mind when he deals with set-ting. Don't oversimplify, and pay attention to what's around you culturally. Awareness of class and culture is money in the bank for a fiction writer.

When I started writing, I paid attention to how characters from different backgrounds interact, and that brought me to stories such as "Dancing with the One-armed Gal" about a Cajun ice-house employee picking up a hitch-hiker who is a recently fired feminist university professor.

Image: In this light, does diversity create conflict?
TG: Right. Take the two conflicting characters in "Welding with Children." Though these two white Protestant men are from the same tiny Louisiana town, they are nothing alike. Bruton is not a churchgoer. He is a welder, a blue-collar shade-tree mechanic. Mr. Fordlyson is a businessman in his sev-enties or eighties, a deacon in the Baptist church. He has an inner compass that tells him what the community values should be. He's also judgmental and tactless. They are from two different levels of society, and everything they say to each other is freighted with the reader's understanding of that fact.

Image: You went to Catholic schools and then Nicholls State University in a Cajun Catholic community. How did the church and school shape your worldview and artistic vision?

TG: I was educated by Marianite nuns in the 1950s and received a very structured view of the world. That order specialized in education in all fields, and in particular in religious instruction. They were great teachers and great people. As a kid, I was pretty rough around the edges and benefited from the notion that I owed a debt of loyalty to the giver of all things. A sense of right and wrong, of self-control, of respect for a religious tradition, an understanding that I can't understand everything in the world and that's all right—these things were like seeds that have matured slowly in me. I would be one unhappy man without them. I feel sorry for kids who are raised without any moral guidance from parents or church, kids who grow up in a vacuum and who are expected to "pick it up when they get to be adults." Maybe drive down to Wal-Mart and buy a gallon of religion. That's like throwing a twenty-six-year-old off an ocean pier and yelling, "Hey, it's called swimming. Pick it up."

Image: In 1977 you studied with Walker Percy at Loyola University in New Orleans. Can you talk about the class and what Dr. Percy was like as a teacher?

TG: Percy selected ten students based on writing samples, and we met every week for three hours and did the usual creative writing workshop stuff. What was special was that this world-famous writer was taking the time to share his notions of good fiction with us. Several people in the class went on to become successful writers. One wound up being the editor of *Newsweek*. Another was the novelist Valerie Martin, one was playwright Larry Gray, and another was famous French Quarter guide and raconteur Kenneth Holditch. Everybody was smart and engaged and felt honored to be in that class. Percy, who had that rare quality of being modest and brilliant at the same time, addressed us like friends. He was generous with his time and tactful and succinct with his criticism. He would take my feeble efforts and mark them up as carefully as if he was a New York editor. For the first time, my fiction was taken seriously, and this helped me take myself seriously as a writer.

In class Percy asked us to question the values of the characters we created: he wanted to know what they were looking for in life, where they wanted to go. For Percy each fictional character was on a quest for truth or happiness or something that would complete him. In an interview he once said that if a piece of fiction didn't in some way concern itself with values, he wasn't interested in it. His own fiction shows him to be worried about American society and how it's affected by materialism, the worst side of

Hollywood, the worst side of the music industry. But in class, he was not cynical. He was a gentle, guiding spirit throughout that semester in 1977. During the class I read all of his fiction, and afterward much else that I read seemed inconsequential and detached from the real world. Reading Percy made me ask questions about narratives: What are the characters looking for? What would make them happy?

Image: In many ways your writing class was like a high school shop class. I mean this in the best way. We received general information, then we went to the shop and built the stories. You taught like a person preparing us to work on machines. Do you think this is an accurate remembrance?

TG: When an instructor asks a student in an introductory creative writing class to write a short story, he is asking him to do something very complex. It is like telling a bunch of people who have never done carpentry at all, "Go home and build me a dining-room table." They have no idea what to do. The first thing the instructor does is break down the task into its composite parts. I would tell them what kind of lumber to buy and then how to plane it, how to glue the boards together and then how to sand and stain and varnish it. You spend one week on each process. That student of furniture-making can build a table because he comes to understand that it is not an incomprehensible mass of activity, it's an ordered series of steps. It's the same with fiction writing. Instead of lecturing on wood and varnish, I explain about plot, character, conflict, and setting. I try to give students the tools with which they can build a story, along with a few exercises so they can practice using the tools. The aim is to get them rolling, to give them some feeling of control, some orientation to the task at hand. If a teacher merely tells a class to go home and write a story, he's wasting his students' time and his own. He'll mostly get in a bunch of prose units as rough as a table built out of demolished chicken coops.

Image: Could you talk about two or three of the main notions you like to communicate to would-be writers in your short-story workshop?

TG: In regards to the short story form, the simple stuff is the most important: "To open parachute, pull this ring."

First, if there is no conflict, there is no story. A story doesn't exist until there's conflict. Everything seems to grow out of it. It brings plot into being. Character is defined by it. Conflict generates theme out of thin air. The initial conflict the author chooses is what is developed all the way through the tale. It's the nervous system of the story. Eventually there is going to be an epiphany or a climactic moment or an anti-climatic moment that relates to that conflict. Every part of the story is informed and united by the struggle between two forces. To use a homely metaphor, a loaf of bread, anywhere you sample it with a pinch, is a loaf of bread. A story about a struggle between a man and his wife, anywhere you sample a piece, will taste of the struggle between this man and his wife. If it tastes of something else, you're writing two different stories at the same time.

The second thing I like to talk about is the personal territory of a writer. Young people find it hard to believe that they have a personal territory. They don't find their own experience interesting and don't consider certain things as foundations for stories, things like their own personal fascinations, their family's dynamics, stories, legends, the old folks, weird folks, history, the streets of their neighborhood, values of their county or region—in short, all the stuff the Faulkners and Cormac McCarthys of the world wove into their greatest work. One reason the fiction of the average college sophomore is so dreadful is that they don't listen to the tales those old boring people in their family tell, the grandparents and great-uncles and aunts. So where do they go for story ideas? They borrow from TV and movies. The result is a weak copy of a New York detective drama written by someone raised on a dairy farm by deaf Iranian parents on the banks of the Mississippi River in Arkansas.

Well, I'm exaggerating. What about the kid who was raised in a typical subdivision outside Atlanta? He thinks writing about such a raising is dull, because all subdivisions are the same, right? One day I challenged one of these uninteresting kids. "What is the subdivision next to yours?" "Azalea Acres," she said. "And that place is exactly like your area?" "Oh, no," she said. "Half of those people don't even have pools. We're much better off than they are." "But the kids there are as good as you are?" She hesitated, but only a bit. "They're a pretty rough crowd and ride around in those loud little trucks." What's the next subdivision past them?" "That'd be Pine Hill." "Just like yours?" "God no. Those families think they're royalty. Even the kids drive BMWs and the little girls wear designer flip-flops to the country-club pool!" There are indeed great differences even between subdivisions in the same community. There is a pecking order. There is a culture war between subdivisions worth writing about.

What I want students to understand is that wherever they've lived, that's their territory. They know that area better than any outsider. They know the idiom, the values, the social structures, the different coexisting cultures. A lot of young writers don't understand that every place is unique and that they own the places in which they were raised as far as writing is concerned. Something, maybe TV or Hollywood, gives them the idea that one place in America is just like another. That's a lie. Many writers sometimes don't realize this lie until they're in their forties and start looking back and composing stories and building characters out of their own personal history, set where they were raised. Can you do research and set a story in New York City if you are from Baton Rouge? Sure. A master writer like Annie Proulx does extensive research when she produces her western fiction. But it is a hard way to go, and when a writer ignores his own territory, he does so at his own peril, because unless he is a born researcher, what he discovers will never be as authentic as his impressions of his family and culture witnessed in childhood. What you discover will never be as good as your own background.

I gave this spiel to a class one semester and a student went home and wrote about his subdivision. He lived in one of the New Orleans neighborhoods which experienced terrible soil subsidence. All the homes were built on slabs. The homes built on pilings were three feet up in the air after twenty years because the soil had withered away beneath them. The ones not built on pilings had broken slabs, which caused the living room to lean fifteen degrees one way and the bedrooms to tilt the other. The student invented a dysfunctional family and placed them in one of these houses. It was hilarious because the characters were as warped as their environment. Throughout the story things were sliding off tables and pianos rolled on their own across the rooms. Pets and baseballs would get lost under the marooned slabs. It was a great story, and all the student did to get it was to go home and look around.

Image: I've noticed that you don't seem to put writing above your "real" life.
TG: I don't know if that was any conscious decision on my part. I just learned along the way that writing comes from living. Living doesn't come from writing. The best way to learn how to write about children is to have a couple of your own. You have to go through the struggle of raising them. It's hard, not ever having kids, to sit down and imagine child characters that are going to be believable. If a writer sets a tale on a farm, it seems like he ought to have spent some time on one to figure out the animals and machinery and planting techniques, the little bits and pieces woven into such a narrative that give it some sense of realism. If a guy thinks he's just going to sit in a garret somewhere and write great fiction without being connected to the sources of fiction, he's a fool.

What's important is not so much the act of writing but the stuff that generates your writing, that is, the details of day-to-day life, the physical world, the objects we touch and study every day. I am always out in the yard working on stuff. I live on five wooded acres here; I'm always cutting trees, splitting firewood (with a hydraulic log splitter nowadays), burning brush, or repairing my broken-down tractors. If the weather's bad, I love going into my barn workshop and tinkering with stuff. Last year I was working on pocket watches; the year before it was antique clocks; the year before that, antique shotguns. I just love objects, not just to own them and brag, but to see how they work and the way they are made.

My personal fascinations bleed into my fiction. Much of my writing is full of machinery, sometimes as simple setting detail, sometimes as metaphor. When I write about a character repairing an old engine, it is not something I got from research or conjured out of thin air. It comes from the experience of taking apart and repairing a John Deere two-cylinder tractor or a lovely old Parker shotgun. If a writer understands the source of good fiction—the people, plants, and things he touches in daily living—he won't have any trouble keeping his writing in perspective.

Image: "Welding with Children" is one of your most compelling stories. At one point Mr. Fordlyson says, "Bruton, everything worth doing hurts like hell." I see this a lot in your work: redemption comes at a price.

TG: It's not exactly a secret that important achievements happen after a long payment plan. That "everything worth doing hurts like hell" is a simple law of physics, an obvious rule, and it applies to writing as well as all other arts. It certainly applies to characters who are trying to set their lives straight. In "Welding with Children" Bruton has not done a good job of giving his daughters much of a value system. Now he's got to do it with a set of grandchildren, and it's a mountainous task. It won't be easy, and it'll take the rest of his life. But he has hope that they'll turn out better than his daughters did.

Sometimes I wonder if we are all gradually being babied into the notion that earthly existence is heaven. That life is something perfectible. People lose sight of the notion that sometimes life is still good when it is not so comfortable and not so perfect. An athlete goes through a lot of pain and failure to be a winner. So does a musician or a writer. Every great achievement involves sacrifice and pain and repetition and denial and failure. Everything worth doing hurts like hell. It seems like a lot of people run away from any painful endeavor. They just don't want to deal with it. The lucky ones eventually come to realize that it's okay to sweat.

Image: Humor is a big part of your fiction. Often the humor involves children and old people. Tell us why.

TG: I'm not quite sure myself. Humor is just a tool writers use to make a story work. Shakespeare used it in his tragedies to balance them. Flannery O'Connor used irony and parody to bring tension to her narratives. In a recent story I wrote, a character walks up to a store's community bulletin board and tacks up an advertisement for a carpenter. He places the notice next to another that says, "Free rattlesnake to good home." You might ask why I put that in there. For several reasons: It tells us a little something about the story's setting. Also it gives the reader a little chuckle, and the story needs one at that point. It's a pinch of yeast that I added to give it some buoyancy.

I can't imagine writing a story, even a very sorrowful story, without humor in it. If you read Walker Percy you will see gentle humor. If you read Flannery O'Connor you see a masterful blend of humor and tragedy, sometimes a razor sharp, painful humor. It is something the writer has to know how to use. There is nothing more boring than a story about a tragedy that has absolutely no humor at all. It becomes whining, depressing. Who would want to read such a thing?

You asked about humor with children and old people. Kids and geezers are off of life's script. In the middle of a person's life, he's supposed to behave a certain way: have a career, kiss the wife, argue with the kids, pay his taxes, keep his job, behave, watch what he says. Very old people and very young people ignore all conventions and behave how they want. That's what's so delightful about them, and that's what offers so many opportunities for the writer.

Image: Your novel *The Missing* is rich and compelling, a big canvas. Assuming there is such a thing as a Catholic novel or a Christian novel, I believe you've written it. You have illustrated the Socratic notion—which has its fulfillment in the teachings and life of Jesus—that it is better to suffer wrong than to do wrong to others. Between your earlier novel *The Clearing* and *The Missing*, I see a change. The earlier book shows the damage of war and violence. However in *The Missing* violence is to be avoided even when it seems warranted. Sin is its own punishment. Why did this artistic shift occur?

TG: Actually, they are the same type of novel. What happens in a narrative is dictated by who the main character is. The notion of nonviolence in *The Missing* is dictated by Sam Simoneaux, a guy raised by a loving Catholic uncle in west Louisiana. He was brought up to believe that violence doesn't cure anything, but that belief is also born into him by the mystery of the draw. I think his mild nature is a gift. Once I figured out in the first couple chapters what Sam's personality was, his character was going to propel the entire novel. No matter what happens in *The Missing*, Sam is not going to kill anybody.

It was a delight to write *The Missing* because it goes against contemporary American culture, and against our worst nature. It goes against everything on American television, where cops and bad guys alike are blowing people apart with pistols and assault rifles every hour, on the hour. *The Missing* goes against almost everything Hollywood teaches, with the exception of the recent Clint Eastwood movie, *Gran Torino*, which I thought was a very brave and realistic film. The way that movie ends suggests what I was after in *The Missing:* The path of self-sacrifice was chosen to great purpose.

The Missing builds toward the expectation of a big shootout. When it didn't happen, I know some readers were disappointed. I expected this from day one. Americans have been programmed to a template of offense followed by justified violence. This is a cliché, and a simple-minded notion. I hope *The Missing* sets some writers free from the idea that if offense is given then offense must be taken.

Image: In some ways *The Missing* is an antiwar novel. Were you aware of that element when you started writing it?

TG: I did not go into the writing of *The Missing* wanting to make an antiwar statement. That said, the facts of World War I speak for themselves. It was a war designed and directed by imbeciles. Growing up, I was surrounded by old uncles who had survived it, and that encouraged me to do some research on the conflict. If there is any antiwar sentiment in *The Missing* and *The Clearing*, it is specifically against World War I, which was a mismanaged conflict driven by ego and paranoia. It should never have happened. The only thing it accomplished was to prepare the way for World War II.

Image: You worked on *The Missing* for quite a while. Describe the process of writing and researching the book.

TG: Much of *The Missing* happens on a twenties-era excursion boat. The action could have been framed in other contexts, but I used one of my personal fascinations, inland river history. My father was a tugboat captain on the Mississippi River and its tributaries. My grandfather was a chief engineer on steamboats. I came to *The Missing* with thousands of facts already embedded in my brain about the Mississippi and Ohio Rivers, about the excursion-boat trade, about the music played on the boats. I was practicing what I preach in class, that if a fiction writer has a passion for something, be it mountain climbing or dog grooming, he can use that specialized knowledge to form his fictional world.

I did some reading to brush up on World War I–era artillery. I had to consult war maps to make sure the narrative was set in the right area of France and that sort of thing. To my knowledge there's only one book dealing with riverboat music explicitly, and one on the excursion-boat trade. Not a lot is known about American jazz on the river. It is a tremendous and important chapter of American music history that's been unvisited by scholars. When the old passenger and freight steamers stopped operating around 1900 because of a lack of trade, some of them were bought, their passenger cabins stripped out, and their main decks replaced with hardwood dance floors and bandstands. These boats hired the best orchestras around and paddled from town to town through the length of the Ohio and Mississippi systems offering day excursions and nighttime dance trips. Eventually some of the boats hired African American bands in New Orleans, and this is how jazz began to be heard up and down the Mississippi Valley, before records and before radio. The heyday of these boats ended in the 1940s.

Image: Did members of your family tell you about the old boats?
TG: Oh yes, my mother went to dances on the *Sidney* and the old *Capitol* when she was a teenager and heard the best jazz in the world. Louis Armstrong was playing on the boats in those days. All the famous legends of New Orleans jazz, the guys who invented jazz back in the teens or before, were steamboat musicians.

Image: Both *The Clearing* and *The Missing* were published by Knopf and edited by Gary Fisketjon. What did you learn from the process of working with Fisketjon, and how has it made you a better writer?
TG: Among other things, Gary is concerned with readability. He wants language to be accessible, economical, and lucid. He is expert at finding all the goofs that an author overlooks, all the overwriting and redundancy, wobbly logic, inelegant phrasing, tedious passages. Since I've been working with him I find myself more aware of what I'm doing. He's one of the last great editors in New York. I've come to understand that a certain kind of clean

composition that doesn't sacrifice originality of utterance is a great way to write. What I'm impressed with most is how seriously and energetically he pursues his craft of editing. I take all of his suggestions to heart and follow a great many of them.

Image: Your recent short story "Idols," published in the *New Yorker*, is a real departure. It's set in north Mississippi and Memphis, and it picks up where two of Flannery O'Connor's stories, "Parker's Back" and "Everything That Rises Must Converge," end. Obadiah Parker has found redemption, but Julian Smith has not. Please tell us about writing the piece.

TG: "Idols" is sort of a continuation and parody of the two O'Connor tales. The editor I worked with was expert and thorough, and we went through the story several times over a period of a few weeks. I had to explain a lot of the southernisms to get to keep them in the story. One editor wanted to call the character Mr. Poxley simply by the name of Poxley. I had to explain that in a small, deep South town, a man in his seventies or eighties who owns a substantial business is always addressed and referred to as "Mr."

"Idols" is one of the only things I've done set outside Louisiana. I got a good feel for north Mississippi when I was visiting writer-in-residence at the University of Mississippi for a semester in 1996. I was always tempted to write a story that sprang out of that region.

I was sitting in my office at home one day and Tommy Franklin called from Oxford, Mississippi, and said he and William Gay were thinking of putting together an anthology of stories that gave tribute to Flannery O'Connor. He asked if I had a story that might fit. "You mean stories that sound like O'Connor's writing?" I asked. He said yes. I said, "Maybe stories that use an O'Connor character?" He said, "I guess that's one way you could do it." I said, "Okay, I'll see what I can do." I chose two characters and started writing to see what was going to happen. Of course the magic is always in seeing what's going to happen. Every story is a gift.

Image: What are you reading now?

TG: I read books that come my way by accident. I picked up a free book at the library giveaway in Jefferson, North Carolina, a novel by Carolyn Chute, who wrote *The Beans of Egypt*. This was called *Letourneau's Used Auto Parts*. I was floored by the energy and drive, and the insanity. It was a convincing interpretation of backwoods folks in Maine, a whole class that has fallen through the cracks of America's golden streets. The characters are fleshed-out originals, and reading what happens to them was like watching a house burn down in slow motion. I couldn't put the book down, and I am looking forward to reading others of her works. It's not for the faint of heart, but interesting stuff. What she has done is embrace her territory, as all good writers do. I think she knows the woods of Maine better than anybody else in the solar system.

Image: Are you writing anything currently? Is there a trilogy in the works, with *The Missing* and *The Clearing*?
TG: It might seem that way, but it's not going to happen. I do have another novel in mind, something funny and energetic. I hope to get it done in a couple of years, not my usually four or five or six years. I'm also putting together another collection of short stories. I think everything I write is going to be set in Louisiana, but I'm going to try to get away from local characters a little, and write about people who are not from Louisiana but currently living there. I think that would be a way of broadening the scope of the tales.

Image: Besides collecting and restoring antique machinery, you volunteer as a machinist and fireman of steam locomotives at the Tennessee Valley Train Museum in Chattanooga. How did you get involved with the museum?
TG: I'm a lifelong railroad buff. Railroad buffs tend to seek out any operating steam locomotive. I went by there and met a few of the staff members and rode in the locomotive cab and saw what a fine organization it is. I made the acquaintance of one of the engineers, who encouraged me to become a member of the staff and take training as a steam locomotive fireman. For that I am very grateful.

This hobby reflects my lifelong interest in antique machinery. When I was five or six years old and a steamboat would come to town—there still were a few paddle-wheelers in those days—my father would hear the whistle and put me in the car and bring me down to the waterfront in Morgan City and show it to me. If he knew anybody on the boat's crew, he would get me on board and we would walk through the engine room and listen to the machines, smell the hot valve oil and glossy enamel, and these old guys would tell me about steam engines. Dad would do the same thing when he'd spot an old steam tug on the river in New Orleans. Several times we walked the wharves to take pictures of a sizzling Bisso Towboat Company tug or one of the old paddlewheel steam ferries. He knew the era of steam machinery, the stuff that built this country out of nothing, was passing and would soon be gone forever. Indeed by 1960 or so, most of it was.

Tim Gautreaux's *The Missing*

Tom Ashbrook/2009

From *On Point with Tom Ashbrook* (8 April 2009). Copyright © 2011 Trustees of Boston University. Used courtesy of WBUR, 90.9 FM Boston and WBUR.org.

Ashbrook: From WBUR Boston and NPR, I'm Tom Ashbrook and this is *On Point*. Louisiana writer Tim Gautreaux is son of a tugboat captain, grandson of a riverboat captain, and author of a new novel set on the Mississippi that follows the steamboat not in Mark Twain's day but in the rough and tumble, down and dirty age of the 1920s. World War I is the backdrop, a kidnapping in New Orleans is the plot starter, and the themes are wide and deep as the river. Loss, reparation, the pull of vengeance, jazz is new, human nature is old, and the river rolls. Up next, *On Point*, a different life on the Mississippi and Tim Gautreaux's *The Missing*.
[music]
From WBUR Boston, I'm Tom Ashbrook and this is *On Point*. Louisiana author Tim Gautreaux's new novel *The Missing* opens in war-torn France at the end of World War I. It ends in dark swamps and backwoods Arkansas. In between, it churns the Mississippi in a four-deck three-hundred-foot sternwheel steamboat, not in Mark Twain's time, but in the Roaring Twenties, with jazz, moonshine, a kidnapping, reckoning. This hour *On Point*, we're going over the river and into the woods rough with Louisiana's Tim Gautreaux. You can join the conversation. Have you read Gautreaux? Do you know this river, these woods, the urge for vengeance? Joining me now from KSLU in Hammond, Louisiana, is novelist and short story writer Tim Gautreaux. He's a Louisiana native, grew up the son of a tugboat captain; he's writer-in-residence and professor emeritus at Southeastern Louisiana University in Hammond. His new novel is *The Missing*. The *New York Times* calls Gautreaux a "spinner of yarns with a moral" and *The Missing* "moving

and resonant." The *Times-Picayune* calls *The Missing* Gautreaux's "master-piece." Tim Gautreaux, welcome to *On Point*. Thanks for being here.
Gautreaux: Hi Tom.

Ashbrook: It's wonderful to have you. I wish you'd just start off by introducing us to your main character here, Sam Simoneaux, and just sort of the salient key facts of his early birth that lead to his uncle finding him in a bit of a bad and tragic situation.
Gautreaux: Tom, actually Sam Simoneaux is a person I got out of the police reports in the *Times-Picayune*. That's how I get the seeds for a lot of my narratives. I read the police reports. I read about a kidnapping in which a child was almost abducted out of a retail center. I began to think, what would that security guard who foiled a kidnapping feel like if he hadn't succeeded? And for the rest of his life he had to wonder about this child that he was partly responsible for losing. That went into the heart of Sam Simoneaux, the character, as I put him together. He was the guy with this sense of duty. And the whole story grew out of this particular seed. Sam Simoneaux the character is born and raised in my imagination in southwest Louisiana, in the Cajun culture, grew up speaking French. But he understood that he had a certain amount of musical talent and he wanted to move off the farm and go to New Orleans when he was about sixteen. Then he goes off to war. The book actually starts in France. He arrives in France on the day that the Armistice is signed, and so the people there nickname him Lucky. He keeps this name throughout the novel—this is his nickname, this is a kind of ironic nickname, of course, as the narrative turns out.

Ashbrook: He goes off to war just as the war ends, and that's kind of a pattern that occurs again and again here. This shocking infancy of Sam Simoneaux where his entire family, it's not clear early in the book why, but his entire family is slaughtered, and his father pokes him into a cold cast iron stove just before the slaughter begins. He's the only one to survive.
Gautreaux: Right. He has a lot of baggage that follows him through life.

Ashbrook: Yeah I guess!
Gautreaux: The normal archetype in American fiction and American narrative is for some sort of tremendous amount of revenge to occur. And I thought what would it be like to construct a narrative in which this didn't exactly happen. I was reading the last Sunday's book review in the *New York*

Times, and the lead sentence was, "While violence never fails to provoke and disturb, it's the absence in its wake that continues to affect us." And that struck me as being a pretty lucid understanding of one of the key points of the novel that if you are left behind, the people who are left behind, are left with this giant hole in their lives, whenever someone in their family is killed. And of course Sam's entire family is wiped out. He's raised by a very loving uncle, and that affects the rest of the narrative. When he gets back to New Orleans, he gets a job as a floorwalker, which in 1921 is a good job for a farm boy because you're inside; you're not being baked by the sun.

Ashbrook: It's kind of a security guard in a department store.
Gautreaux: Exactly, exactly. I guess floorwalkers went out in the forties. But this scene is set in 1921 on Canal Street in New Orleans. And a young girl is kidnapped on his watch. And he's sort of blamed for it—he didn't follow the correct procedures for finding a lost child in the big department store, so he's fired. Ostensibly he goes off to look for this child because his boss tells him, "Well, if you find the kid, we'll give you your job back." But there are many other motivations which have to do with his personal history, of course, that make him go off and look for the child. And the whole novel is this search.

Ashbrook: All of that puts him on the river. I think the opening twist for an awful lot of readers is that when you think steamboat and Mississippi and riverboat and river life, Americans almost automatically think of Mark Twain in the nineteenth century, but you're in the 1920s here.
Gautreaux: Right.

Ashbrook: We should just kind of paint the mural of the Mississippi river life, the steamboat life in the twenties compared to the archetypal Mark Twain images people may have in their minds, Tim.
Gautreaux: Right, well, Mark Twain, of course, was on boats that were actually engaged in interstate commerce. They were hauling freight and passengers. They were building America. They were running where the railroads didn't run. All of that trait played out in the late 1890s. But there were a lot of old big steamboats around that really didn't have much to do. There were some routes that ran as late as the 1930s, but there were very few, and generally on the upper Ohio. Boats could be bought for a song. And someone got the idea of taking out the entire second deck of cabins—that's where your dining room and all your passenger state rooms were—and installing

a 300-foot-long maple dance floor and showing up at towns after, of course, the town had been prepped by an advance man putting up all sorts of posters and hiring the best dance orchestra you could possibly find in the region and then running moonlight cruises for dancers. This was a phenomenally successful trade, particularly after the boats that were based in New Orleans would hire local African American jazz bands, because it was an extremely danceable music. And so from really, say, 1910 all the way to 1940, there was this big era in American music history that a lot of people don't know about, where there were these excursion steamers, made out of these old packet boats, going up and down the Mississippi and the Ohio Rivers, all the way from New Orleans to Pittsburgh, or New Orleans to as close as they could get to Minneapolis, generally Davenport. And they would go from town to town, they would land, and they would run day excursions, generally for church groups or benevolent associations. And then at night was the big dance cruise—at 8:30 at night, a moonlight cruise. They would go out. There was hot dance music and waxed down 300-foot-long dance floor; there were setups for drinks during Prohibition. The owners of these boats sort of winked at the fact that people brought on a lot of home-made liquor during Prohibition. And some of the boats had a few slot machines sprinkled around when the sheriff wasn't looking.

Ashbrook: Just maybe. You know the way you describe it—moonlight cruises and church groups—makes it sound sort of elegant. But there's some pretty rough trade—this kind of a floating saloon environment at the same time.

Gautreaux: It depended on the town. If you landed at a big urban center like Pittsburgh or Cincinnati or New Orleans, you would get civilized crowds. People would dress to the nines, especially for the day excursions. And they would come out—the young swains would use the cruises for courting opportunities. But sometimes that boat would tie up at a really rough town like a mill town, or an industrial town, or a town that was nothing but chemical factories, and they would entertain those people, and those were different crowds. Sometimes there were big brawls, big fistfights. So the boats always hired several bouncers and made sure that the busboys were big and burly so they could pull apart these brawls.

Ashbrook: And all of this, more or less, runs in your blood. Your father a tugboat captain, but your grandfather was a riverboat captain. Did stories get passed down?

Gautreaux: To a certain extent. I was the youngest child of a youngest child, so my aunts and uncles were very old when I was a child. I was born in '47, and my mother was born in 1907. And one of their big entertainments, the fondest memories of youth, was going on the dance boats for the moonlight cruises out of New Orleans or Baton Rouge. They would dance to Fate Marable, the music of Louis Armstrong, all sorts of people who were putting together the jazz idiom in America at the time. As a child, there was still an old steamboat running in New Orleans. It wasn't a tramping boat that went from town to town, but it stayed anchored in New Orleans, the old *President*, which was a big side-wheel steamboat that was originally a packet, named the *Cincinnati*. And she would go out on dance cruises, and my aunts took me along on several of those cruises when I was very young. I can remember the machinery, and how the boat felt, and how the whistle sounded, and what the officers were like as they ran the thing, and what the crowds were sort of like. It was sort of a window into the very early part of American history.

Ashbrook: We're going to learn more about that history and the story and themes in Tim Gautreaux's new novel *The Missing*. Behind us right here "Steamboat Stomp," 1926, from Jelly-Roll Morton. Listeners, you can join the conversation. Can you picture this life on the Mississippi? Not exactly Huck Finn days. I'm Tom Ashbrook. This is *On Point*. We'll be right back. [music]

Ashbrook: I'm Tom Ashbrook. This is *On Point*. We're talking this hour about life and death on the Mississippi and the steamboat era you've probably never thought of. Not Mark Twain days, but the 1920s. A new novel built around kidnapping and loss, it's *The Missing* by Tim Gautreaux. He joins us from Hammond, Louisiana. And it's getting just rave reviews. You can join in the conversation. Are you a Tim Gautreaux fan from his earlier work, novel, short stories? What do you hear in this floating Mississippi world in the Roaring Twenties? Tim, I wonder if you'd read a little bit for us. You've got a passage here where this side-wheeler, sternwheeler, the *Ambassador* is loading up for a moonlight cruise, dance trip early on in the book. Sam has just joined up to work on the riverboat, hoping to find this kidnapped girl. Could you read a bit for us, Tim?

Gautreaux: Sure. Be glad to. "Late in the day it was still hot. Sam stood on the wharf and directed jostling couples up the steamboat stage plank to the ticket booth on the main deck. The calliope began gargling, the high notes singing flat until the whistles warmed up. Fred Marble, the pianist with the black orchestra, wearing a slouch hat and gloves against the flying steam, tickled out 'Ain't We Got Fun' on the roof, the instrument's wincing notes sailing upriver over the French Quarter. Couples in their twenties and thirties began showing up, then what looked like a small men's club, everybody in seersucker and straw boaters. For the most part, people were well dressed, the young women in thin drop-waist dresses, the men in summer suits. The calliope music stopped with a yodel, and out of the long curving line of open windows above Sam the band began to pour a thumping-loud rendition of 'When My Baby Smiles at Me' in a rattling-good dance tempo, the music coming down on the crowd like peppery candy for the ears. Customers began to back up on the broad stage plank, and as departure time drew close they were stacked three abreast, grinning and craning their necks at the big white apparition. Sam palmed a nickel-plated counter, and when he checked it, it read 1,255. Four deckhands shuffled down to stand by their bitts and the boat's steam whistle let out a deep, river-filling chord. Ralph Brandywine would pilot the *Ambassador* through the city river traffic, and he leaned out the wheelhouse window holding a megaphone and yelled down to Sam to hustle the last customers on board. The paddlewheel began to turn slowly, the half-ton deck bell banged three times, and a crush of customers bunched up on the stage as though afraid of being left behind on the wharf—the worst thing that could happen to anybody, to be left out of the steamy cloud of music and fun. Sam began to enjoy paddling the people on board, calling out for everyone to step up, thumbing his little counter device, getting lost in the excitement and the smell of vanilla, witch hazel, jasmine dusting powder, and Sen-Sen. Two minutes later the steam capstan sputtered the stage plank aboard and the mob of latecomers jammed against the ticket booth on the first deck as the boat backed away in earnest, steam spuming from vent pipes in the hull, engine-room gongs cracking alive like fight bells, and above it all big mossy gouts of coal smoke roiling from the stacks. Sam looked back across the wharf and saw, two hundred yards off, three teenaged girls running in heels through the falling light, hands on hats, purses flying out from their elbows, the hems on their short dresses shimmying with the white reciprocal blur of their knees, but it was too late, and he didn't want to think about what was in their girl hearts as the big boat turned out under the early stars: an image of romance, hot dance music, or just dumb human fun based on the necessary mystical imagining that things in general just ain't so bad all the time."

Ashbrook: Tim Gautreaux reading from his new novel *The Missing*. You can join the conversation. Do you know this terrain? Your dad was a tugboat captain. I guess that means not on the river, but down what, around New Orleans or on out? Not towboat we're talking here, but tug?

Gautreaux: Well, he worked both, but he was mainly a towboat captain. He worked the inter-coastal canal and very often he was on the Mississippi River. I would ride with him as sort of an auxiliary wheelman and sometimes go up to Baton Rouge, a little further on.

Ashbrook: And your grandfather's riverboat days, were those Mississippi or . . .

Gautreaux: He was in the Atchafalaya basin. He ran lumber steamers. Sometimes he would get out onto the big river. Engineers tended to go from job to job in those days. He was chief engineer on steamboats, passenger and freight steamers.

Ashbrook: I read that your family came to New Orleans all the way back in 1785 with a group of Acadians. Does that make you Cajun, or how does that work exactly?

Gautreaux: I guess you could call it that. The Gautreaux line goes back to 1785 in New Orleans. We were banished from Nova Scotia and went back to France for thirty years, but the Acadians that went back to France did not assimilate. The Spanish government needed farmers desperately in 1785, so they bankrolled that batch of Cajuns to come over and set up farmsteads.

Ashbrook: I wonder how it feels: you've written short stories for a long time and some very well-received novels—*The Next Step in the Dance* in 1999 and *The Clearing* in 2003. The *Times-Picayune* calls this one, *The Missing*, your "masterpiece." After a lifetime of writing, how does that feel to have it received that way? Do you look at it that way, I wonder?

Gautreaux: Well, who knows what's to come. I hope to get better and better. Things seem to be getting better. So who knows what's down the line. It took a long time to write *The Missing*. A lot of work went into it. Maybe it's the most researched book, but a lot of it is personal history, just as in *The Clearing*, a lot of that was family legend and history.

Ashbrook: Let's get a call from Juanita in Shenandoah Valley, Virginia. Juanita, you're on the air with Tim Gautreaux.

Juanita: Hi! I grew up in Louisiana. And I can remember going as a high school group on the *President* for a dance. It was very exciting. And the band that was playing for us was Pete Fountain, before he became famous.

Ashbrook: Sure, and this is the big boat tied up right there in New Orleans, Juanita?
Juanita: Exactly, the *President.*

Ashbrook: So, in a way you're part of this history that Tim Gautreaux's writing about here.
Juanita: I absolutely am. In fact, my family owned four weekly newspapers in different parts of Louisiana. So I have never read any of his novels, but now hearing this, I'm going to look for the latest one.

Ashbrook: That's great. Thanks for calling, Juanita. Tim, were you out there yourself on some of these late midnight, moonlight cruises?
Gautreaux: Mainly I would take the day trips with my aunts. It was in the 1950s and '60s when I did that. But the *President* was steam all the way up until 1979 and still exists somewhere. They don't use it anymore, but I think it's tied up in Alton, Illinois.

Ashbrook: So, what, did they just keep running these steamboats, shoveling the coal in until they fell apart, and diesel took over just by the exhaustion of the old boats?
Gautreaux: Basically, a lot of the old boats were wooden hulled, and they babied them along. The *Capitol*, for example, ran all the way I think until 1942, '43, and she was ancient by then. She was probably the last of the first generation boats. Of course, the *President* was originally the *Cincinnati*, which was a packet, and she was built in 1924.

Ashbrook: I remember what I guess must have been replicas, much later, all the way up the river in Hannibal, sort of day trip steamboats that would take folks around. What about the music? Juanita mentions Pete Fountain, but you've got a lot of music, and music plays an important role in *The Missing*. It's representing a new kind of music, jazz, which had all kinds of very, very clear racial and sort of edgy tones about it in this time, in the 1920s. Tim, give us some of that sense.
Gautreaux: Well, Sam Simoneaux is a pianist; he's sort of a so-so pianist, and he gets a job on this boat because the little girl that was kidnapped was part of an act. She was three-and-a-half years old. She was just joining her

parents as a little singer. She had a little bell-like voice; she was a very special child.

Ashbrook: Her parents are musicians on the boat.
Gautreaux: Yeah, they're musicians on the boat, white musicians, and he goes along with them, because they figure that somebody who saw the little girl's act somewhere on the boat's route was responsible for her kidnapping. That's why he's in this whole milieu. As far as the history of jazz music on the riverboat scene, the Streckfus line in particular, which was a line of excursion boats, would recruit bands in New Orleans. Legend has it that they went out one day in about 1917 or 1918 with two bands on one excursion. They had a really ritzy white orchestra on the main dance deck, and upstairs on the Texas deck, which had some open area, they put an African American New Orleans jazz band. And by the middle of the cruise, all the dancers were outside in the dark dancing to the African American band, and almost nobody was dancing to the big fancy orchestra. Right then it was decided that this is the band that they ought to recruit for the young people. Jazz music of course in 1920 was revolutionary. Dixieland was hot music that generated all sorts of new dance steps, and young people just went wild for it. Louis Armstrong in 1919 or '20 or '21 was like the Rolling Stones in 1966.

Ashbrook: Right, right.
Gautreaux: That's how they looked at it. The only way you could get jazz music in the early days if you lived in Davenport or Vicksburg or Memphis was off an excursion steamer that showed up and could put 2,500 people on board.

Ashbrook: You use it kind of interestingly as a literary catalyst here, because it came with all kinds of racial resonance; it almost had an edge like we think of hip hop, I don't know, twenty years ago. It mixed things up when jazz came on the scene, especially steaming up there through the heart of old Dixie.
Gautreaux: Yeah, one of the big worries of the early excursion boats was landing at a rural town, filling the boat up with 2,500 white people, and then presenting the music by an African American orchestra because many of these people had never seen an African American with a suit and tie on before. And of course these orchestras were very well dressed. So there was always that kind of a worry how are the people here going to respond to this particular type of music, because it was so revolutionary. But it was also extremely danceable, and that's what ultimately won people over, and it

was better music than the white bands could put out in that particular era, particularly in '17, '18. So naturally jazz began to spread and many orchestras sprang up.

Ashbrook: It's about as rich an environment as we can picture when we put that whole gumbo together. The *Times* and others describe you, Tim Gautreaux, as an "old-fashioned story teller," a "spinner of yarns with a moral." How do you feel about that? Do you set out to bring a moral to it? Does it just happen for you as a writer?

Gautreaux: Oh no, that type of stuff comes out of an author, no matter what he writes. I could write a letter to my insurance company, and it would probably have some sort of a moral fundamental working there.

Ashbrook: So tell us about what some of the moral quandaries are at work in this book—the issue of vengeance comes up and comes up very strongly, not just from the kidnapping but from Sam Simoneaux's very, very earliest years as we heard earlier. And he's there also in a war environment where he sees the havoc, the devastation, left behind by the World War I that he just misses in France. How do you begin to turn over those themes of violence, vengeance, and the emptiness that can come along? Tim Gautreaux.

Gautreaux: Without giving the novel away, all I can say is something sort of general. I noticed that the archetype, the template, so to speak, the way that Americans look at any type of injury that is done to someone, or any type of tragedy that happens, that there should be some sort of a recompense, some sort of a vengeance. Americans are very Old Testament when it comes to vengeance, and I didn't want to write a book like that. The book is an exploration of how one-for-one vengeance really is sort of beside the point. Many people lose people in this book, or briefly mention people who are missing in their lives. I guess that's where the title came from, *The Missing.* At one point in the novel, a character says, "When somebody is killed, you don't lose just that person but you lose everything he or she can do for an entire lifetime." And so *The Missing* is about this big vacuum, this big emptiness that is left behind when somebody is lost. That's one of the things it's about.

Ashbrook: There are holes in the lives of this book, and bullet holes in the wall. Tim Gautreaux joins us from Hammond, Louisiana. Let's get a call from Bill in Sudbury, Massachusetts. Bill, you're on the air.

Bill: Hi, Tom—thanks for taking my call. Hi, Tim—Bill Dowey here.

Gautreaux: Good to see you.

Bill: I just wanted to make the point that I grew up in New Orleans, too, and went on the *President* myself. I think I probably went on it later than you did, Tim. I loved that dance floor—it was so huge and so smooth. It was an incredible dance floor there on the *President*. I also wanted to say that a lot of people don't know that Tim Gautreaux is a pretty good dancer. He and his wife Winborne do a lot of Cajun two-step and step out all the time. Hey, Tim, how's it going?

Gautreaux: I'm doing fine. Couldn't be better.

Ashbrook: He's doing very well with this new book. Bill, what did you feel that you were a part of when you were dancing on the steamboat there, tied up at New Orleans? What kind of tradition did it feel like you were a part of, Bill?

Bill: Well, actually, for me it goes back to when I was in eighth grade in grammar school, my grammar school class had an outing on the *President*, so there was always even as I grew up as an adult, they still continued to have musical ventures, all sorts of different types of music on it. The last time I remember going on was—Tim said it was still operational as late as 1979—I think it was probably '78 that I remember going on around Mardi Gras time. At that time, they had two or three different groups that would play one after the other. It was great fun not only being there, but then going out at night time above board, looking at the stars if you didn't want to continue dancing all the time. It was a great variety, lots of fun.

Ashbrook: It sounds like a great setting for romance, or if you're at one of the more rough and tumble locations up the river for some trouble. Bill, thank you very much for calling. Tim, is that right: you and Winborne, your wife, out there cutting up the rug or the waxed floor?

Gautreaux: Oh, yeah, we took jitterbug classes forty years ago or so, thirty years ago. Of course, dancing is very much in Louisiana culture, southwest Louisiana and in New Orleans culture. People just like to dance.

Ashbrook: Absolutely. This is from 1924, we'll go out here, with "Frankie and Johnny" from Fate Marable. Tim Gautreaux is with us. His new novel is *The Missing* set on the Mississippi of the 1920s. You can join the conversation. I'm Tom Ashbrook; this is *On Point*. We'll be right back.
[music]
Ashbrook: I'm Tom Ashbrook. This is *On Point*. We're talking this hour about life and death on the Mississippi, in a steamboat era, not Mark Twain's, but the Roaring 1920s in a new novel built around a kidnapping dealing with

loss there. Tim Gautreaux is the author. He joins us today from Hammond, Louisiana, and the book is *The Missing.* Jazz, murder, vengeance, loss, all going on here around a kidnapping of a three-year-old girl. You can join the conversation. What do you make of Tim Gautreaux's take on vengeance, its allure, its ultimate emptiness? And is this the American journey of self-discovery up the river on a quest on a riverboat, with jazz, dancing? We have a call right here from Louisiana, Port Allen, Louisiana. And Ron. Hi, Ron. You're on the air with Tim Gautreaux.

Ron. Hi, Tom. Hi, Tim. Tim, I just wanted to call and mention to you that I think you're from Morgan City originally?

Tim: Yes. That's a fact.

Ron: I married a girl from Morgan City and lived there many years myself. I came across a collection of your short stories a few years back. I'm in the car, so I can't go find it. I had not read fiction in quite a while, and I picked up a collection of your short stories. The descriptions of the countryside in southwest Louisiana and the people have stayed with me. You're just a fabulous writer.

Gautreaux: Well, thank you.

Ron: I've always wanted a chance to tell you that.

Gautreaux: Thank you.

Ashbrook: Ron, that's great. I appreciate your call. Morgan City is kind of a gritty town. Do you think Tim caught it, that area?

Ron: Well, it isn't anymore, but at one time it was. And there was surely some material for books and short stories down there at the time that I lived down there.

Ashbrook: Tim Gautreaux?

Gautreaux: To say the least.

Ashbrook: Yeah, to say the least. That's great. Ron, thank you very much for calling. Let's get another call right here from Buffalo, New York. And Harold. Harold, you're on the air with Tim Gautreaux.

Harold: Hi, Tom. How are you? Hi, Tim.

Ashbrook: Very well.

Gautreaux: Hey.

Harold: Comment ça va, Tim? I taught at Lafayette, Louisiana, for seven years at USL, the university there. And I got steeped in Cajun culture and actually taught Cajun culture, even though I wasn't a Cajun. I wanted to say two things to you, Mr. Gautreaux. One is I just read your *Times* book review this morning because it's the first chance I had to actually look at it. I was very happy to see what you had to say, and especially what you said this morning about two things. The missing idea of how when somebody dies in our lives, all the things that they could have done are now no longer there. My uncle died in Normandy in World War II, and I wish that he was there for me when I was growing up. Every day I wish for that. I'd go out to his grave and place flowers on his grave. I wish he was here. The second thing is that, yeah, vengeance is an afterthought. It's something else that happens, and I wanted to give you kudos on that remark. I look forward to buying your book and reading it. Thank you so much, sir.
Gautreaux: Thank you.

Ashbrook: Thank you very much for calling, Harold. That vacuum that never goes away from those who are dead, the missing. And also, vengeance. We don't need to give the plot away at all, but I wish if you'd just share some of your thoughts on vengeance with us, Tim, and why it ends up in your telling such a dry hole. What is it about human nature, life, the cosmos, that makes vengeance . . .
Gautreaux: I guess it is kind of a cosmic concern. My original take on vengeance is very superficial. I just got tired of seeing so many bloody TV dramas and so many bloody movies where people are wronged and then they go out and they do the Clint Eastwood thing. They kill a whole bunch of folks.

Ashbrook: Rambo.
Gautreaux. Right, right. And this is supposed to give you closure and this is supposed to do this and do that and have all these beneficial and analgesic effects on your soul. But in truth I don't see it and I don't buy it. Even I think Hollywood is turning around on this a little bit. If you saw the latest Clint Eastwood movie, *Gran Torino*, the opposite happens there really. I won't give that ending away—of course, everybody has seen the movie—but in the end of that movie we have kind of a reversal of the whole notion of vengeance. There's a shootout, but it's not what you would think. And really the villains in *The Missing* get their comeuppance, but not in the way you'd normally expect it, the big bloodbath of a gunfight.

Ashbrook: Those kinds of things happen in stories and movies and life all over this country, but I wonder what you think as a Southern writer. In some ways I have a strong association with the South as well as a culture of honor, the culture of arms, the readiness for bloodshed. It may change in Clint Eastwood's latest movie, but do you see your region changing when it comes to that kind of kind of cultural instinct and heritage?

Gautreaux: No, not really. But see, I'm not from the Protestant culture of the Deep South. I'm from really the French Catholic culture. And Cajuns, as it says in the book somewhere, very often were just too poor to afford a grudge, and they really weren't big on vengeance because the results of vengeance are something that hurt the family, and Acadians have always been very family oriented. Why perform an act of violence that's going to land you in jail if you have children to support? That is sort of the Acadian take on violence and vengeance.

Ashbrook. Life is already tough enough. I read somewhere that you were describing one of your dad's first jobs out in the cypress swamp, cutting down cypress trees that were five feet through the middle, standing in waist deep water, with snakes and leeches and a crosscut saw in 95 degree heat. You don't need more trouble if that's your day job.

Gautreaux. Right. Course a lot of people worked hard like that, but I think it's a cultural difference, sort of a life-view that most south Louisiana Acadians have.

Ashbrook: Let's get a call from Sarasota, Florida, and Tanka. Tanka, you're on the air.

Tanka: Oh, hi, Tom. I started my college career at Southeastern Louisiana College, when it was Southeastern Louisiana *College*.

Ashbrook: Yeah, great.

Tanka: Also, the *President*, my mother was a cashier on the boat for many years. And I would ride the day trips, and I would ride some night trips and fall asleep on those gliders near the dance floor. Remember those? Pretty cool. My father and my husband are both riverboat engineers. I was thinking about the so-called six degrees of separation, and I think this is much less. I'm so looking forward to your book. It sounds exciting.

Gautreaux: Thank you.

Ashbrook: That's great, Tanka. The riverboat engineers, the actual machinery of the river is something you're clearly kind of in love with, Mr. Gautreaux. Tim, this machinery, something about machinery, just grabs you as a writer, it seems to me.

Gautreaux: Yeah, I'm interested in obsolete machinery; it's a genetic defect. Maybe it's a carry-over from what my grandfather was interested in. Yes, I have a big collection of steam whistles and steam gauges. I'm a fireman at the Tennessee Valley Railroad Museum. My wife says the only reason I write fiction is so I can tell people about obsolete machinery.

Ashbrook: We love reading about it; it sure brings this to life. There's another point: we keep getting steamboat calls, and why not? The allure is pretty strong.

Gautreaux: It's amazing that we've gotten several calls on the old *President*, but then I'm sitting here and realizing that she was an excursion boat from 1934 until even after she was dieselized, in maybe 1990. So millions and millions of people have been on the old *President*.

Ashbrook: Right. I wish you'd read just a little bit more for us from *The Missing*. We've got a reading a little bit later in the book where there's a brawl on the riverboat where it's not one of the fancier, more elegant cruises. This one turns pretty rough on the *Ambassador*; it's pulled into a rough town. The boat crew had trouble with those brawls. You've got a fight scene here that takes place after they've loaded up at a factory town you've called Bung City. They've headed out for a Mississippi cruise. Could you read a bit for us, Mr. Gautreaux?

Gautreaux: Sure. Sam Simoneaux's job on this boat is a misery. He works sixteen hours a day. He's a bouncer; he gets beat up on every cruise. They run three or four cruises a day every day. So this is a tough, tough job. This is where they land I think at a little town in Arkansas, which is a factory town, totally made up of course.

"He walked across the dance floor and saw two groups of men pointing fingers and complaining loudly that the band didn't know how to play any reels. Zack Stimson studied his abusers and tentatively began to strum 'Under the Double Eagle.' The band fell in behind him, and nearly a hundred and fifty couples started to dance three hundred different ways. The water-tank factory workers, mostly in hobnail brogans, tried to form two lines for a clomping Virginia reel, while the creosote workers, mainly in pressed overalls, were dancing deluded buck-and-wings, clog steps, or lunging polka stomps deadly to their partners' toes. Pinwheeling dancers broke through the Virginia reel lines like crazed mules spinning out of a flaming barn. By the middle of the tune half the dancers were capsized on the floor and a general stomp-and-gouge had broken out. Charlie Duggs, Sam, and Aaron waded in and began pulling scuffed and screaming women out of the fray; then they began shoving apart the fighters and getting knocked around for their trouble. The biggest waiters waded in next, pulling hair and kicking, and the orchestra kept playing, as if trying to remind everyone what they were there for. A little man pulled a knife, and Charlie slapjacked him on the top of his head. Someone knocked down a tin lantern and a big fellow fell on it, crushing open the fuel tank, and women shrieked as he caught fire, then leapt up and ran, a flaming cross flying down the middle of the dance floor. Men stopped fighting to knock him over, everyone suddenly mad to get at him, a flurry of sympathetic hands rolling him like a barrel across the dance floor as he hollered and cursed. A man in overalls dumped a pitcher of water over his length, and suddenly the battle was finished. People from all sides grabbed the smoking man's singed hands in congratulation and hauled him to a chair. Most of his hair was gone, and his face was blacked, but a woman came down from the café and gave him a stick of butter and when a water-tank worker handed him a full glass of whiskey, the victim gave the room a bald-faced grin. Couples re-formed, a few started to dance again, and there was a general search for hats and eyeglasses."

Ashbrook: Tim Gautreaux reading from a raucous moment there in his Mississippi riverboat mystery, tale, *The Missing* just out and quite a book, set in the Roaring Twenties with life on the Mississippi. Before it's all over, your protagonist Sam Simoneaux is off the river and into the deep woods of Arkansas, back in the swamps of Louisiana. I wish you could give us a sense of the cultural boundary between those two zones. When you get off the river, when he heads into Arkansas, what's he passing from and to?
Gautreaux: Well, he's going off of a mildly civilized milieu of the boat, which is its own floating little civilization, and he's going into the Deep South of the early 1920s. Some people imagine that America was totally civilized and structured by that time. They think of the cities—they think of St. Louis or Boston or Atlanta—places that were paved and all connected up with telephones, but the rural areas were not like that at all. In, say, 1921 rural Arkansas or Louisiana or Mississippi was very much like it was in the 1870s. And with isolation, if you've ever read *Heart of Darkness*, comes a certain amount of degeneration.

Ashbrook: And a kind of clan rule as you depict it.

Gautreaux: Yeah. Law enforcement in the rural areas was spotty at best. In some places, you had to write a letter if you wanted a lawman to show up. And this is the milieu that he goes in to. A man controlled his own destiny when he was trying to look for somebody to be dealt with back in the woods.

Ashbrook: It's compelling terrain, and you bring it over compellingly. Walker Percy once said famously that as a southern writer you've got to be careful that you don't think too much of yourself as a southern writer or make that the frame of your work, or you will end up, he said, in the business of "amazing Yankees," sort of telling stories that will make Yankees' jaws drop.
Gautreaux: That's one of my favorite Percy quotes.

Ashbrook: That's just fantastic. It feels to me that while you're bringing on all this color and all this culture, I don't see you quite dropping yourself in that pigeonhole, Tim Gautreaux.
Gautreaux: You have to look at your region's history. Of course, I've lived here all my life, sixty-one years. You have to develop an ear for the false step, the mistake. When you go over the top, you have to see that; you've got to revise it out of your manuscript. I think it's really bad to consider yourself a certain type of writer. People ask me all the time, "Are you a southern writer?" And I say, "No, I'm a writer who happens to have been born in the South, and whatever territory you have, that's what you make use of as a writer." But if you actually consider yourself on the grits and gravy train, what's going to happen is you're going to come across as a big cliché-monger, and you're just going to pack your prose with all sorts of overused stuff.

Ashbrook: You've taught a lot students, no small number of them southern young men and women in your time. Do you see a different sensibility coming up in the twenty-somethings, following you into that literary realm, Tim?
Gautreaux: Not really. What you have to do is just get the student to understand what his territory is, whether it's a subdivision in New Orleans or Atlanta. That's his territory. Or if it's a farm in Minnesota or whatever, that's his territory, because students don't think territorially anymore. They think we're all part of one similar civilization, that people in Utah think exactly the same way as people in Biloxi, Mississippi. And if you've got a head shop and a record story in a community, then it's totally integrated with pop culture, and nothing is further from the truth.

Ashbrook: When you push them in that direction, are they willing to go there, turn around and really think about the gritty reality of the place, the space they're from?

Gautreaux: No creative writing student is ever worth a damn until he's middle-aged.

Ashbrook: So maybe it doesn't matter. When they get there, they'll be lucky if they had you back in the day.

Gautreaux: Right, you have to plant the seeds.

Ashbrook: It's great. Tim Gautreaux, it's a wonderful tale and a wonderful novel. We're grateful to you for taking your time out of Hammond, Louisiana, and KSLU to join us today. Mr. Gautreaux, author of *The Missing*, thank you very much for joining us this hour.

Gautreaux: Thank you.

Ashbrook: We'll go out with "New Orleans Shout," 1929, King Oliver. I'm Tom Ashbrook. This is *On Point*.

[music]

Index

Dodd, Susan, 67

Dubus, Andre, 70, 130

Dufrense, John, 77

Eastwood, Clint, xvii, 160, 176–77

Eliot, T. S., xiv, 44; *The Waste Land* xiv, 44–45

excursion boat, 126, 138, 143, 160–61, 167, 172, 178

Exxon *Valdez*, 33

Faulkner, William, xvii, 30–31, 46, 54, 61, 82–83, 88–89, 105, 110, 145–46, 148, 151, 156; *Absalom, Absalom!*, 145; "A Rose for Emily," 145–46

Fitzgerald, F. Scott, 65

Florida, 143, 177

Fountain, Pete, 171

France, xvii, 138–39, 161, 164–65, 170, 173

Franklin, Tom, 71, 81, 162

French, xi, 29, 37, 46, 53–54, 59–60, 69–70, 77–78, 104, 107–8, 115–16, 118, 128, 153, 165, 177

French Quarter, New Orleans, 61, 154, 169

frontier tradition, vii, 9, 19, 38

Frost, Robert, 59

Gaines, Ernest, 10, 37, 76, 110–12, 114, 135, 146, 151

Gautreaux, Tim: editing process, ix–x, 11–12, 34, 48–49, 66, 77, 103, 161–62; family, viii, x, xv, xxi, 6, 18, 22–23, 26–27, 32, 37–39, 45–46, 54–56, 59–60, 64, 67, 69–70, 76–79, 96–98, 100–101, 104, 107, 109, 114, 116, 122, 124, 129, 133, 138–39, 142, 144, 146–48, 152–53, 160–61, 163–64, 167–68, 170, 178; Tiger Island, 22, 45, 92, 110
Works:
Black Bayou (unpublished), 47
"The Bug Man," xxi, 149

The Clearing (originally *Victrola Souls*), xiv–xvii, xxii, 54, 66, 70–71, 73, 75, 78–79, 81, 86, 87, 90, 97, 100–103, 105, 107, 110, 119, 121, 124–26, 128, 131, 138–40, 143–44, 152, 159–61, 163, 170; Nimbus, 85, 102; point of view, xiv, 77, 79, 100–101, 140, 143; *characters:* Buzetti, xv; Byron Aldridge, xiv–xv, xvii, 54, 70, 79–80, 100–102, 125, 138–40, 143; Crouch, xv; May (housekeeper), 80, 82, 103, 144; Randolph Aldridge, xiv, 79–80, 100–101, 103, 125, 139–40, 143

"The Courtship of Merlin LeBlanc," 49, 60, 91, 148

"Dancing with the One-Armed Gal," xxii, 123, 153

"Deputy Sid's Gift," 33, 46, 143

"Died and Gone to Vegas," xxi, 28, 38, 58, 60

"Easy Pickings," xxii, 61

"Floyd's Girl," 60

"Good for the Soul," xxii, 93

"Idols," 162

"License to Steal," 49

"Little Frogs in a Ditch," xxii, 13–14

The Missing, xvi–xviii, xxii, 119, 126, 128, 131, 138, 141–42, 144, 152, 159–61, 163, 164–65, 168, 170–71, 173–76, 178–79, 181; *character:* Sam Simoneaux, xvii, 138, 141–42, 144, 159–60, 165–66, 168–69, 171, 173, 178–79

The Next Step in the Dance (originally *Machinery of Dreams*), x, xiii–xiv, xxii, 6, 8, 17, 21, 22, 25, 33, 35–36, 45–46, 49–51, 54, 58–60, 69, 73, 77, 87–90, 97, 101, 107, 109, 110, 114, 116, 118–19, 120, 124, 128, 130, 135, 137, 140, 152, 170; *characters:* Colette Thibodeaux,

Printed in the USA
CPSIA information can be obtained
at www.ICGtesting.com
CBHW022027230524
8914CB00001B/3